3895

Bloom's Modern Critical Interpretations

The Adventures of
  Huckleberry Finn
The Age of Innocence
All Quiet on the
  Western Front
Animal Farm
As You Like It
The Ballad of the
  Sad Café
Beloved
Beowulf
Billy Budd, Benito
  Cereno, Bartleby the
  Scrivener, and Other
  Tales
The Bluest Eye
Brave New World
Cat on a Hot Tin
  Roof
The Catcher in the
  Rye
Catch-22
Cat's Cradle
The Color Purple
Crime and
  Punishment
The Crucible
Daisy Miller, The
  Turn of the Screw,
  and Other Tales
Darkness at Noon
David Copperfield
Death of a Salesman
The Divine Comedy
Don Quixote
Dracula
Dubliners
Emma
Fahrenheit 451
A Farewell to Arms
Frankenstein
The General Prologue
  to the Canterbury
  Tales

The Glass Menagerie
The Grapes of Wrath
Great Expectations
The Great Gatsby
Gulliver's Travels
Hamlet
The Handmaid's Tale
Heart of Darkness
I Know Why the
  Caged Bird Sings
The Iliad
The Interpretation of
  Dreams
Invisible Man
Jane Eyre
The Joy Luck Club
Julius Caesar
The Jungle
King Lear
Long Day's Journey
  Into Night
Lord of the Flies
The Lord of the Rings
Love in the Time
  of Cholera
Macbeth
The Man Without
  Qualities
The Merchant of
  Venice
The Metamorphosis
A Midsummer Night's
  Dream
Miss Lonelyhearts
Moby-Dick
My Ántonia
Native Son
Night
1984
The Odyssey
Oedipus Rex
The Old Man and the
  Sea
On the Road

One Flew Over the
  Cuckoo's Nest
One Hundred Years of
  Solitude
Othello
Paradise Lost
The Pardoner's Tale
A Passage to India
Persuasion
Portnoy's Complaint
A Portrait of the Artist
  as a Young Man
Pride and Prejudice
Ragtime
The Red Badge of
  Courage
The Rime of the
  Ancient Mariner
Romeo & Juliet
The Rubáiyát of Omar
  Khayyám
The Scarlet Letter
A Scholarly Look at
  The Diary of Anne
  Frank
A Separate Peace
Silas Marner
Slaughterhouse-Five
Song of Myself
Song of Solomon
The Sonnets of
  William Shakespeare
Sophie's Choice
The Sound and the
  Fury
The Stranger
A Streetcar Named
  Desire
Sula
The Sun Also Rises
A Tale of Two Cities
The Tale of Genji
The Tales of Poe
The Tempest

Bloom's Modern Critical Interpretations

Tess of the
D'Urbervilles
Their Eyes Were
Watching God
Things Fall Apart

To Kill a Mockingbird
Ulysses
Waiting for Godot
Walden
The Waste Land

White Noise
Wuthering Heights
Young Goodman
Brown

Nathanael West's
Miss Lonelyhearts

Edited and with an introduction by
Harold Bloom
Sterling Professor of the Humanities
Yale University

CHELSEA HOUSE
P U B L I S H E R S
A Haights Cross Communications Company®
Philadelphia

Library of Congress Cataloging-in-Publication Data

Miss Lonelyhearts / Harold Bloom [editor].
    p. cm.
  Includes bibliographical references and index.
  ISBN 0-7910-8123-0 (alk. paper)
  1. West, Nathanael, 1903-1940. Miss Lonelyhearts. I. Bloom, Harold.
  PS3545.E8334M5365 2004
  813'.52—dc22
                                    2004024764

Contributing Editor: Pamela Loos

Cover designed by Keith Trego

Layout by EJB Publishing Services

Contents

Editor's Note

My Introduction reads *Miss Lonelyhearts* as an involuntary instance of what the great scholar of Kabbalah, Gershom Scholem, termed Jewish Gnosticism.

Kingsley Widmer describes the book as "a compassionately savage piece of iconoclasm", while Mark Conroy assigns both last laugh and first line to Shrike, master parodist.

Alert to all American apocalypses, Douglas Robinson sees West's novel as akin to Milton's *Paradise Regained*, after which Robert Emmet Long centers on the satire's mingling of horror and comedy.

John Keyes appreciates the marvelous authenticity of the letters sent to Miss Lonelyhearts, while Robert Wexelblatt studies the corrosiveness of West's rhetoric.

Shrike is taken as the true modernist Christ by Beverly Jones, after which the influence of T.S. Eliot's *The Waste Land* on *Miss Lonelyhearts* is traced by Miriam Fuchs.

Literary tradition as West's context is invoked by Richard Lynch, while Marion Crowe concludes this volume with an analysis of West's parodies of Christian iconography.

HAROLD BLOOM

Introduction

I

Nathanael West, who died in an automobile accident in 1940 at the age of thirty-seven, wrote one remorseless masterpiece, *Miss Lonelyhearts* (1933). Despite some astonishing sequences, *The Day of the Locust* (1939) is an overpraised work, a waste of West's genius. Of the two lesser fictions, *The Dream Life of Balso Snell* (1931) is squalid and dreadful, with occasional passages of a rancid power, while *A Cool Million* (1934), though an outrageous parody of American picaresque, is a permanent work of American satire and seems to me underpraised. To call West uneven is therefore a litotes; he is a wild medley of magnificent writing and inadequate writing, except in *Miss Lonelyhearts* which excels *The Sun Also Rises*, *The Great Gatsby*, and even *Sanctuary* as the perfected instance of a negative vision in modern American fiction. The greatest Faulkner, of *The Sound and the Fury*, *As I Lay Dying*, *Absalom, Absalom!* and *Light in August*, is the only American writer of prose fiction in this century who can be said to have surpassed *Miss Lonelyhearts*. West's spirit lives again in *The Crying of Lot 49* and some sequences in *Gravity's Rainbow*, but the negative sublimity of *Miss Lonelyhearts* proves to be beyond Pynchon's reach, or perhaps his ambition.

West, born Nathan Weinstein, is a significant episode in the long and tormented history of Jewish Gnosticism. The late Gershom Scholem's

1

superb essay, "Redemption Through Sin," in his *The Messianic Idea in Judaism*, is the best commentary I know upon *Miss Lonelyhearts*. I once attempted to convey this to Scholem, who shrugged West off, quite properly from Scholem's viewpoint, when I remarked to him that West was manifestly a Jewish anti-Semite, and admitted that there were no allusions to Jewish esotericism or Kabbalah in his works. Nevertheless, for the stance of literary criticism, Jewish Gnosticism, as defined by Scholem, is the most illuminating context in which to study West's novels. It is a melancholy paradox that West, who did not wish to be Jewish in any way at all, remains the most indisputably Jewish writer yet to appear in America, a judgment at once aesthetic and moral. Nothing by Bellow, Malamud, Philip Roth, Mailer, or Ozick can compare to *Miss Lonelyhearts* as an achievement. West's Jewish heir, if he has one, may be Harold Brodkey, whose recent *Women and Angels*, excerpted from his immense novel-in-progress, can be regarded as another powerful instance of Jewish Gnosis, free of West's hatred of his own Jewishness.

Stanley Edgar Hyman, in his pamphlet on West (1962), concluded that, "His strength lay in his vulgarity and bad taste, his pessimism, his nastiness." Hyman remains West's most useful critic, but I would amend this by observing that these qualities in West's writing emanate from a negative theology, spiritually authentic, and given aesthetic dignity by the force of West's eloquent negations. West, like his grandest creation, Shrike, is a rhetorician of the abyss, in the tradition of Sabbatian nihilism that Scholem has expounded so masterfully. One thinks of ideas such as "the violation of the Torah has become its fulfillment, just as a grain of wheat must rot in the earth" or such as Jacob Frank's: "We are all now under the obligation to enter the abyss." The messianic intensity of the Sabbatians and Frankists results in a desperately hysterical and savage tonality which prophesies West's authentically religious book, *Miss Lonelyhearts*, a work profoundly Jewish but only in its negations, particularly the negation of the normative Judaic assumption of total sense in everything, life and text alike. *Miss Lonelyhearts* takes place in the world of Freud, where the fundamental assumption is that everything already has happened, and that nothing can be made new because total sense has been achieved, but then repressed or negated. Negatively Jewish, the book is also negatively American. Miss Lonelyhearts is a failed Walt Whitman (hence the naming of the cripple as Peter Doyle, Whitman's pathetic friend) and a fallen American Adam to Shrike's very American Satan. Despite the opinions of later critics, I continue to find Hyman's argument persuasive, and agree with him that the book's psychosexuality is marked by a repressed homosexual relation between Shrike and Miss Lonelyhearts. Hyman's Freudian observation that all the suffering in the book is essentially female seems valid, reminding us that Freud's "feminine masochism" is mostly encountered among men, according to Freud himself. Shrike, the butcherbird impaling his victim, Miss Lonelyhearts, upon the thorns of Christ, is himself as much an instance of "feminine masochism" as his victim. If Miss Lonelyhearts is close to pathological frenzy, Shrike is also consumed by religious hysteria, by a terrible nostalgia for God.

The book's bitter stylistic negation results in a spectacular verbal economy, in which literally every sentence is made to count, in more than one sense of "count." Freud's "negation" involves a cognitive return of the repressed, here through West's self-projection as Shrike, spit out but not disavowed. The same Freudian process depends upon an affective continuance of repression, here by West's self-introjection as Miss Lonelyhearts, at once West's inability to believe and his disavowed failure to love. Poor Miss Lonelyhearts, who receives no other name throughout the book, has been destroyed by Shrike's power of Satanic rhetoric before the book even opens. But then Shrike has destroyed himself first, for no one could withstand the sustained horror of Shrike's impaling rhetoric, which truly can be called West's horror:

> "I am a great saint," Shrike cried, "I can walk on my own water. Haven't you ever heard of Shrike's Passion in the Luncheonette, or the Agony in the Soda Fountain? Then I compared the wounds in Christ's body to the mouths of a miraculous purse in which we deposit the small change of our sins. It is indeed an excellent conceit. But now let us consider the holes in our own bodies and into what these congenital wounds open. Under the skin of man is a wondrous jungle where veins like lush tropical growths hang along overripe organs and weed-like entrails writhe in squirming tangles of red and yellow. In this jungle, flitting from rock-gray lungs to golden intestines, from liver to lights and back to liver again, lives a bird called the soul. The Catholic hunts this bird with bread and wine, the Hebrew with a golden ruler, the Protestant on leaden feet with leaden words, the Buddhist with gestures, the Negro with blood. I spit on them all. Phooh! And I call upon you to spit. Phooh! Do you stuff birds? No, my dears, taxidermy is not religion. No! A thousand times no. Better, I say unto you, better a live bird in the jungle of the body than two stuffed birds on the library table."

I have always associated this great passage with what is central to West: the messianic longing for redemption, through sin if necessary. West's humor is almost always apocalyptic, in a mode quite original with him, though so influential since his death that we have difficulty seeing how strong the originality was. Originality, even in comic writing, becomes a difficulty. How are we to read the most outrageous of the letters sent to Miss Lonelyhearts, the one written by the sixteen-year-old girl without a nose?

> *I sit and look at myself all day and cry. I have a big hole in the middle of my face that scares people even myself so I cant blame the boys for not wanting to take me out. My mother loves me, but she crys terrible when she looks at me.*
>
> *What did I do to deserve such a terrible bad fate? Even if I did do some bad things I didnt do any before I was a year old and I was born this way. I asked Papa and he says he doesnt know, but that maybe I did something in the other world before I was born or that maybe I was being punished for his sins. I dont believe that because he is a very nice man. Ought I commit suicide?*
>
> *Sincerely yours,*
>
> *Desperate*

Defensive laughter is a complex reaction to grotesque suffering. In his 1928 essay on humor, Freud concluded that the above-the-I, the superego, speaks kindly words of comfort to the intimidated ego, and this speaking is humor, which Freud calls "the triumph of narcissism, the ego's victorious assertion of its own invulnerability." Clearly, Freud's "humor" does not include the Westian mode. Reading Desperate's "What did I do to deserve such a terrible bad fate?," our ego knows that it is defeated all the time, or at least is vulnerable to undeserved horror. West's humor has *no* liberating element whatsoever, but is the humor of a vertigo ill-balanced on the edge of what ancient Gnosticism called the *kenoma*, the cosmological emptiness.

II

Shrike, West's superb Satanic tempter, achieves his apotheosis at the novel's midpoint, the eighth of its fifteen tableaux, accurately titled "Miss Lonelyhearts in the Dismal Swamp." As Miss Lonelyhearts, sick with despair, lies in bed, the drunken Shrike bursts in, shouting his greatest rhetorical set piece, certainly the finest tirade in modern American fiction. Cataloging the methods that Miss Lonelyhearts might employ to escape out of the Dismal Swamp, Shrike begins with a grand parody of the later

D.H. Lawrence, in which the vitalism of *The Plumed Serpent* and *The Man Who Died* is carried into a gorgeous absurdity, a heavy sexuality that masks Shrike's Satanic fears of impotence:

> "You are fed up with the city and its teeming millions. The ways and means of men, as getting and lending and spending, you lay waste your inner world, are too much with you. The bus takes too long, while the subway is always crowded. So what do you do? So you buy a farm and walk behind your horse's moist behind, no collar or tie, plowing your broad swift acres. As you turn up the rich black soil, the wind carries the smell of pine and dung across the fields and the rhythm of an old, old work enters your soul. To this rhythm, you sow and weep and chivy your kine, not kin or kind, between the pregnant rows of corn and taters. Your step becomes the heavy sexual step of a dance-drunk Indian and you tread the seed down into the female earth. You plant, not dragon's teeth, but beans and greens."

Confronting only silence, Shrike proceeds to parody the Melville of *Typee* and *Omoo*, and also Somerset Maugham's version of Gauguin in *The Moon and Sixpence*:

> "You live in a thatch but with the daughter of a king, a slim young maiden in whose eyes is an ancient wisdom. Her breasts are golden speckled pears, her belly a melon, and her odor is like nothing so much as a jungle fern. In the evening, on the blue lagoon, under the silvery moon, to your love you croon in the soft sylabelew and vocabelew of her langorour tongorour. Your body is golden brown like hers, and tourists have need of the indignant finger of the missionary to point you out. They envy you your breech clout and carefree laugh and little brown bride and fingers instead of forks. But you don't return their envy, and when a beautiful society girl comes to your hut in the night, seeking to learn the secret of your happiness, you send her back to her yacht that hangs on the horizon like a nervous racehorse. And so you dream away the days, fishing, hunting, dancing, kissing, and picking flowers to twine in your hair."

As Shrike says, this is a played-out mode, but his savage gusto in rendering it betrays his hatred of the religion of art, of the vision that sought a salvation in imaginative literature. What Shrike goes on to chant is an even more effective parody of the literary stances West rejected. Though Shrike calls it "Hedonism," the curious amalgam here of Hemingway and Ronald Firbank, with touches of Fitzgerald and the earlier Aldous Huxley, might better be named an aesthetic stoicism:

> "You dedicate your life to the pursuit of pleasure. No overindulgence, mind you, but knowing that your body is a pleasure machine, you treat it carefully in order to get the most out of it. Golf as well as booze, Philadelphia Jack O'Brien and his chestweights as well as Spanish dancers. Nor do you neglect the pleasures of the mind. You fornicate under pictures by Matisse and Picasso, you drink from Renaissance glassware, and often you spend an evening beside the fireplace with Proust and an apple. Alas, after much good fun, the day comes when you realize that soon you must die. You keep a stiff upper lip and decide to give a last party. You invite all your old mistresses, trainers, artists and boon companions. The guests are dressed in black, the waiters are coons, the table is a coffin carved for you by Eric Gill. You serve caviar and blackberries and licorice candy and coffee without cream. After the dancing girls have finished, you get to your feet and call for silence in order to explain your philosophy of life. 'Life,' you say, 'is a club where they won't stand for squawks, where they deal you only one hand and you must sit in. So even if the cards are cold and marked by the hand of fate, play up, play up like a gentleman and a sport. Get tanked, grab what's on the buffet, use the girls upstairs, but remember, when you throw box cars, take the curtain like a dead game sport, don't squawk.'"

Even this is only preparatory to Shrike's bitterest phase in his tirade, an extraordinary send-up of High Aestheticism proper, of Pater, George Moore, Wilde and the earlier W.B. Yeats:

> "Art! Be an artist or a writer. When you are cold, warm yourself before the flaming tints of Titian, when you are hungry, nourish yourself with great spiritual foods by listening to the noble periods of Bach, the harmonies of Brahms and the thunder of Beethoven. Do you think there is anything in the fact that their names all begin with a B? But don't take a chance, smoke a 3 B pipe, and remember these immortal lines: *When to the suddenness of melody the echo parting falls the failing day*. What a rhythm! Tell

them to keep their society whores and pressed duck with oranges. For you *l'art vivant*, the living art, as you call it. Tell them that you know that your shoes are broken and that there are pimples on your face, yes, and that you have buck teeth and a club foot, but that you don't care, for to-morrow they are playing Beethoven's last quartets in Carnegie Hall and at home you have Shakespeare's plays in one volume."

That last sentence, truly and deliciously Satanic, is one of West's greatest triumphs, but he surpasses it in the ultimate Shrikean rhapsody, after Shrike's candid avowal: "God alone is our escape." With marvelous appropriateness, West makes this at once the ultimate Miss Lonelyhearts letter, and also Shrike's most Satanic self-identification, in the form of a letter to Christ dictated for Miss Lonelyhearts by Shrike, who speaks absolutely for both of them:

> *Dear Miss Lonelyhearts of Miss Lonelyhearts—*
> *I am twenty-six years old and in the newspaper game. Life for me is a desert empty of comfort. I cannot find pleasure in food, drink, or women—nor do the arts give me joy any longer. The Leopard of Discontent walks the streets of my city; the Lion of Discouragement crouches outside the walls of my citadel. All is desolation and a vexation of spirit. I feel like hell. How can I believe, how can I have faith in this day and age? Is it true that the greatest scientists believe again in you?*
> *I read your column and like it very much. There you once wrote: 'When the salt has lost its savour, who shall savour it again?' Is the answer: 'None but the Saviour?'*
> *Thanking you very much for a quick reply, I remain yours truly,*
>
> *A Regular Subscriber*

"I feel like hell," the Miltonic "Myself am Hell," is Shrike's credo, and West's.

III

What is the relation of Shrike to West's rejected Jewishness? The question may seem illegitimate to many admirers of West, but it acquires considerable force in the context of the novel's sophisticated yet unhistorical Gnosticism. The way of nihilism means, according to Scholem, "to free oneself of all laws, conventions, and religions, to adopt every conceivable attitude and to reject it, and to follow one's leader step for step into the abyss." Scholem is paraphrasing the demonic Jacob Frank, an eighteenth-century Jewish Shrike who brought the Sabbatian messianic movement to its final degradation. Frank would have recognized something of his own negations and nihilistic fervor in the closing passages that form a pattern in West's four novels:

> His body screamed and shouted as it marched and uncoiled; then, with one heaving shout of triumph, it fell back quiet.
>
> The army that a moment before had been thundering in his body retreated slowly—victorious, relieved.

(*The Dream Life of Balso Snell*)

> While they were struggling, Betty came in through the street door. She called to them to stop and started up the stairs. The cripple saw her cutting off his escape and tried to get rid of the package. He pulled his hand out. The gun inside the package exploded and Miss Lonelyhearts fell, dragging the cripple with him. They both rolled part of the way down the stairs.

(*Miss Lonelyhearts*)

> "Alas, Lemuel Pitkin himself did not have this chance, but instead was dismantled by the enemy. His teeth were pulled out. His eye was gouged from his head. His thumb was removed. His scalp was torn away. His leg was cut off. And, finally, he was shot through the heart.
>
> "But he did not live or die in vain. Through his martyrdom the National Revolutionary Party triumphed, and by that triumph this country was delivered from sophistication, Marxism and International Capitalism. Through the National Revolution its people were purged of alien diseases and America became again American."
>
> "Hail the martyrdom in the Bijou Theater!" roar Shagpoke's youthful hearers when he is finished.
>
> "Hail, Lemuel Pitkin!"
>
> "All hail, the American Boy!"

(*A Cool Million*)

He was carried through the exit to the back street and lifted into a police car. The siren began to scream and at first he thought he was making the noise himself. He felt his lips with his hands. They were clamped tight. He knew then it was the siren. For some reason this made him laugh and he began to imitate the siren as loud as he could.

(*The Day of the Locust*)

All four passages mutilate the human image, the image of God that normative Jewish tradition associates with our origins. "Our forefathers were always talking, only what good did it do them and what did they accomplish? But we are under the burden of silence," Jacob Frank said. What Frank's and West's forefathers always talked about was the ultimate forefather, Adam, who would have enjoyed the era of the Messiah, had he not sinned. West retains of tradition only the emptiness of the fallen image, the scattered spark of creation. The screaming and falling body, torn apart and maddened into a siren-like laughter, belongs at once to the American Surrealist poet, Balso Snell; the American Horst Wessel, poor Lemuel Pitkin; to Miss Lonelyhearts, the Whitmanian American Christ; and to Tod Hackett, painter of the American apocalypse. All are nihilistic versions of the mutilated image of God, or of what the Jewish Gnostic visionary, Nathan of Gaza, called the "thought-less" or nihilizing light.

IV

West was a prophet of American violence, which he saw as augmenting progressively throughout our history. His satirical genius, for all its authentic and desperate range, has been defeated by American reality. Shagpoke Whipple, the Calvin Coolidge-like ex-President who becomes the American Hitler in *A Cool Million*, talks in terms that West intended as extravagant, but that now can be read all but daily in our newspapers. Here is Shagpoke at his best, urging us to hear what the dead Lemuel Pitkin has to tell us:

> "Of what is it that he speaks? Of the right of every American boy to go into the world and there receive fair play and a chance to make his fortune by industry and probity without being laughed at or conspired against by sophisticated aliens."

I turn to the *New York Times* (March 29, 1985) and find there the text of a speech given by our President:

But may I just pause here for a second and tell you about a couple of fellows who came to see me the other day, young men. In 1981, just four years ago, they started a business with only a thousand dollars between them and everyone told them they were crazy. Last year their business did a million and a half dollars and they expect to do two and a half million this year. And part of it was because they had the wit to use their names productively. Their business is using their names, the Cain and Abell electric business.

Reality may have triumphed over poor West, but only because he, doubtless as a ghost, inspired or wrote these Presidential remarks. The *Times* reports, sounding as deadpan as Shrike, on the same page (B4), that the young entrepreneurs brought a present to Mr. Reagan. "'We gave him a company jacket with Cain and Abell, Inc. on it,' Mr. Cain said." Perhaps West's ghost now writes not only Shagpokian speeches, but the very text of reality in our America.

KINGSLEY WIDMER

The Religious Masquerade:
Miss Lonelyhearts

THE DOUBLE PLAY OF PROFOUNDITY AND PATHOLOGY

*M*iss *Lonelyhearts* (1933),[1] West's second novella, is often, and I think rightly, viewed as his finest work. Possibly some of its superiority to his first novella can be related to the more serious pessimism and concern with commonplace suffering of the depression during which it was written. Certainly it attempts far more than the solipsistic dream-onanism of art of *The Dream Life of Balso Snell. Miss Lonelyhearts* is a richly aslant religious fable. The entitling figure, a twenty-seven-year-old newspaper reporter, remains otherwise unnamed than by his advice column appellation, probably to emphasize the forced role he plays. Midway in the narrative, Lonelyhearts tries to explain to his conventional fiancée, Betty, his dilemma:

> A man is hired to give advice to the readers of a newspaper. The job is a circulation stunt and the whole staff considers it a joke. He welcomes the job, for it might lead to a gossip column, and anyway he's tired of being a leg man. He too considers the job a joke, but after several months of it, the joke begins to escape him. He sees that the majority of the letters are profoundly humble pleas for moral and spiritual advice, that they are inarticulate expressions of genuine suffering. He also discovers that his

From *Nathanael West.* © 1982 by Twayne Publishers.

11

correspondents take him seriously. For the first time in his life, he is forced to examine the values by which he lives. This examination shows him he is the victim of the joke and not its perpetrator.

Betty still does not understand his anguish, and in her naive but not altogether imperceptive way, thinks that he is sick, suffering from "city troubles," an unhealthy life. But at this point the reader may also not quite understand this slightly stiff passage of the reporter's schematic rationalization. A larger and more perplexed personal and cultural "joke" has also been made evident under the guise of this role-playing.

Part of the Lonelyhearts' victimization comes from responding to the "profoundly" pathetic pleas, the self-parodying letters to his advice column of physical and psychological cripples crying for help: "Desperate, Harold S., Catholic-mother, Broken-hearted, Broad-shoulders, Sick-of-it-all, Disillusioned-with-tubercular-husband," and the many other laments, "all of them alike, stamped from the dough of suffering with a heart-shaped cookie knife." But his situation, on an exploitative periodical in a megapolitan wasteland and under an hysterical cynical-mocking feature editor, Willie Shrike (perhaps named after the predatory bird), makes acceptance nearly impossible, even if he had moral clarity and religious solace to offer.

Nor is any real alternative presented by his fiancée, Betty, "the girl in the party dress" who believes in curative chicken soup, therapeutic visits to nature, boy buys girl a soda, an ordinary dishonest job in advertising, and conventionally cute suburban marital bliss and order. She cannot understand the Lonelyhearts dilemma, nor can all the Betty-moralists of the bland world. For, as Lonelyhearts comments, her "answers were based on the power to limit experience arbitrarily. Moreover, his confusion was significant while her order was not." As long as he takes his role at all seriously, he feels the demands of real suffering. And the lack of adequate answers to it.

West seriously presents the Lonelyhearts dilemma of solacing commonplace anguish; he is a self-defined tormented "humanity-lover." But he is also presented as a grotesque joke, a victim of his own, and traditional Christianity's, pathology. In the third of the fifteen brief chapters that make up the fiction, "Miss Lonelyhearts and the lamb," some of the religious mania appropriate to the "born-again Christian" (as we now call it) is compactly annotated. Lonelyhearts has returned to his rather monastic room, solely decorated with "an ivory Christ that hung opposite the foot of the bed," nailed directly to the wall with large spikes, and reads from Dostoyevsky's *The Brothers Karamazov* a passage by the saintly Zossima advocating "all embracing love." Reflecting on his sense of "vocation" as son of a New England Baptist minister, he recalls that "something stirred in him when he shouted the name of Christ, something secret and enormously powerful." Now he knows what the "thing" is—"hysteria, a snake whose scales are tiny mirrors in which the dead world takes on a semblance of life. And how dead the world is ... a world of doorknobs. He wondered if hysteria were really too steep a price to pay for bringing it to life." Though his intelligent self-consciousness seems considerably greater than the usual born-again religious devotee, the next dozen chapters provide the logic, of his dilemmas and his compulsions, for the concluding "Miss Lonelyhearts has a religious experience" where he feverishly reaches the hysteria of "Christ! Christ!" and "his identification with God was complete." He turns his doorknob and goes forth to "perform a miracle" to test his "conversion," to embrace not only a confusedly vengeant cripple but to "succor ... with love" all the suffering. But the immediate grotesque result is his semiaccidental death and the messing up of several lives since there is no place for the Christ-vision in the real modern world. Such hysteria really is too steep a price for bringing the world to purposive life since it entails madness, death, and further suffering.

Conversion to faith is the snake-induced sin in our dead world. Lonelyhearts's religious experience comes from a self-cultivated hysteria, aided by fasting, fever, psychic paralysis, hallucinations, added to his personal history of an obsessional "Christ-complex" (his phrase), a tormenting sexual ambivalence, and genuine moral anguish. Also in the third chapter, where Lonelyhearts still just plays with his conversion hysteria, he cuts short his chant of "Jesus Christ" when "the snake started to uncoil in his brain," and pushes himself into an amnesiac sleep. There, however, he dreams that he is "a magician who did tricks with doorknobs ... [which] bled, flowered, spoke." His dream then shifts from such Daliesque surrealism to a Buñuelish hyper-realism in which he recapitulates a college prank. He and several student buddies had argued all night about "the existence of God," then drunkenly gone out to barbeque a lamb, though on Lonelyhearts's "condition that they sacrifice it to God" first. Singing an "obscene version of 'Mary had a Little Lamb,'" they take one purchased alive to a field where Lonelyhearts botches the butchering and the injured lamb escapes. Deserted by the others, he has to messily smash the lamb with a stone, ending with a grotesque Beelzebub image of gruesome sacrifice with flowers, blood, and flies. That stone he will later metaphorically translate into the "rock of faith" so that he can sacrificially offer himself to botched suffering.

Underneath, then, the earnest newspaper columnist resides a sick Jesus-freak, as we would now say. Clinically astute West emphasizes other pathological elements in his protagonist, especially his sexual contradictions.

Not only has Lonelyhearts identified with his womanish role-name as lovelorn columnist but his relation to women is peculiar. Much of his treatment of fiancée Betty is hostile, from pinching her nipples to meanly ignoring her to making the virginal girl pregnant to savagely putting her down. Clearly, he does not really like her. He also rather passively lets himself be seduced by an impotent cripple's unfeminine wife, Fay Doyle, though a gross character whom he finds repulsive and frightening (her "massive hams ... were like two enormous grindstones"; "she looked like a police captain"; etc.). She sexually exhausts him, and later arouses his total revulsion. In a final scene with her, supposedly acting out one of his Christian love-roles, he ends roughly dropping her to the floor and blindly beating her "again and again" in the face before fleeing.

He had previously focused on her husband, Peter Doyle, as his Christian love-object, solacing him and holding hands. All Lonelyhearts's sexuality seems messily ambivalent. With Mary Shrike, sex-teasing (and apparently frigid) wife of his editor, he hypes himself into compulsive but always failing attempts at seduction. Several peculiar obscenities appear here, including perhaps an Oedipal twisting, as in paternalistic Willie Shrike's complaining to his reporter of his wife's sexual coldness before sending her off with him. Apparently, also, in sly lubricity, Mary has Lonelyhearts pet her into sexual response, and then runs in to her waiting husband. But even when thinking of Mary, Lonelyhearts "felt colder than before he had started to think of women. It was not his line." His sexual line seems to be disguised and displaced homoeroticism.[2] While his warmly holding hands with the crippled Peter Doyle might be taken as confused Christian compassion, or at least playing at it, an earlier chapter emphasizes something else. In "Miss Lonelyhearts and the clean old man," the protagonist, after leaving the girl friend he was abusing, goes to Delehanty's, a bar frequented by newspaper people (a pre-1933 prohibition "speakeasy"), where he listens to other reporters tell stories of gang rapes of resented female writers. Then, with another drunken reporter, he torments a gay elderly man they forcibly pull out of a public toilet. Lonelyhearts ends up twisting and twisting the screaming "old fag's" arm until someone smashes him in the head. The sexual fascination has turned into guilty rage. Various other detailing also underlines the sexual ambivalence, such as Shrike shrewdly noting, earlier, to Lonelyhearts, "so you don't care for women, eh? J.C. is your only sweetheart, eh?" (With bemused double play, which West frequently uses, the woman, Farkis, who shows up for Shrike's predatory ministrations right after this is described as an exaggeratedly mannish figure.) As one can confirm in the often effete iconography of the Protestant churches of West's time, much about the traditional Jesus might appropriately suggest a covertly homosexual response. That, of course, should not be separated from the general sexual repression of puritanized Christianity, especially strong in that direction in America, or from the admixture with a guiltily sadistic misogyny. Thus West has larger grounds for strongly implying homoeroticism in the love of Jesus, including the longing for sexual mergence for the born-again in the guise of submission to compassionate feeling. When Lonelyhearts is being most Christian, as with Peter Doyle, he is also being most homoerotic. J.C. does become this terribly ambivalent fellow's deathly sweetheart.

Before turning to other aspects of West's analysis of the Lonelyhearts's syndrome, including the compulsion to order, the violent self-laceration, and the hallucinatory longings, I think it crucial to emphasize the double nature of West's treatment, some of which I have been summarizing. Lonelyhearts is clearly presented by West as thoughtfully earnest about the serious moral dilemma of how to answer and solace hardly remediable human suffering. Other details and tropes confirm that we are to see the young man as sincerely searching for a religious answer to human anguish and pervasive modern disorder. But the reader is also carefully, indeed almost gleefully, provided with the details of guilty sexual confusion, long inculcated religious hysteria, and a religiousized suicidal loss of all reality. The protagonist, and the issues, must be seen as *simultaneously* morally profound and clinically pathological. A good many misreadings result from failing to recognize the careful and thorough *doubleness* of West's perceptions and art. We must see Lonelyhearts as *both* sick and saintly. To West's sardonic non-Christian eye, Lonelyhearts, and much of his religion, can only be viewed as inseparably earnest and grotesque, a pious illness. Modern religiousness is a sadly serious disease masquerading as an answer to the impossible.

Otherwise put, Lonelyhearts is a "case" of denied and twisted homoeroticism, a compulsive-obsessional neurosis, even finally an hysteric-schizophrenic psychosis—a not untypical "Christ complex." But he also reveals the moral quester, the sensitively compassionate man seeking to answer the deepest moral cruxes of human disorder and suffering. He is, indeed, as I first quoted him, the victim of a bad joke, but it is finally a cultural and cosmic one. I think it is this doubleness of view, however finally dissolving into the ironies of the sick saint,[3] which not only produces the intensely paradoxical stylization of the work—combining earnest speech, gross wisecracks, surreal dreams, illiterate letters, witty conceits, serious cultural critiques, clinical detailing, and religious visions—but which gives it much of its distinctive brilliance of perception.

If one seeks the most pertinent literary analogue (the stock literary criticism device), *Miss Lonelyhearts* might well be viewed as a Dostoyevskian fiction. But this would not relate to the Russian's Christian apologetics (a bit mocked with the Zossima passage quoted earlier) but his feverish atheism. Thus Lonelyhearts parallels in part the "antihero" of *Notes from Underground,* another nameless figure also simultaneously a clinical case (sadomasochistic, sexually troubled, guiltily anguished) and a profound existential metaphysician of the limits of rationality and the nature of freedom in an absurdist universe. Both novellas end without any possibility of redemption or regeneration, paradoxical explorations of a fated modernist self-consciousness.[4]

Where Dostoyevsky provocatively indicted the disease of Western rationality as unable to order the self and the world, West provocatively indicted Christian religiousness as masquerading the self and the world. Double playing his material into both a clinical case and a moral exemplum, into a poignant tale and a horrendous joke, West went deeper than either iconoclasm or compassion. It is a profound response to a central issue of our culture.

THE ORDER OF SUFFERING

Suffering is real. Part of what this means for the author of *Miss Lonelyhearts* is that much of human pain, misery, and despair cannot readily be resolved, ameliorated, cured, solaced, dissolved by usual human efforts. In the novella's first chapter, "Miss Lonelyhearts, help me, help me," part of the issue gets established through West's mimicry of three semiliterate letters to an advice columnist: one from an eight-time pregnant Catholic mother in constant pain from her kidneys but piously denied an abortion; one from a yearning sixteen-year-old girl thinking of suicide because "born without a nose—she wants love but finds that even her mother "crys terrible" when looking at her, her father thinks "maybe I was being punished for his sins," and boys won't go out with her ("although I am a good dancer and have a nice shape") because "I have a big hole in the middle of my face which scares people even myself"; and one from the concerned adolescent brother of a retarded deaf and dumb thirteen-year-old girl, with brutally punitive parents, who has been sexually molested. Later letters in the story come from the wife of an impotent cripple, the frightened wife of an unemployed abusive psychopath, a cripple with an unfaithful wife ("what I want to no is what is the whole stinking business for"), an impoverished widow who has lost her son, and a paralytic boy who wants to be a violinist. The problems given are predominantly female and sexual, around physical or psychological crippling, in a context of the moralistically punitive. Such miseries cannot be readily ameliorated, often not genuinely assuaged, and traditionally call for a religious answer.

Alternatively, we find the typical modern response of viewing all such miseries as "illness" which reduce to ostensible corrections by expertise of therapy, trivial psuedo-change, institutional device, or obtuse pity. So with the figure of conventional order, Betty. Even when Lonelyhearts behaves outrageously to her, she assures him that he is just "sick." All suffering comes from a temporary condition of illness. He shouts back at her in moral-religious indignation, though since it is self-conscious it, too, becomes a forced role-playing "with gestures that were too appropriate, like that of an old fashioned actor"—the always insistent Westean point about masquerading. Says Lonelyhearts, "What a kind bitch you are. As soon as anyone acts viciously, you say he's sick.... No morality, only medicine." This is the modern "liberal" refusal disguised as tolerance, the denial of the moral sensibility and of responding to suffering, the failure to recognize the unredeemable disorder in the moral universe.

The metaphysical pathos of wishing to restore order, which must of course include responding to suffering, also gets presented in a double way by West. His reporter clearly shows a compulsion, in the clinical sense, for order, an obsessional need to ritually compose things, to restrictively confine sensations, to limit reality. For example, in the chapter "Miss Lonelyhearts and the fat thumb," he found himself "developing an almost insane sensitiveness to order. Everything had to form a pattern...," whether personal efforts, objects in hand, or even the view from the window. But such self-conscious mania leads to an insistent rigidity in which things tend to fall, break, clash, go out of control, as, threateningly, all reality does.[5] In the street the "chaos" seems overwhelming once one becomes so sensitive to ordering: "Broken groups of people hurried past.... The lamp-posts were badly spaced and the flagging was of different sizes. Nor could he do anything with the harsh clanging sounds of streetcars and the raw shouts of hucksters. No repeated group of words would fit their rhythm and no scale could give them meaning." Like common little compulsions of counting left steps, avoiding sidewalk cracks, pairing or counting-off objects, etc., the patterned responses will not long hold. The man's awareness of the insistent disharmonies of modern urban sensations is true but has become a madness. All one can finally do with the surreal jumble and cacophony of sights and sounds is, like the desperate Lonelyhearts, try "not to see or hear." Intense awareness, which most of us protectively refuse to have most of the time, becomes a paralyzing condition.

Be it the urban street sights and sounds, a media format (such as the front page of a newspaper, or, now, an ad-announcement-fantasy riddled segment of television programming), or our reality-and-dream garbled mental states, painful chaos threatens if we fully recognize and respond. In a later chapter of despair, "Miss Lonelyhearts and the dismal swamp," the reporter, withdrawn into bedridden physical illness after sex with Fay Doyle, slides into a surreal fantasy, the slough of despond of the modern Bunyan:

> He found himself in the window of a pawnshop full of fur coats, diamond rings, watches, shotguns, fishing tackle, mandolins. All of these things were the paraphernalia of suffering. A tortured high light twisted on the blade of a gift knife, a battered horn grunted with pain.
>
> He sat in the window thinking. Man has a tropism for order. Keys in one pocket, change in another. Mandolins are tuned G D A E. The physical world has a tropism for disorder, entropy. Man against nature.... Keys yearn to mix with change. Mandolins strive to get out of tune. Every order has within it the germ of destruction. All order is doomed....
>
> A trumpet, marked to sell for $2.49, gave the call to battle and Miss Lonelyhearts plunged into the fray. First he formed a phallus of old watches and rubber boots, then a heart of umbrellas and trout flies, then a diamond of musical instruments and derby hats, after these a circle, triangle, square, swastika. But nothing proved definitive and he began to make a gigantic cross. When the cross became too large for the pawnshop, he moved it to the shore of the ocean. There every wave added to his stock faster than he could lengthen its arms. His labors were enormous. He staggered from the last wave to his work, loaded down with marine refuse....

His psychological tics of compulsion, brilliantly extended in conceits by West, merge with religious mania, the phallus become a cross, and all reality "the paraphernalia of suffering" in a grandiloquent attempt to order our trashy world. Sex and religion and junk become one tidal-wash of chaos. Against our pathetic futility of order, entropy wins.

While this compulsion to order comes close to madness, yet the mania also should be seen as heroic, ideal. In an earlier episode, Lonelyhearts recalled an incident from his adolescence with his younger sister in which "he had gone to the piano and begun a piece by Mozart.... His sister left her picture book to dance to his music. She had never danced before. She danced gravely and carefully, a simple dance, yet formal...." Though drunk in a speakeasy, Lonelyhearts is also having a vision: "swaying slightly to the remembered music, he thought of children dancing. Square replacing oblong and being replaced by circle. Every child, everywhere; in the whole world there was not one child who was not gravely, sweetly dancing." The attempt in this, as in the previously quoted passage, to give geometrical shape and a lyrical and symbolical ordering, Mozartean or Christian, aesthetic and religious, to our messy world serves high poignancy. And gross irony, since Lonelyhearts gets in an accidental bar brawl in the middle of his meditations, and the main real shaping is that his "anger swung in large drunken circles." He ends up gruesomely assaulting someone, beaten, hungover. Formal and sweet order can have little place in this world.

A psychologically forced ordering provides the substitute. Religion, in a view such as West's, provides some of the most ornate forms of a compulsion mania, as with hypnotically chanting the holy name (Jesus),[6] imposing on all the flotsam and jetsam of disintegrating reality the symbolic self-castrating form (a phallus become a cross), and shaping anxiety with a ritualized routine (the imitation of Christ). By the thirteenth chapter, after ragingly beating Fay Doyle in sexual revulsion (and perhaps for not responding to his guilty role-playing with the "love-fruit" of Christian rhetoric), Lonelyhearts retires to his bed for a purgative three days, living on crackers, water, cigarettes, and hysteria. In religious crisis and personal breakdown, he attempts to heighten the paralytic Christian humility he took on a few days earlier by identifying himself as the impervious "rock of faith." No longer responding with anger, sex, pity, thought, he wills but one thing in mad purity of heart, his compulsive rockness. Humility, as so often, has become hardness. In the extended play with the conceit of the rock, West suggests how self-demands based on compassionate sensitivity become its antithesis. Part of the technique here is to sympathetically see most of the compulsions from inside, from Lonelyhearts's viewpoint (as with most of the narration, with the early exception of the physical-religious description of him, and the late exception of Shrike's last party after Lonelyhearts leaves— both rather pat foreshadowing devices).

In one of Shrike's shrewd but flamboyantly self-parodying metaphors, Lonelyhearts has become a rock-head, a "swollen Mussolini of the soul." (Fascist dictator-poseur Mussolini had a very large, completely bald, and imperviously arrogant dome.) Lonelyhearts's caring self has become untouchable—it was only "his mind that was touched, the instrument with which he knew the rock"—so all subserves the compassionate mania to escape from compassion's suffering. His "rock of faith" extends the earlier "stone" of Shrike's advice: when your readers "ask for bread, don't give them crackers as does the Church, and don't, like the State, tell them to eat cake. Explain that man cannot live by bread alone.... Teach them to pray each morning, 'Give us this day our daily stone.'" Lonelyhearts's daily "stone that had formed in his gut" of moral anguish defensively becomes an all-consuming petrification disguised as faith. He can now desperately but blandly play the calm martyr with all his mockers, even masquerade as the charmingly conventional husband-to-be in advertising-and-suburb with Betty. The obsessional image protects him from all mere reality. "He did not feel guilty. He did not feel. The rock was a solidification of his feeling, his conscience, his sense of reality, his self-knowledge. He could have planned anything." With an amazing doubleness of empathy and mockery, West shows how the call to feeling and genuineness gets compulsively transposed into nonfeeling and masquerade.

In sympathetically savaging the Lonelyhearts mania, West also double plays the culminating religious experience. Back in his ascetic bed and desperation in the final chapter, Lonelyhearts's quest-compulsion reaches madness in which he "welcomed the arrival of fever. It promised heat and mentally unmotivated violence. The promise was soon fulfilled; the rock became a furnace." He is disassociating, a very sick man, and a mystic. The compulsion to order becomes hallucinatory. The decorative Christ figure on his wall becomes moving, animate, Lonelyhearts's "life and light," even apparently his pattern of nerves, as well as the "bright bait" for the dead fish things of this world. Then "the room was full of grace," and he becomes, heart and mind, the fresh "rose" of the mystic tradition of beatitude (and of feminine vulnerability to the masculine deity), and thus completes his "identification with God." The beatitude turns, of course, into a regressive oneness which denies all discrimination of reality and must be fatal.

As I read the Westean metaphors, drawn from the ecstatic Christian tradition, they are both earnest in their intensity and ironic in their jumbling (Christ is bait instead of fish; what the quester seeks is more feverish violence than true serenity; God becomes an approving editor). Lonelyhearts's compulsive imposition on himself of metaphors of divine order complete, he goes forth to impose them on the world, to embrace the crippled Peter (Doyle), the impotent phallus he has betrayed with his wife, arriving on the stairs to threaten Lonelyhearts with a gun to play-the-man in retaliating for the misunderstood beating of Fay Doyle. That, indeed, will be the "miracle" of love. Doyle, confusedly caught between the ecstatic Lonelyhearts he does not understand and the arrival of Betty, accidentally fires the gun, finishing off Lonelyhearts in the gratuitously grotesque way which is the only final order in this world. Compulsive manias, such as born-again religion, can only feverishly disguise the world until violence sunders all, returning the masquerade to the reality of suffering.

THE SOLACE OF FANTASY

Along the way of his quest for religious transformation, and the fatal masquerade of personal and social realities, Lonelyhearts tries a pastoral recuperation, a few days in the country with Betty, at her insistence. Returning from that, especially when they "reached the Bronx slums," he knew that she and nature "had failed to cure him" of his vision of human suffering and the need to answer it:

> Crowds of people moved through the street with a dreamlike violence. As he looked at their broken hands and torn mouths he was overwhelmed by the desire to help them, and because this desire was sincere, he was happy despite the feeling of guilt which accompanied it.
>
> He saw a man who appeared to be on the verge of death stagger into a movie theater that showed a picture called *Blonde Beauty*. He saw a ragged woman with an enormous goiter pick a love story magazine out of a garbage can and seem very excited by her find.
>
> Prodded by his conscience, he began to generalize. Men have always fought their misery with dreams. Although dreams were once powerful, they have been made puerile by the movies, radio and newspapers. Among many betrayals, this one is the worst.

This point about the violence implicit in ordinary suffering (the hyperbolic surreal images) is presented seriously. Since Lonelyhearts feels himself "capable of dreaming the Christ dream," once one of the most serious, he has a fervent stake in the solacing process, and, as a yellow journalism advice columnist, a guilty share in its corruption.

Dream-fantasies, whether of art (the preceding *The Dream Life of Balso Snell*) or of the American gospel of success (the following *A Cool Million*), dominate West's concern. *Miss Lonelyhearts* does not confine itself to the central Christian fantasy; it also surveys, as part of its imaginative argument, other dream escapes. The main vehicle for this is Lonelyhearts's editor, Shrike, a somewhat diabolical hysteric-cynic, a compulsive machine for making jokes—a not uncommon repressed type—who exacerbates the Christ-complex by making Lonelyhearts the butt of ornate parodies, though hardly more grotesque than the commonplace scene just quoted.[7] Shrike, too, insists on the fusion of the great dreams of the culture and the debasing media—the "Suzan Chesters, the Beatrice Fairfaxes and the Miss Lonelyhearts are the priests of twentieth-century America," which we might update with the whole range of nostrum peddlers of religiosity and psychiatry. Shrieking Shrike is the angry-hurt idealist about it.

And it is Shrike who, at the end of the opening chapter, mockingly dictates the start of an alternative column of advice: "*Art Is a Way Out.*" Eight chapters later, in a series of parody dream-escapes, Shrike proposes more personally to Lonelyhearts "Art! Be an artist or a writer. When you are cold, warm yourself before the flaming tints of Titian, when you are hungry, nourish yourself with great spiritual foods by listening to the noble periods of Bach ...," and so on through a nonsense purple-passage and Beethoven and Shakespeare as compensation for poverty and crippling. Thus West continues the mockeries of cultural pretension he presented with his *Balso Snell*, but now the psuedo-compensatory media culture is viewed, as in the earlier quote above, as gross "betrayal." The exploitative debasement so integral to most of modern culture-marketing has, as with the Christ dream, essentially destroyed the ideal possibility for both actor and audience. Thus we generally recognize that however important the fantasies, the religious, the romantics, the aesthetes, etc., do not really lead lives much different than the rest of us. The great cultural ideals come out as mere diversions, entertainments, psychic and moral masturbations. But is this the "worst" of all the many "betrayals" of our humanity? As his examples suggest, West further indicts the processed culture, the exploited fantasy, for a denial of actual reality, of authentic being. Religion, art, and other fantasies now become vicious masquerades in the deepest sense, denying recognition and change of the self and the world.

Denatured religion and art falsify all. So do the other fantasy-answers (though oddly West leaves out our processed politics). Shrike, in the same section as on art as a way out of actual miseries, also provides Lonelyhearts sick-a-bed with other burlesqued escape alternatives. The life of "the soil": "You are fed up with the city and its teeming millions. The ways and means of men, as getting and lending and spending ... are too much with you" and so you go back to the ancient rural ways and "sow and reap and chivy your kine, not kin or kind, between the pregnant rows of corn and taters. Your step becomes the heavy sexual step of a dance-drunk Indian and you tread the seed down into the female earth...." The hyped-up euphoniousness, the aslant allusions (including Wordsworth, Tolstoy, and Hart Crane), and the emphasis on sexual displacement are all heavily self-parodying. So, too, with escape to the South Seas: "You live in a thatch hut with the daughter of the king.... Her breasts are golden speckled pears, her belly a melon.... In the evening, on the blue lagoon, under the silvery moon, to your love you croon in the soft sylabelew and vocabelew ... and when a beautiful society girl comes to your hut ... you send her back to her yacht that hangs on the horizon like a nervous racehorse...." (Allusions here may include several pop songs of the period and a standard romantic movie formula.) Shrike concludes that the South Seas stuff is done with and that "there's little use in imitating Gauguin" anymore—just more arty masquerade. But let us "now examine Hedonism, or take the cash and let the credit go.... Then follows a cataloging of what we might now call "The *Playboy* Philosophy," with superficial doses of sports, stock vices, faddish paraphernalia, and trite culture ("You fornicate under pictures by Matisse and Picasso, and often you spend an evening beside the fireplace with Proust and an apple.") For your last party, "the table is a coffin carved for you by Eric Gill" (an early twentieth-century English craftsman of neo-medievalizing piety), and you finish with a speech: "'Life,' you say, is a club ... where they deal you only one hand and you must sit in. So even if the cards are cold and marked by the hand of fate ... play up like a gentleman and a sport. Get tanked, grab what's on the buffet, use the girls upstairs, but remember ... don't squawk." Shrike annotates for Lonelyhearts this parody (it may partly mock Hemingwayesque American he-man-stoicism) with "you haven't the money, nor are you stupid enough to manage it."

Then follows the parody of art as compensation and passing references to the options of suicide and drugs, concluding, "God alone is our escape. The Church is our only hope, the First Church of Christ Dentist, where He is worshipped as Preventer of Decay...." (While Christian Science provides the shape of the rhetoric, many varieties of faith-healing and escapist rhetoric are at issue, here and elsewhere.) Shrike finishes with a parodistic letter to J.C., the "Miss Lonelyhearts of Miss Lonelyhearts," decrying the difficulty of faith and life "in this day and age," and jokily begging for reassurance.

While this mockery of escapist fantasies has its points, the burlesque testifying to mass-culture vulgarization and exploitation, the manner seems a bit thick, too much in the style of collegiate humor, or *Saturday Night Live*, or certain stand-up comedians. It is an hysterically compulsive humor, a mechanical jokiness—as Lonelyhearts elsewhere comments on professional-journalist humor—out of control in pathetic disillusionment. While appropriate to Shrike in his sexual and moral hysteria (and also to part of the known character of Nathanael West), it is too shallow, too pat, to be really witty.

Shrike's "thick glove of words," typical to a stock type of compulsive joker, self-revealingly culminates in his role as Lonelyhearts's alter ego in his charade party, "Every man his own Miss Lonelyhearts." Also pathetically anxious sore-rubbing are Lonelyhearts's other desperate efforts at escapism—drunkenness, predatory sex, psychosomatic illness, violent outbursts. In his messy little effort at revenge against the tormenting Willie Shrike, he takes Mary Shrike to a nightclub, El Gaucho. He recognizes the phony romantic atmosphere as "part of the business of dreams," of the exploited fantasies of those "who wanted to write and live the life of an artist," or other fantasy modes of adventure, prowess, beauty, success, love— just variations on "those who wrote to Miss Lonelyhearts for help." Mary's insistent fantasized tales of her past and her heritage are just another sad effort at "something poetic" in a meanly empty life. With mechanical desperation, she would do anything to be "gay" (in the older sense)— "Everyone wants to be gay—unless they're sick"—in that saddest of all fantasy compulsions, the anxious search for a "good time." For Lonelyhearts, and the perceptive reader, such efforts can only heighten the "feeling of icy fatness."

Part of the persuasiveness, the seriousness, of the figure of Lonelyhearts comes from West giving him his own sharply intelligent sense of our fraudulent mass culture. Though West shortly later went to work in the Hollywood dream factory, his sense of the "betrayal" by sleazy romanticizing remained constant—the genuine evil which encourages masquerading.

To pursue romanticizing in a slightly different sense, West, in the chapter following Shrike's burlesque of the escape fantasies, "Miss Lonelyhearts in the country," has his protagonist try Betty's therapy of a few spring days with her at an unused farm, her childhood home in Connecticut. This pastoral interlude, which is also the only bit of affectionate sex in West, is more positive than any other scene. Even so, Lonelyhearts finds in a walk in the spring woods destructive entropy at work: "in the deep shade there was nothing but death—rotten leaves, gray and white fungi, and over everything a funereal hush." And even at Lonelyhearts's most vital moment, his copulating in the grass with virginal "little girl" Betty (thus seeing her, he escapes feminine power), he also notes that the small green leaves hung in the hot still day "like an army of little metal shields," and he heard a singing thrush sound like "a flute choked with saliva." While this may partly be understood as West's further characterization of Lonelyhearts's megapolitan morbidity even when in a pastoral love scene, I think it also typically reveals the Westean sensibility. No nature-romantic, he insistently, even incongruously, displays modernist sensibility in its concern with entropic mechanisms.

The pastoral-sexual peace, of course, can only be a regenerative interlude—that is the nature of pastoral—and one hardly answering the "Bronx slums," the letters witnessing horrible commonplace anguish, the betrayed culture, and the megapolitan malaise. A series of ironically surreal scenes in a "little park" in New York City reenforces the point with "waste land" imagery. The park was a self-parody of one, desolate, its ground "not the kind in which life generates," its "gray sky looked as if it had been rubbed with a soiled eraser. It held no angels, flaming crosses, olive-bearing doves, wheels within wheels. Only a newspaper struggled in the air like a kite with a broken spine." For Lonelyhearts, it is a dead land (properly marked by spineless media) but full of inhuman crucifying threats. As he walks through the park, even the shadow of a lamp post "pierced him like a spear." In another nightmarish extension of his anguished psyche in the park, looking toward a memorial obelisk he saw its "rigid shadow ... lengthening in rapid jerks"; looking at the monument itself, it "seemed red and swollen in the dying sun, as though it were about to spout a load of granite seed." Waiting another sexual rendezvous near the obelisk, "he examined the sky," with the continuation of the same metaphor he had been applying to a woman (a recurrent psychological point in West) "and saw that it was canvas covered and ill-stretched." Trying to fathom its unnaturalness, he "examined it like a detective who is searching for a clue to his own exhaustion." In the "tons of forced rock and tortured steel" that makes up the menacingly surrounding skyscrapers, he discovered his "clue." "Americans have dissipated their radical energy in an orgy of stone breaking ... hysterically, desperately, almost as if they knew the stones would some day break them." Lonelyhearts's tortured psyche reflects the hard hysterical reality, its revulsive stone becoming the rock that will break him. The park, like the dreams, provides no real solace, only frightening human constructs, stone city and stoned soul.[8]

The mechanically hard and violent order overwhelms all. The solacing fantasies of religion provide no exception. The obsessive Shrike produces a news clipping in a bar—"ADDING MACHINE USED IN RITUAL OF WESTERN SECT.... *Figures Will be Used for Prayers for Condemned Slayer of Aged Recluse. ...*" Dreams of hope have turned into mechanical bad jokes, media hypes like the Lonelyhearts column, willed and destructive hysteria like the Lonelyhearts "religious experience." They are also grotesquely irrelevant to most of actuality which West, with the pessimistic refusal of solace central to modernist sensibility, sees as harsh, random, breaking.

VIOLENT TROPES

One of the most striking characteristics of *Miss Lonelyhearts*, it should be evident, is the drastic metaphor, the shocking figure of speech. To note a few more. When Lonelyhearts's smug colleague Goldsmith smiled, he was "bunching his fat cheeks like twin rolls of smooth pink toilet paper." When the crippled Doyle hobbled across the barroom, "he made many waste motions, like that of a partially destroyed insect." When hostile-joker Shrike, whose "dead pan" face has been geometrically as well as punningly described, finishes his preliminary seduction speech (religious parody, of course) to a Miss Farkis, he "buried his triangular face like the blade of a hatchet in her neck." Later, when the hysterically joking Shrike tries to persuade the near-catatonic Lonelyhearts, now rocklike in faith, to play one of his mocking games, he "was a gull trying to lay an egg in the smooth flank of a rock, a screaming, clumsy gull." When Lonelyhearts despairingly looks out the window after failing to polish off his column (partly because his religious rhetoric is too drippingly artificial to even be convincing to himself), a "slow spring rain was changing the dusty tar roofs below him to shiny patent leather ... slippery ... he could find no support for either his eyes or his feelings." Often surrealistically hyper-lucid and extreme, the tropes resonate with the themes of mechanical artifice, hysterical masquerade, and violent breakdown.

A number of West's metaphors are extended, in the sense of seventeenth-century poetic conceits. Bemusedly, we hear gross Fay Doyle undressing in the dark for sex: "She made sea sounds; something flapped like a sail; there was the creak of ropes; then he heard the wave-against-a-wharf smack of rubber on flesh. Her call for him to hurry was like a sea-moan, and when he lay beside her, she heaved, tidal, moon driven." And then, as they say of comic routines, the topper: "Some fifteen minutes later, he crawled out of bed like an exhausted swimmer leaving the surf...." (Some critics, again missing the mockery and West's double play, have earnestly misread the metaphoric point as sexual vitality or the maternal sea, but most of West's maritime figures are negative, here and elsewhere, ironic play with the inhuman and gratuitous.)

Some figures more slyly continue. When Lonelyhearts fails to communicate with the embittered Doyles though he has hysterically poured out his Christian-love message (ironically, a parody of Shrike's parodies), he "felt like an empty bottle, shiny and sterile." Half a dozen paragraphs later, his message totally misunderstood by the lascivious and voracious Fay, she attempts to sexually arouse him and he "felt like an empty bottle that is being slowly filled with warm, dirty water." He finally overflows with violent rage.

The elaboration of metaphors, whether of the psyche-stone-skyscraper-city-religious-rock, of the compulsive metaphysic of geometrical and symbolic shapes, of Lonelyhearts phallic fears, breast fixations and homoerotic confusions, or of the parodistic images of media romanticism and debased religiosity, heightens, incises, almost takes over the fiction. Highly artful work, we can certainly believe the reports that West rewrote and rewrote *Miss Lonelyhearts* with a rather un-American sense of craft quite antithetical to the vulgar romanticism of pouring out warmly dirty "self-expression." Curiously, he countered "confessional" subject matter—the dream life of the artist, religious conversion, fantasy-dominated people—with rigorous craft. Almost uniquely in his time and place, West combined self-conscious strict artistry with intense immediate concern.

Some of that self-consciousness deserves further emphasis. West's writing shows an exacerbated visual imagination, beyond his evident fascination with painting, especially surrealism. The hyper-lucid visualization organizes, disciplines, objectifies the concern with extreme subjectivity. Aesthetically, no doubt, West is heir to the symbolists' "correspondences" (Baudelaire), the modernist Anglo-American poets' "objective correlative" (Eliot), and the surrealists' disjunctive images of "dream lucidity" (Breton). But those are pedantic considerations. More interestingly, the self-conscious tropes do something else; they carry out and reenforce the dominant issue of self-consciousness, which is what forces the masquerading. I have noted a few instances in which Lonelyhearts, for all his sincere anguish, is so aware of what he is doing that he has taken on a pose, actor's gestures, a willed role. Even his final desperate escape from consciousness and role-playing by hysteria and hallucination seems incomplete, yet more wilful masquerading. Still another example: in one of his most sincere conversations with fiancée Betty, Lonelyhearts plays what he acknowledges to be a "trick" in speech; "he stumbled purposely, so that she would take his confusion for honest feeling." Ironically, she is too simple and sincere to be taken in. Of course part of Lonelyhearts's difficulty in role-playing here (and with Mary Shrike and Fay Doyle) comes, as I noted earlier, from hostility to women and ambiguous homoeroticism. But it clearly goes beyond that. His self-induced hysterical conversion experience attempts to break through his tormenting self-consciousness in costuming as Miss Lonelyhearts. If he can only become the true believer, the ultimate Miss Lonelyhearts, J.C., he can become real and one, transcend the masquerade.

This I take to be West's crux. Whether Lonelyhearts holds Doyle's hand as expression of compassion, pursues sex, advises the lovelorn, plans the future with Betty, or withdraws to his rock of faith, he is, as an examination of each scene will show, role-playing, masquerading. The ills of such divided consciousness, and the consequent forced pretending of a role, apply, of course, to Lonelyhearts's alter ego, Shrike, and his ornate joking, gaming, parodies. The "acting" also applies to others, even the inchoate simple cripple Doyle (his pretense at a leering manner in the speakeasy, his playing "dog" for his wife, his later playing the injured husband). Lonelyhearts also applies the point to the disillusioned tough-guy pretenses of the other reporters in the speakeasy. They return the perception by seeing Lonelyhearts's religiousness as put on, made up, "too damn literary." In both details and style West ironically confirms their point. One of Lonelyhearts's colleagues notes that even if the character were to achieve "a genuine religious experience, it would be personal," only, and thus end up "meaningless," incomprehensible, which in fact it does. Another replies that the trouble with Lonelyhearts, "the trouble with all of us, is that we have no outer life, only an inner one, and that by necessity." Then the reporters turn back to compulsively defensive jokes as usual disguises for their irrelevant feelings. But that division between inner and outer life, between human feeling and the compulsive order surrounding it, remains central throughout the novella as the condition of anguished self-consciousness and consequent role-playing—theirs, Shrike's, Lonelyhearts's, and not least the oh-so-self-consciously artful author's. Our world violates us and we escape into unreality.

Miss Lonelyhearts is also full of small and large violence; stylistically as well as dramatically.[9] Violence marks the essential breaking out of self-consciousness and through the masquerade, a desperate assertion against alienation, helplessness, inauthenticity. In his final effort toward religious experience, as I previously noted, Lonelyhearts explicitly wants "unmotivated violence" to restore life to the dead world. And he gets it. Earlier, despairingly drinking and thinking of sex, he summarizes: "Only friction could make him warm or violence make him mobile." And in yet another passage, he notes of himself: "With the return of self-consciousness, he knew that only violence could make him supple."

Alive, "mobile," "supple"—these are, in the biblical phrase, the difference between "the quick and the dead." West, preoccupied with violence in all his works, which he presents as quintessentially American, serves it as the assertion of life against suffering: as when Lonelyhearts recalls accidentally stepping on a frog, and then frenziedly eliminating its misery by crushing it, or when he smashed with a stone the misbutchered lamb, or when he twists and twists the arm of "the clean old man," or when his suffering over his failure of charity with the Doyles turns to his ragingly beating Fay, or when his guilty misery over Betty turns to giving her pain ("like a kitten whose soft helplessness makes one ache to hurt it"), or when his compassion for the hurt in the lovelorn letters turns to rage, or when his own total misery leads to the violent denial of himself. This violently hallucinatory denial of all reality is the destructive religious fallacy. Violence becomes the crucial assertion through suffering of life, only to end as its final masquerade, death.

Among the masquerades which West pursues, one of the most violating tropes, of course, is the entitling one—the hysterical need for the ultimate Miss Lonelyhearts. That savage metaphor for Christianity is truly violent to the heritage, a really "sick" joke. I suppose that in a vestigially Christian culture it should be offensive to many—if they do not willfully misread or disguise their responses—perhaps even more so than the fervent blasphemy in D.H. Lawrence's *The Man Who Died* (a novella written not long before *Miss Lonelyhearts*) where a Christ copulates on an altar with a priestess. Perhaps West's more cynical fiction also offends more supposedly tolerant folk, those from the likes of William James (*Varieties of Religious Experience* was one of West's acknowledged sources) to current agnostics. These would grant that religious fervors have a decently pragmatic side; it is nice to believe: it may help one feel good, or bear the world, or endure suffering, or "get through the night," or add other poetic flavor to existence. Nonsense. For from the Westean view, they may discover that the joke is on them. Betraying self-consciousness and inauthentic role-playing will result in a cosmic pratfall.

While West may be no more sardonically atheistic in his savaging of religious grotesquery than some of his fine artistic contemporaries (for example, Céline or Buñuel), he leaves no room for displaced piety. The role-playing religious order madly violates the (dis)ordering that is. Religion, by the same logic with which it provides acceptance or solace, anesthetizes the essential human and defeats the actual. Instead of answering misery, despair, unmerited suffering, suicide, religion often creates them. To be "born again," as was Miss Lonelyhearts, is to be dead—and quite literally—to the truth. It destroys him, hurts others, answers nothing. Faith is a grotesque disease, however much we are aware, as West was, of the poignant imperatives to it. To falsely order suffering takes the heart out of the human, which would better remain lonely in its unacceptable universe. That is the unmasqueraded message of *Miss Lonelyhearts*.

Miss Lonelyhearts is an exceptionally intense very short novel, yet in the fundamental sense Nathanael West's largest work. Appropriately to its time of depression disillusion (perhaps *the* twentieth-century revelation, so far, that the American system doesn't work), and to its place as a somewhat marginal American's response to the mainline mythologies (Menckenism cum brilliance?), it is a compassionately savage piece of iconoclasm. At the level of stock cultural history, I suppose it can be viewed as combining the zesty art of negation that partly characterized the 1920s with some of the more grimly sordid realities of the following time. As with many of the more interesting achievements in literary history, it does not quite categorize and can be viewed in later perspective as a document of cultural "transition." It seems to precariously fuse two kinds of sensibility—a "hinge" work—with

both the artful modern expressiveness of the period after the Great War and
the depressed social actualities of the following period—a literary flying fish.

But more importantly, *Miss Lonelyhearts* may be *sui generis*, a striking
literary act intriguing in its very exceptionalness for both the times and the
author. West's novella may be one of those unique works (one thinks of
others by Laclos, Corbière, Lermontov, Zamiatin, Melville, and Hart Crane)
which stands beyond its genesis, beyond its author—a one-time only
achievement, the small odd masterpiece. Indeed, to continue a discussion of
West beyond *Miss Lonelyhearts* must have more than a little of the tone of
anticlimax. West was never again to achieve such shaping intensity. *Miss
Lonelyhearts* might thus be said to overreach its author as well as times,
arriving at that kind of impersonality which certain self-contained works
seem to acquire. The "Miss Lonelyhearts" paradigm, as it were, remains a
permanent expressive accounting of the religious masquerade, and its
relentless unmasking.

NOTES

1. *Miss Lonelyhearts* in *The Complete Works of Nathanael West* (New York, 1957), pp.
63–140. For West's periodical versions of some of the chapters, see the primary
bibliography, below, and for comparison with the books, see Carter A. Daniel, "West's
Revisions of *Miss Lonelyhearts*," *Studies in Bibliography* 16 (1963): 232–43.

2. I am not, of course, suggesting that all homosexualities are pathological. As my
colleague Karl Keller expertly points out, the Lonelyhearts problem is less homosexuality
than the denial of it. The homosexuality issues have been much disputed in the criticism.
Early on, Stanley Edgar Hyman made a more or less traditional Freudian diagnosis of
Lonelyhearts's Oedipal condition, *Nathanael West* (Minneapolis, 1962), pp. 22–23. Victor
Comerchero extended this in *Nathanael West, The Ironic Prophet*, pp. 84 ff. Randall Reid
caught them out in overreadings (after all, we have almost nothing about the protagonist's
early life), but in throwing out the critics' Freudian literalism he also foolishly threw out
the crucial sexual ambivalence (*The Fiction of Nathaniel West*, pp. 73 ff). Others have
followed Reid in denying the obvious, such as Miles D. Orvell, "The Messianic Sexuality
of Miss Lonelyhearts," *Studies in Short Fiction* 10 (Spring 1973): 159–67. The fullest
discussion is James W. Hickey, "Freudian Criticism and *Miss Lonelyhearts*," in *Nathanael
West*, ed. David Madden, pp. 111–50. While he makes some interesting points, he
essentially reduces the figure to an "hysteric-schizophrenic"; this undermining of larger
human relevance in the art is, of course, characteristic of thorough-going Freudian
criticism. Perhaps most importantly, Lonelyhearts's sexual ambivalence takes
sadomasochistic displacements, including Christianity.

3. I am here elaborating the doubleness I noted in an earlier essay (1967). West, in
"Some Notes on Miss L" (1933), had defined the fiction as "the portrait of a priest of our
time who has a religious experience. His case is classical and is built on all the cases in
James's *Varieties of Religious Experience and Starbuck's Psychology of Religion*" (reprinted in
White, *Nathanael West*, p. 166). I suspect that West was defending himself against his
protagonist being taken as a mere freak. The saint/psychotic doubleness is spelled out in
terms of the sources (primarily James) by Marcus Smith, "Religious Experience in *Miss*

Lonelyhearts," *Contemporary Literature* 9 (Spring 1968): 172–88. On the other hand, there are those, from James Light on, who ignore the pathological and take the Christianity too literally, such as Thomas M. Lorch declaring that Lonelyhearts "goes to his death in the fullness of Christian faith, charity and hope" ("Religion and Art in *Miss Lonelyhearts,*" *Renascence* 20 [Autumn 1967]: 13). See also his "West's *Miss Lonelyhearts*: Skepticism Mitigated?" *Renascence* 18 (Winter 1966): 99–109, which dismisses West's mockery of Catholic mysticism (as in the opening Shrike parody prayer using Loyola's "Spiritual Exercises") and also denies the Jamesian influence. Little better, of course, are readings which take a purely pathological emphasis, as in Gerald B. Nelson's erroneous and hyped-up "Lonelyhearts," in *Ten Versions of America* (New York, 1972), pp. 77–90. Others have more sensibly taken some double view of the protagonist, within the atheistic context, as with Mike Frank, "The Passion of Miss Lonelyhearts According to Nathanael West," *Studies in Short Fiction* 10 (Winter 1973): 67–73. There are some good comments on the human incompleteness of all the characters and the resulting manias in Roger D. Abrahams, "Androgynes Bound: Nathanael West's *Miss Lonelyhearts,*" in *Seven Contemporary Authors*, ed. Thomas B. Whitbread (Austin, 1966), pp. 49–72.

4. I analyzed *Notes from Underground*, and also related it to the Lonelyhearts atheistic analogue, in my *Edges of Extremity: Some Problems of Literary Modernism* (Tulsa, Okla., 1980).

5. West's double plays on "order" are also sometimes misunderstood. Robert D. Richards, Jr., thinks that West is praising the desire for order when he is exposing it as a compulsion in a universe lacking any human, and humane, order ("Miss Lonelyhearts," *University Review* 33 [December 1966]: 151–57).

6. I am suggesting a word change for West here; my researches indicate that in the 1930s, as well as the present, Christian hysterics did not chant "Christ" or "Jesus Christ," as West has it, but the more personal (and erotic?) "Jesus." Is this a Jewish slip? Some of West's aslant Jewishness appears in the pastoral chapter where the man at the "Aw-Kum-On Garage" in rural Connecticut "said there was still plenty of deer at the pond because no yids ever went there. He said it wasn't the hunters who drove out the deer but the yids." Some displaced mocking Jewish touches may include *shiksa* Betty's belief in therapeutic soup and the fearful fascination with Christian lunacy.

7. Many critical discussions overdo the wickedness of Shrike, though he is but a pathetic and hysterical alter ego of Lonelyhearts (speeches given to Shrike were originally given to Lonelyhearts in the earlier versions published as periodical stories). In the overall Westean pattern, Shrike stands as one of a series of faltering verbal-sadistic clowns, a masquerader gone compulsive. J.A. Ward suggests that Shrike derives from Groucho Marx, for whom West's brother-in-law Perelman wrote scripts ("The Hollywood Metaphor: The Marx Brothers, S.J. Perelman, and Nathanael West," *Southern Review* 12 (July 1976): 659–72). Mary Shrike may also be viewed as a painfully comic automation in her fantasy spiels, sexual teases, and "mechanical" appearance (a "tight, shiny dress that was like glass-covered steel"), a parody mechanism of lascivious frigidity.

8. West's urban "waste land" is even more barren than the more "optimistic" one of Eliot's poem suggested Edmond L. Volpe in a series of loose comparisons ("The Waste Land of Nathanael West," *Renascence* 13 (1961): 61–77). Incidentally, Volpe interprets the two narrative shifts away from the protagonist as a faltering in West's feelings, but I think they may be more simply explainable as somewhat awkward plot devices used to reinforce the ironic failures of communication.

9. In a brief piece written in the same period, West insists "In America violence is idiomatic." Much ahead of the more general consciousness of the centrality of violence to

the American psyche, he simply refers it to our realities and our media fare ("Some Notes on Violence" (1933), reprinted in White, *Nathanael West*, pp. 162–64). For a detailed discussion of the psychodrama of violence with Lonelyhearts, with repressed sensory responses leading to aimless aggression which becomes regressive self-destruction, see Lawrence DiStasi, "Aggression in Miss Lonelyhearts: Nowhere to Throw the Stone," *Nathanael West*, ed. Madden, pp. 83–101. He informed me that the argument could be understood as a Marcusean dialectic about pseudo-sublimation in a deceitfully controlling cultural order.

MARK CONROY

Letters and Spirit in
Miss Lonelyhearts

I. INTRODUCTION: THE SCENE OF TYPING

An advice-to-the-lovelorn columnist whose advice is often worse than no advice, and who knows it, has many reasons to want to escape into daydream. This pastor's son has as his most significant dream that of salvation through, and ultimately as, Jesus Christ. But before that consumes his life, there are smaller dreams, and although their goal is to take him out of an imprisonment, they often return him there more forcibly. In Nathanael West's novel *Miss Lonelyhearts*, all the title character's dreams, all his forms of escape, have a way of doing that.

One of the strongest dreams occurs as Miss Lonelyhearts, in typical paralysis before the newsroom typewriter where he produces his columns, sits and thinks instead of a desert:

> A desert ... not of sand, but of rust and body dirt, surrounded by a back-yard fence on which are posters describing the events of the day.... Inside the fence Desperate, Broken-hearted, Disillusioned-with-tubercular-husband and the rest were gravely forming the letters MISS LONELYHEARTS out of white-washed clam shells, as if decorating the lawn of a rural depot.[1]

From *The University of Windsor Review*, vol. 17, no. 1 (Fall–Winter 1982). © 1982 The University of Windsor Review.

"Desperate," "Broken-hearted" and the rest are of course the letter writers that send queries to his columns; but their names are monikers created by and for the newspaper, and the fence that rings them in with the day's events is the newspaper itself: that which imprisons both the columnist and the readers, and binds them to one another. They exist for him only through their letters, he for them only in his replies. Yet not content with the stories these characters invent for themselves, he invents his *own* for them. In his story, they spell out his name as an object of worship—which means, ironically, that they are as much Miss Lonelyhearts' creators as his dupes. In dreaming his readers' dreams of him, Miss Lonelyhearts realizes that their dreams allow "Miss Lonelyhearts" to exist as a name, and its bearer to pursue his trade.

Paradoxically, this scene recalls him to his task; after all, the readers' faith in his name requires Miss Lonelyhearts to help them form its letters by forming his own letters. His typing, however, is again interrupted:

> He could not go on with it and turned again to the imagined desert where Desperate, Broken-hearted and the others were still building his name. They had run out of sea shells and were using faded photographs, soiled fans, time-tables, playing cards, broken toys, imitation jewellery—junk that memory had made precious, far more precious than anything the sea might yield. (26)

The column, it appears, consists of the mutual effort of writer and reader to construct a saving name, not from nature but from the runic fragments of discourse and human fabrication: timetables, photographs, playing cards. The name they build must somehow yield the meaning of the junk of its decay.

The prospects for genuine redemption, as opposed to temporary balm, are not good, though, because Miss Lonelyhearts soon has another dream of detritus, and here it is *he* who does the forming, not his readers. His daydream features the cultural remnants similar to those of the earlier dreams. He finds himself "in the window of a pawnshop full of fur coats, diamond rings, watches ... the paraphernalia of suffering" (30). They are not such in themselves, certainly, but only by virtue of their situation in the pawnshop. Still, Miss Lonelyhearts, sensing a "tropism for disorder" among these objects, joins battle with chaos:

> First he formed a phallus of old watches and rubber boots, then a heart of umbrellas and trout flies.... But nothing proved definitive and he began to make a gigantic cross. When the cross

became too large for the pawnshop, he moved it to the shore of the ocean. (31)

This dream, parallel with the first, makes it clear that Miss Lonelyhearts is a Miss Lonelyhearts reader. Like the others, he uses the "paraphernalia of suffering" of a pawnshop to erect a variety of symbols by which the suffering can be redeemed: a project for forming legible meaning from the spoor of failure. He carries his readers' projects of redemptions back to the life-giving sea, in an attempt to transcend the desert of the newspaper office; and his way of getting there begins with a sexual symbol and ends with a religious one—a development that will be seen to mime that of the book as a whole. Whether in practice he ever actually gets to the life-giving sea of renewal we explore below.

In addition to the fact that Miss Lonelyhearts' way of retrieving meaning from cultural debris is the same as his readers', the setting is also very similar, the pawnshop suggesting the newspaper office as did the fenced-in desert. This columnist's fantasy visions, whether of his readers' attempts to give meaning to their suffering or his own, can only exist within the prison of the newspaper office. He can be a saviour, they a faithful flock, only insofar as the paper allows both to exist linguistically, as words. Indeed, whenever Miss Lonelyhearts confronts his readers in the flesh, the results are disastrous.

The pawnshop image itself is a clue as to why this dream may well end in disaster. A pawnshop is a place where its customers' misfortunes are exploited for money, just as the Miss Lonelyhearts column has its origin as a cynical circulation gimmick, where his replies to his readers' problems are cruel jokes that function as further posters on the fence of the desert. Thus does every attempt to escape this doomed condition return Miss Lonelyhearts all the more forcibly to it.

II. THE WORLD ACCORDING TO SHRIKE: ORIGIN AS PARODY

The dreams may be Miss Lonelyhearts' invention, but his column is not. It is the brainchild of the newspaper's city editor, Willie Shrike, to whom Miss Lonelyhearts owes his name (and so his identity); and like his name, the words he writes are not his, though he writes them, owes his existence to them. His first reply in the novel, in fact, is dictated by Shrike:

"'*Art is a Way Out.*

"'Do not let life overwhelm you. When the old paths are choked with the debris of failure, look for newer and fresher paths. Art is just such a path. Art is distilled from suffering ...

"'For those who have not the talent to create, there is appreciation ...'" (4)

It is ironic that Shrike emphasizes Miss Lonelyhearts' bondage by dictating a letter that speaks of a spurious "way out" through suffering; doubly ironic that he dictates a recommendation of the saving, creative power of art. It is a complete perversion of the "personal expression" in language that not only Miss Lonelyhearts but also his colleagues and his boss once believed in

> At college, and perhaps for a year afterwards, they had believed in literature, had believed in Beauty and in personal expression as an absolute end. When they lost this belief, they lost everything. Money and fame meant nothing to them. They were not worldly men.

At the newspaper they are as far removed from personal expression as possible; the relentless mechanism of the paper and its cynical relation to its audience are personified by Shrike, and the other newspapermen are the objects of his sinister ventriloquism: "Like Shrike, the man they imitated, they were machines for making jokes. A button machine makes buttons, no matter what the power used, foot, steam or electricity. They, no matter what the motivating force, death, love or God, made jokes" (15). They all imitate Shrike as machines would, but Shrike himself is a kind of mechanism: all are caught in the infernal machine of the paper.

Miss Lonelyhearts' project is to forge from this empty language the possibility of genuine redemption: if the cynical fictions he is required to write are actively taken over by the writer, then perhaps they will be rendered true. The relentless machine of the typewriter must be sublated, and the Promethean pen must replace subservience before the typewriter (where an earlier draft of this novel has a bemused Miss Lonelyhearts mention he composed his first love letters!).[2] If the joke can, by a change of intention, cease to be a joke, then the writer's pledges can be redeemed along with the suffering of his readers, in the same way that the paraphernalia of suffering in a pawnshop can be redeemed.

That this change of heart might not succeed in reversing the columnist's role from victim to saviour is clear from another dream, related to those above, where Miss Lonelyhearts is a magician who makes doorknobs flower and speak at his command. But when it comes time to "lead his audience in prayer," ventriloquism once again intervenes: "But no matter how hard he struggled, his prayer was one Shrike had taught him and his voice was that of a conductor calling stations" (9). Not only Miss Lonelyhearts' language but also the circumstances in which he enunciates it are determined by Shrike (or rather, by the same cynical exigencies that determine Shrike's behaviour). However sincere, his prayers come out as Shrike has dictated them.

Shrike constantly refers to the need for the circulation to multiply; Goldsmith, one of Shrike's imitators, tells Miss Lonelyhearts to respond to a sexually frustrated letter writer by determining to "get the lady with child and increase the potential circulation of the paper" (26). The reproduction of life is to serve the newspaper rather than vice versa. And indeed the general pattern in this text is that the manic productivity of civilization has produced no spiritual regeneration. The protagonist sees the explosion of productivity that produced the city as destructive frenzy: "an orgy of stonebreaking," he calls it. And the existing civilization is the stone that "would someday break them [i.e., the Americans]" (27). Many of Miss Lonelyhearts' readers have also been financially and psychologically broken by the repetitive activity of the economic system; one thinks of Doyle the cripple, and also, inevitably, of the text's 1932 publication date.

Miss Lonelyhearts, then, is broken like the readers of his columns, but over his typewriter, not the wheel. The same mechanism that can reproduce language to infinity without sympathy or even comprehension adheres to Shrike's own discourse, machinelike letter without spirit. Shrike's name is already, of course, a parodic anagram for "Christ," but he is not sufficiently demonic to be an anti-christ: he is at best, as one of the chapters calls him, a dead Pan.[3] The nickname works on two levels, since in Shrike one finds the incarnation of the boundless capacity for parody and joke-telling founded on the failure of Eros. If his practical jokes seem to have an air of the sadistic, this should not be surprising; they are used as compensation for the lack of true sexual power, in a pattern that Miss Lonelyhearts also imitates (at least at first). Shrike's relation to his wife bears out this sadistic hint: unable to please her himself, he still maintains dominion over her, in a parody of the male role. As Mary Shrike tells Miss Lonelyhearts:

> "Do you know why he lets me go out with other men? To save
> money. He knows that I let them neck me and when I get home
> all hot and bothered, why he climbs into my bed and begs for it.
> The cheap bastard!" (22)

Shrike's lovemaking at best pleases himself at the expense of frustrating both his wife and her other men; and it is a question whether it even pleases Shrike. ("Sleeping with her is like sleeping with a knife in one's groin," he tells Miss Lonelyhearts (21).) Shrike's victimage and his glib rhetoric are of a piece, and his sadistic ironies shield his own impotence.

In taking out Shrike's wife, Miss Lonelyhearts indulges in a bit of sadism himself; one suspects the real quarry here is Shrike rather than Mary. But the columnist becomes a part of the scheme whereby Shrike, in his own inadequacy, victimizes others in turn. As Miss Lonelyhearts attempts to "drag Mrs. Shrike to the floor," she demands to be released: "Then he heard footsteps ... the door opened and Shrike looked into the corridor. He had on only the top of his pajamas" (24). It seems that even in his off hours, Miss Lonelyhearts still works for Shrike, is still his victim.

This sadism has as its condition the unredemptive, unregenerative sexuality that is imaged in the text by various distortions of nature: "... there were no signs of spring. The decay that covered the surface of the mottled ground was not the kind in which life generates" (5). The Eliotic wasteland imagery has been remarked by other critics, and the title character in this text bears some resemblance to Eliot's Fisher King.[4] One could even say that Shrike is a walking wasteland of cultural detritus, though that fact indicates some of the difference between West's world and Eliot's. Whereas in Eliot the reclamation of the Indo-European cultural heritage would revivify the wasteland with the "peace which passeth understanding," West by contrast presents a universe where that attempt has already fallen under the ban of Shrike's sterile parody. Though the iconography remain, it cannot inspire the belief of other times. The fragments Miss Lonelyhearts has shored against his ruin are themselves already ruins.

The fact that the culture is decaying would explain the decay Miss Lonelyhearts finds in his urban park near the office: the little park that he says needs a drink. For all his girlfriend Betty's conviction that his problems are city problems, their weekend in Connecticut confronts images that partake of the city park: "Although spring was well advanced, in the deep shade there was nothing but death—rotten leaves, gray and white fungi, and over everything a funeral hush" (38).

To bring renewal to this decay, Miss Lonelyhearts wishes his readers would "water the soil with their tears. Flowers would then spring up, flowers that smelled of feet" (5). This comic image is an ironical use of what like the sea are potent symbols of regeneration. The agent of this flowering is his readers' tears, suffering its own means of redemption. Indeed, the park vision in its essence is feminine: not only because of the Mary Magdalene image of tears and feet, but also because it is initiated by the "shadow of a lamp-post" that pierces him "like a spear" (4). But this confusion is a part of his dilemma: how to make passive suffering the agent of overcoming. The appeal of Christ as a model for this *via negativa* is obvious, and upon returning from

Connecticut Miss Lonelyhearts endeavours to propose the Christ vision explicitly, but cannot: "He snatched the paper out of the machine. With him, even the word Christ was a vanity." (39)

Christ's name is early on identified with the redemptive power of language: "... something stirred in him when he shouted the name of Christ, something secret and enormously powerful" (8). He also figures the triumph of the soul through suffering, of course; and Miss Lonelyhearts hopes that his linguistic bondage to the repetitive dead language of the paper will yield redemptive discourse not only because his own suffering makes him similar to his readers, but also because remorse over his own complicity in their exploitation will bring the necessary humility to accept the mystical solution. If those two reasons sound contradictory, they are; but both spring equally from a situation of writing that breeds suffering equal to that of his correspondents. Still, it is his complicity in the initial exploitation that keeps Miss Lonelyhearts from really fusing with his readers; true, he suffers as his readers do, but for him suffering is indissociable from guilt. The readers are unknowing victims, but the columnist is knowing: a party to his own exploitation, and to the same extent, that of his readers. His female name expresses the predicament: he is the perpetrator of a hoax, but also a passive sufferer under it.

The price, then, of bondage to Shrike is an emasculated language which increasingly takes over Miss Lonelyhearts' life. The fraudulent discourse becomes its own curse after a while. (As mentioned earlier, his colleagues are also riddled with self-contempt. The revealing exchange where various newspapermen at the speakeasy fantasize "gang bangs" of famous women novelists is fitting, since for a woman to attain something of their own forsaken ideal of personal expression must be further unwanted proof of their linguistic emasculation!) The glib rhetoric and endless punning of Shrike signify the same impotence as that displayed by the readers with their "inarticulate and impotent" (18), and ungrammatical, letters. His abdication of any true self-expression is the precondition for Shrike's sterile patter. In a way, the empty articulateness of Shrike or Miss Lonelyhearts is more severe a condition than the words of the letter writers, or the balletic hands of Doyle as they shadow forth his suffering. At the least, they give some voice to grief. Shrike, by contrast, manages this only once, in evoking the true hell of life with Mary. But both glibness and inarticulateness contain formidable latent aggressions, as becomes clear below.

Miss Lonelyhearts is different from Shrike in that he wishes to break through glibness and cliché to some ideal of authentic speech. When he attempts such speech, though, his tongue becomes a "fat thumb" (11). Like his readers, he loses the ability to articulate his thoughts at precisely the moment when they are most important to him: as he is explaining to Betty his position on the newspaper and his attitude toward it. He begins to "shout at her, accompanying his shouts with gestures [that resemble] those of an old-fashioned actor" (12). This scene is repeated later when he is at home with Betty, and Betty advises him to stop "making a fool of yourself" by avoiding his job. He replies with his own Miss Lonelyhearts story, told in the third person, recapitulating his absurd vocation to the point where he "discovers that his correspondents take him seriously. For the first time in his life, he is forced to examine the values by which he lives. This examination shows him that he is the victim of the joke and not its perpetrator" (32). Though more articulate than his first attempt, it is still blunted on Betty ("he saw that Betty still thought him a fool" (32)).

Like his dreams, the story he tells Betty is an approach to his predicament. He is not usually in the position of asking for advice or expressing suffering, as he here does; more typically he gives advice or alleviates suffering (in theory). The column begins as exploitation disguised as service; but his encounter with his victims as individuals gives his own culpability some clarity. This is why his formulation that he is victim and not perpetrator could be amended; he is both victim *and* perpetrator, indeed victim *insofar* as perpetrator.

Ironically, this figure is seen by Shrike as a priest of twentieth-century America (44); his characteristic posture is that of hearing confession. In a society where failure is sin, advice for its banishment is absolution. But if Miss Lonelyhearts could genuinely absolve his readers with healing speech, his own pain would be removed along with theirs. The trouble is that the remedy has been poisoned before the fact by its origin as parody. Much as he mocks Betty's belief that all evil is sickness to be cured ("No morality, only medicine" (13)), her medicinal approach is not far from his own naivete in assuming that words infused with the proper spirit can heal.

When Miss Lonelyhearts tries to transmit his own belief in the efficacy of suffering for redemption, he becomes inarticulate like his readers, but in his case it takes the form of the slick rhetoric of the column. His readers' tongue-tied sincerity wars against the cynical patter of Shrike, producing a strange combination. He sees it at one point as owing to his avoidance of Christ: "... he had failed to tap the force in his heart and had merely written a column for his paper" (49). Yet when he tries to bring up Christ at the Doyles', the results are even worse: "This time he had failed still more miserably. He had substituted the rhetoric of Shrike for that of Miss Lonelyhearts" (50). The figure of Shrike and the column provide the measure of his failure to give genuine healing through speech. It is not that his hysterical speeches to the Doyles are not sincere, just that their form has already been inscribed by the pen (or typewriter) of Shrike's paper. When the columnist attempts to play his savior-role straight, the conventions within which he must do it—determined by the newspaper's management and ratified, despite the falsity of those conventions, by the readers—betrays the pathos of that role. When he tries to legitimate his false role toward his audience, it becomes only more false. This is the paradox concealed in the fact that it is only when he understands that he is being *taken seriously* by his letter writers that he realizes he is also the victim of the joke he has helped to perpetrate.

III. STAGES ON MISS LONELYHEARTS' WAY

Given this understanding of his own position as a writer addressing an audience under false pretenses, is there a pattern to Miss Lonelyhearts' attempts to work through the predicament that haunts his dreams, daydreams and language?

The fitful alternation between frantic activity and catatonic passivity in the character of Miss Lonelyhearts has been noted by others.[5] Some have traced this trait to that psychology associated with hysteria, that "snake whose scales are tiny mirrors in which the dead world takes on a semblance of life" (9). The violent imagery of West seems to support this view.[6] One of the commentators on *Miss Lonelyhearts*, Randall Reid, has pointed out that the febrile imagery is not only indicative of the protagonist's hysterical state, but also of a genuine state of affairs; so what Reid calls hysteria, and what we might call passive-aggressive behaviour, reflects Miss Lonelyhearts' imprisonment in a situation that requires him to parody a redeemer's role.[7] We argue that it is his status as a writer that compels his behaviour: behaviour which oscillates between passive withdrawal and active delusion in an attempt to transcend an enforced false relationship with his readership. Roughly speaking, there are five stages that lead up to the protagonist's final ironic apotheosis:

1. Anger at his impotence in the face of Shrike and his paper, with two results: the attempt to use his position to sexual advantage, and sadism directed against various targets. (The two are related, since sex, as we have seen, is generally used here in an aggressive way.) He tries unsuccessfully to seduce Shrike's wife in an indirect foray against the editor, but this sally only confirms his bondage to and victimage by Shrike. The second, more fateful, attempt involves a letter writer, Fay Doyle.

With Fay's letter, a complaint about being married to a cripple, the prospect of spiritual nourishment looms again in adulterous sex. This time he is successful, though Fay is as much the seducer as seduced: "He had always been the pursuer, but now found a strange pleasure in having the roles reversed" (28). Mrs. Doyle is a sea image, of course. (Miss Lonelyhearts crawls out of bed "like an exhausted swimmer leaving the surf" (28)). Thus, when he cannot advance his own aggressive interests on those who have rhetorical and institutional power over him, he practices his designs on a reader, over whom *he* has some power. But even this sadistic move is only partly successful, ending with a lengthy tale of woe related by Fay, to which, as usual, Miss Lonelyhearts must listen sympathetically. The climatic incident in the speakeasy with the Clean Old Man brings these sadistic impulses to a head, as Miss Lonelyhearts viciously twists the old man's arm to torture him into telling the "story of your life" (17). The frustration and sadism of the columnist's role are clearest at this point, and the scene will be echoed later in the text.

2. Attempt to escape the columns and the attendant sense of futility: what could be called the "suburban solution." He retreats first to his room (in the chapter "Miss Lonelyhearts in the Dismal Swamp"), then to Connecticut with Betty. Of course, Shrike, who bursts into Miss Lonelyhearts' sickroom before he leaves, has already satirized this possibility of escape (along with the escapes of hedonism, the South Seas, suicide, art and drugs) in a series of bombastic set pieces (35).

Despite Shrike's malediction, Miss Lonelyhearts and Betty go to Connecticut for a pseudo-pastoral interval. It is not only nature but nature's story that is competing with his gloom, as Betty's stories of her childhood on a farm are proffered as an antidote to his own story (32, 36). This itself gives a clue to the failure of nature as an escape: Betty has already made a cliché of nature, one which has been parodied by Shrike. Nature as an imagined scene of plenitude is a figure of cultural fantasy, and so his union with nature and its story, figured in his sexual union with Betty—now "wholesome" rather than "sick" sex—is still not proof against the Bronx slums through which they return from Connecticut's impossible suburban space.

3. Decision to use the new fully conscious sense of his own degradation to effect his readers' salvation. He feels at this stage that he has not allowed the Christ dream to emerge "not so much because of Shrike's jokes or his own self-doubt, but because of his lack of humility" (39). He begins cultivating this humility, and avoiding Betty as well. His visit to the Doyles is the culmination of his attempt to bring the message of suffering as redemption through Christ. It is initiated by accident and ends in disaster. Miss Lonelyhearts is trying to read the cripple Doyle's letter, which he has been handed, when their hands inadvertently touch:

> He jerked away, but then drove his hand back and forced it to
> clasp the cripple's. After finishing the letter, he did not let go, but

pressed it firmly with all the love he could manage. At first the cripple covered his embarrassment by disguising the meaning of the clasp with a handshake, but he soon gave in to it and they sat silently hand in hand.

This kind of grotesquely painful social awkwardness is something that initiates the elaborate series of false steps and misinterpretations between Miss Lonelyhearts and Doyle that melodramatically recurs in the last chapter. Nor do the cross-purposes augur well for the session at the Doyles where, amid the couple's ill-concealed mutual hatred, Miss Lonelyhearts tries to "find a message" to give them. It is at this point that he realizes he has only written a column for the newspaper and imitated, against his intention, the rhetoric of Shrike.

   4. A second retreat from the column, this one more severe. It is this sequence that is presided over by the image of the rock: a metaphor for passive withdrawal. When Shrike bursts into Miss Lonelyhearts' room during his hideout, as is Shrike's wont, Miss Lonelyhearts does not yield: "Shrike dashed against him, but fell back, as a wave that dashes against an ancient rock, smooth with experience, falls back" (51).

   The nature of Miss Lonelyhearts' withdrawal, his passivity, is worthy of note: a withdrawal from speech and specifically from the narratives of his column. The false reciprocity of his column has been a story of redemption in exchange for a story of woe, but by this point Miss Lonelyhearts has clearly abdicated his part of the exchange. In the chapter entitled "Miss Lonelyhearts Attends a Party," he utters not a recorded word. But then the party is just another ploy to humiliate him, in the form of a game called "Everyman his own Miss Lonelyhearts," which involves a batch of his (presumably as yet unanswered) letters from the cityroom. Says Shrike: "'First, each of you will do his best to answer one of these letters, then, from your answers, Miss Lonelyhearts will diagnose your moral ills'" (52). It so happens that the letter he distributes to Miss Lonelyhearts is Doyle's death threat, prompted by his wife's contention—which ironically is untrue—that Miss Lonelyhearts tried to rape her. The letter is read by Shrike, because the letter's intended recipient has silently left the party without removing the letter from its envelope.

   In rejecting the letters, in refusing to read the message and abdicating his Miss Lonelyhearts role, he does not "get the message" of his own peril. The letter is a prediction, the more because its addressee has not read it. Everyone in the book has a Miss Lonelyhearts story, including columnist and editor. Both the columnist's professional and his sexual lives have relied upon an exchange of stories: Mary Shrike has a tale of woe, Betty a tale of innocence, etc. In the wake of failure as a healer, he is now weary of the surfeit of narratives that endlessly repeat the stories of the tellers' lives without ultimate cure. So he withdraws—from the letters, from his professional position, and from his own past exploitation. This break with his past writing situation he sees as a way of detaching himself from Shrike's joke.

But his refusal to be the butt of Shrike's joke only insures that he will be the victim of a more earnest joke with a fatal punch-line. Miss Lonelyhearts has refused to read the story of his own life: of his past complicity in the deceptions that made his linguistic life possible, and of his future peril from an admirer who has discovered his fraudulence and illegitimacy. (Fay's rape story is a lie, but its profounder truth is that Doyle has been cuckolded in a sexual betrayal that is also a linguistic one: Doyle could, after all, be any reader whose trust Miss Lonelyhearts has transgressed.) His renunciation of the letter in favour of the spirit of a Christ that he will not have to "handle ... with a thick glove of words" seals his doom (33). His own past is inscribed in Doyle's letter and, because the message is not received, his atonement as well.

In the subsequent chapter, Miss Lonelyhearts' conversation with Betty only confirms his divorce from language. Although he does speak with her, he blandly fobs her off with things he feels she wants to hear: he tells her he is working for an ad agency, he begs her to marry him, for this reason (55). He feels guiltless about this because his withdrawal from language (that is, from any connection between language and truth) is complete: "He did not feel guilty. He did not feel. The rock was a solidification of his feeling ..." (56). Ironically, this dialogue with Betty is a further negation of his own past ties to his earlier aggressive sexuality. In this sense, his position parallels that of Betty, who offers to abort their illegitimate child, and so remove a reminder of the common burden of their past.

5. Miss Lonelyhearts' momentary dyslexia now culminates in what West acidly calls a "religious experience." In another failed dialectical reversal, he rises, after lying abed for three days, on the third day and foresees a new career as Miss Lonelyhearts, only now twice-born. His call to grace takes the form of a repetition of his previous writing situation, with God taking Shrike's position:

> God said: "Will you accept it, now?"
> And he replied, "I accept, I accept."
> He immediately began to plan a new life and his future conduct
> as Miss Lonelyhearts. He submitted drafts of his column to God
> and God approved them. God approved his every thought.

Miss Lonelyhearts' letter to Christ—dictated by Shrike earlier in the text—has now been answered. The passive-aggressive oscillation now swung back to frenzied acceptance of the columnist-savior role, but on a mystical plane that will somehow transform shoddy advice into revelation: in the extreme of his delusion, Miss Lonelyhearts is indistinguishable from God. ("His heart was one heart, the heart of God. And his brain was likewise God's (57).) The aggressiveness of his mission is signaled by the "mentally unmotivated violence" that changes the rock into a furnace (56).

The promise is fulfilled by the arrival of the cripple Doyle, but lacking the message of Doyle's note, Miss Lonelyhearts radically misconstrues the meaning: "God had sent him so that Miss Lonelyhearts could perform a miracle and be certain of his conversion. It was a sign" (57). A sign it surely is, but of rather a different sort. How different becomes clear when one sees that this ironic climax is the repetition of the climaxes of two previous chapters: chapters that suggest the dissonance between the true import of Doyle's actions and the victim's interpretation of it.

Doyle's act itself and its intent have been prefigured in the sordid close of the "Clean Old Man" incident. That scene directly depicts the frustrated sadism practiced by Miss Lonelyhearts at first against his editor, his fiancée and, of course, his readers. His seduction of Fay belongs to this early phase, though it occurs before he meets her husband. Doyle's revenge is thus the mirror of Miss Lonelyhearts' earlier impotent rage, and is also the fulfilment of a chain of events begun by Fay's seduction.

Miss Lonelyhearts sees his role as the opportunity, in the fullness of his divinity, to enact fully what he only awkwardly enacts in the scene where he and the cripple meet. He thinks: "He would embrace the cripple and the cripple would be made whole again, even as he, a spiritual cripple, had been made whole" (57). As he was at the beginning, so now the born-again columnist is confronting his specular image in that of his readers; but he assumes that he has been healed, and so misreads the nature of his resemblance to Doyle. To be specific, this misconception allows him to ignore the "something wrapped in a newspaper" that Doyle is carrying, which is a pistol (57). His ignoral is symptomatic of his refusal to acknowledge the aggression lying within his own writing position, along with the equally aggressive consequences. (It is not surprising that, deluded as he is, Miss Lonelyhearts is incapable of "reading" what is really in the newspaper.)

Trapped in the narrative of the Christ story, he does not recognize the story he is really in: the oldest story in the book, the adulterous triangle. He misunderstands Doyle's warning as a cry for help. His attempt to escape his past involvement with stories takes the form of another story, the Christ legend, which he persists in enacting and which only causes him to misread his own peril. His fate is a parody of the Christ story where resurrection on the third day is followed by crucifixion: the Christ story as Shrike no doubt would have written it. Miss Lonelyhearts is most completely the victim when he believes himself the saviour, and he is, of course, never more distant from his readers (whom Doyle represents) than when approaching his mystical union.

In *Miss Lonelyhearts*, the central narrative of Western culture produces no revivification, only the bloom of fever. It only makes possible the endless parodic repetitions of Shrike (who is conscious of the parody) and the manic delusions of Miss Lonelyhearts (who at the last is not). Miss Lonelyhearts' Christ dream betrays him as much as Shrike's Christ joke has betrayed his readers; he is in this respect as well, Doyle's *semblable*. Rather than allowing Miss Lonelyhearts to exchange his soulless typewriter for a Promethean pen producing lifegiving language, it leads him only to repeat Christ's role and his own subservient columnist's role, and the two roles fail to cohere. Like the many narratives Miss Lonelyhearts tries to escape, the Christ legend is doomed to the same fraudulence; as long as Miss Lonelyhearts is who he is, even the Christ dream is compromised fatally, like a compulsively recurring dream that ends only with the end of the dreamer.

The stories we tell ourselves, like the stories we tell others, are as necessary as they are fraudulent; and the more irrelevant they become, the more necessary they may well seem. The narrative of *Miss Lonelyhearts* is the story of this cruel calculus. It is a tale where Shrike has the last laugh, because he has already written the first line.

NOTES

1. Nathanael West, *Miss Lonelyhearts and The Day of the Locust* (New York: New Directions, 1969); pp. 25–26.

2. In Robert I. Edenbaum, "To Kill God and Build a Church," from *Twentieth Century Interpretations of Miss Lonelyhearts*, ed. Thomas H. Jackson (Englewood Cliffs, N.J.: Prentice-Hall, 1971); p. 62.

3. Robert Andreach, in his article "Nathaniel West's *Miss Lonelyhearts*: Between the Dead Pan and the Unborn Christ," gives this Pan motif about as thorough a treatment as one could want. (Cf. Jackson, pp. 49–60.)

4. Edmond L. Volpe has argued that *Miss Lonelyhearts* constitutes an implicit if not intentional reply to Eliot's poem. Cf. "The Waste Land of Nathanael West" in Jackson, pp. 81–92. Though I would suspect West's first novel, *The Dream Life of Balsa Snell*, is a likelier candidate for this honor than *Miss Lonelyhearts*, the intertextual contrast is an illuminating one. Volpe demonstrates that in West's pessimistic vision, the option of mysticism held out by Eliot is foreclosed. It would be of interest to pursue the intercalation of the two works even further than Volpe, since he does not have much to say about either the specific role of cultural reclamation in Eliot's project of spiritual renewal or the way

this is satirized by West. One way to approach this would be to argue that for Eliot the great cultural tradition is still a living alternative to the banalizing influence of mass culture, whereas for West, mass culture's reign is harder to question.

5. Randall Reid, in his book *The Fiction of Nathanael West* (Chicago: University of Chicago Press, 1967), speaks of the final "hysteria" of Miss Lonelyhearts, though he argues as well in other places that psychological categories should be taken with large grains of salt when studying West (pp. 95–96).

6. West himself has spoken of this rendering of hysteria as a goal of *Miss Lonelyhearts'* style. Cf. Nathaniel West, "Some Notes on *Miss Lonelyhearts*," *Contempo*, III (May 15, 1933). Reproduced in Jackson.

7. Reid discusses the way West's images reflect not only the inner reality of hysteria as Miss Lonelyhearts may be said to experience it, but also the objective conditions that give grounds for that hysteria and desperation (p. 90).

DOUGLAS ROBINSON

The Ritual Icon

*M*iss *Lonelyhearts* is, at one level, an attempt to mediate allusively between two biblical texts, the apocalypse and the temptation of Christ in the wilderness; as such, it stands as a kind of American *Paradise Regained,* which also mediates between those two texts by internalizing the restoration of paradise, displacing the raising of Eden "in the waste wilderness" into the divine mind of Jesus Christ.[1] The parallels between West's novel and Milton's brief epic are in fact striking enough to be taken seriously: whereas Milton has Satan describe Jesus as "Proof against all temptation as a rock / Of adamant, and as a center firm" (4:533–34), West tells us that "Miss Lonelyhearts stood quietly in the center of the room. Shrike dashed against him, but fell back, as a wave that dashes against an ancient rock, smooth with experience, falls back. There was no second wave."[2] As in *Paradise Regained,* this rocklike immovability is Miss Lonelyhearts's only successful defense against a satanic Shrike: "'Don't be a spoilsport,' Shrike said with a great deal of irritation. He was a gull trying to lay an egg in the smooth flank of a rock, a screaming, clumsy gull" (132). Milton's Satan is of course the same kind of master-rhetorician as Shrike—opposing to Christ "Not force, but well-couched fraud, well-woven snares" (1.97) by "the persuasive rhetoric / That sleeked his tongue" (4.4–5)—but in the end he, too, is profoundly disconcerted by Christ's immovability.

From *American Apocalypses: The Image of the End of the World in American Literature.* © 1985 The Johns Hopkins University Press.

The thematic reduction that this alignment of Miss Lonelyhearts with Christ and of Shrike with Satan immediately suggests, however, is absurd. As John R. May contends, this reading makes Shrike a Satan-figure who tempts Miss Lonelyhearts to presumption ("The rock is the sign of Miss Lonelyhearts' presumption; it is a traditional image for the unchanging fidelity of God"),[3] and if Miss Lonelyhearts is punished for that presumption with death, Shrike's victory signals the "last loosening of Satan," or impending apocalypse.

That this is a false reduction of the novel is evident in West's insistence on aligning his antagonists the other way as well: Shrike, after all—whose name is a near-anagram of Christ—is the one who keeps talking about Christ; and while his is a devastating rhetoric in which the *real* alternative of Christ is destroyed, that rhetoric *becomes* his image of order, his rock, which guarantees his invulnerability throughout the novel. If Milton's Christ throughout *Paradise Regained* remains "unmoved," then Shrike is clearly the dominant Christ figure here; for Shrike is unmoved by the suffering that Miss Lonelyhearts perceives precisely because he can retreat into the illusory world of rhetoric, a paradoxical discovery of order in absence that significantly parallels Christ's own deferral of presential order to an absent future. Shrike's rhetoric, for Miss Lonelyhearts, represents a temptation to order analogous to Betty's more naive belief in order, as well as to his own hopeless wishing for an apocalypse—all temptations he knows he must stay away from, for they will only exacerbate his sickness. Miss Lonelyhearts is driven throughout the novel by an acute perception of suffering that simply will not reduce either to Betty's simplicities or to Shrike's rhetorical sophistication:

> A man is hired to give advice to the readers of a newspaper [he explains to Betty]. The job is a circulation stunt and the whole staff considers it a joke. He welcomes the job, for it might lead to a gossip column, and anyway he's tired of being a leg man. He too considers the job a joke, but after several months at it, the joke begins to escape him. He sees that the majority of the letters are profoundly humble pleas for moral and spiritual advice, that they are inarticulate expressions of genuine suffering. He also discovers that his correspondents take him seriously. For the first time in his life, he is forced to examine the values by which he lives. This examination shows him that he is the victim of the joke and not its perpetrator. (106)

If Milton's Christ represents order and Satan a restless wandering through chaos, clearly West aligns Miss Lonelyhearts with the latter. Miss Lonelyhearts is restless throughout the novel because he sees too well that all order, indeed all *language*, is a wholly unjustified reduction of the human truth of suffering to nonexistence. As a newspaper writer, he deals in words and is taught to manipulate words by his feature editor, Shrike; but that manipulation soon goes sour on him. The letters he receives are "inarticulate expressions of genuine suffering"—which is to say that genuine suffering exposes the reductive dangers of articulation, for to articulate suffering in his responses to the letters is always to falsify the suffering.

West's problem, of course, is that he is writing a novel about the inauthenticity of articulation. His novel launches a powerful assault on the entire Western tradition of the apocalyptic unveiling of order, but by doing so *verbally*, it partakes in the very tradition that West attacks. This is, of course, the central dilemma in American writing: How does one forge an order that will not harden into a rock of repression? By what authority can one destroy all authoritarian images of order? Miss Lonelyhearts undergoes his negative revelation in the end, gives in to the temptation to become "proof against all temptation," and becomes the rock: "He approached Betty with a smile, for his mind was free and clear. The things that muddied it had precipitated out into the rock" (136). But schizophrenia (which we may define as a form of ethical splitting, perhaps) is no answer to the writer's dilemma. Having devalued the apocalyptic transformation of chaos into order, he must seek a new transformation, a new reduction, perhaps, but one that will not falsify the chaotic facts of inarticulate human existence.

Early in the novel, Miss Lonelyhearts has a sudden memory from childhood that seems to offer West a tentative way out:

> One winter evening, he had been waiting with his little sister for their father to come home from church. She was eight years old then, and he was twelve. Made sad by the pause between playing and eating, he had gone to the piano and had begun a piece by Mozart. It was the first time he had ever voluntarily gone to the piano. His sister left her picture book to dance to his music. She had never danced before. She danced gravely and carefully, a simple dance yet formal.... As Miss Lonelyhearts stood at the bar, swaying slightly to the remembered music, he thought of children dancing. Square replacing oblong and being replaced by circle. Every child, everywhere; in the whole world there was not one child who was not gravely, sweetly dancing. (84–85, ellipsis West's)

Miss Lonelyhearts quickly dismisses his memory—"What in Christ's name was this Christ business? And children gravely dancing? He would ask

Shrike to be transferred to the sports department" (85). But the dance remains a possibility—a possible reduction of flux to order in which order is ephemeral, always passing away: "Square replacing oblong and being replaced by circle." The being-replaced of the dance is Yeats's Romantic image for art, of course, repeated in Eliot's *Four Quartets* as "the still point of the turning world."[4] But West, as opposed to Yeats and Eliot, remains profoundly mistrustful of that image; the image, too, West understands, is a falsification of the inarticulate flux of human suffering.

NOTES

1. *The Complete Poetical Works of John Milton*, ed. Douglas Bush (Boston: Houghton Mifflin Co., 1965), 1.7, p. 464. All subsequent quotations are from this edition. References are to book and line. I find, after writing my discussion of *Miss Lonelyhearts*, that Harold Bloom has recently linked West's novel to *Paradise Regained* as well, as a ground for a revisionary reading of the work that, substantially different though it is, finally reaches a position that is not far from my own: that West is seeking to revise the Miltonic rage for order. See Bloom's *The Breaking of the Vessels* (Chicago: University of Chicago Press, 1982), pp. 21–25.

2. *The Complete Works of Nathanael West* (New York: Farrar, Strauss & Cudahy, 1957), p. 132. All subsequent quotations from West's works are from this edition.

3. John R. May, *Toward a New Earth: Apocalypse in the American Novel* (Notre Dame: University of Notre Dame Press, 1972), p. 126. All subsequent quotations are from this edition.

4. T.S. Eliot, *Four Quartets* (New York: Harcourt, Brace & Co., 1943), p. 5. The seminal discussion of the Romantic image of the dance in Yeats and the moderns is Frank Kermode, *Romantic Image* (New York: Chilmark Press, 1961).

ROBERT EMMET LONG

Miss Lonelyhearts:
The Absurd Center of the Dead World

W est's initial conception of *Miss Lonelyhearts* grew out of an incident that occurred in March 1929. S.J. Perelman invited West to join him at Siegel's restaurant in Greenwich Village where he was to have dinner with a newspaperwoman who wrote a lovelorn column for the *Brooklyn Eagle* under the name "Susan Chester." At the restaurant, "Susan Chester" read aloud some of the letters from her readers, thinking that Perelman might be able to put them to comic use. He did not find them especially promising as material for satire, but West was moved, and intrigued, by them; and they became the starting point for his novel,[1] which evolved slowly, passing through six different drafts, before being completed in December 1932.

Although the earliest drafts of the novel have not survived, the later stages of West's revision can be glimpsed in five next-to-final chapter drafts published in *Contact* and *Contempo* magazines in 1932,[2] a year before the publication of the work. They reveal that even in this later stage of composition he was still attempting to resolve the problem of how best to present the protagonist. In the February 1932 issue of *Contact*, the third-person protagonist is called Thomas Matlock, but in the May issue West's narration shifts to the first person, and in the October issue back again to the third. Clearly, a first-person narration would have diminished the author's ironic judgment of the hero—and proved unmanageable at the end, when he is killed. Clearly, too, while using the name Thomas Matlock in the first segment, West had decided to dispense with a name for him at all, other than Miss Lonelyhearts, as the work progressed, thus achieving additional irony— a relentless challenging of the hero's identity.

Another conspicuous feature of West's revision is that in the earlier version Miss Lonelyhearts and Shrike were not as absolutely antithetical as they later became. The earlier Miss Lonelyhearts indulged in moments of self-mockery that, in revision, were rewritten as a mockery of him by Shrike. Indeed, a whole sequence in the first draft of "Miss Lonelyhearts in the Dismal Swamp," in which Miss Lonelyhearts ponders, only to reject as fruitless, avenues of escape from his despair (the South Seas, the arts, the farm), was later given to Shrike. Moreover, this lengthy, rather lushly parodic passage is out of key stylistically with the rest of the work. In rewriting, West reduced the length and tone of the passage considerably, making it suitable to be spoken mockingly by Shrike as Miss Lonelyhearts's alter ego.

West's revisions almost always work toward greater cohesiveness and concreteness, as can be seen in the opening sentences in the February 1932 and April 1933 versions:

February 1932	*April 1933*
Thomas Matlock, the Miss Lonelyhearts of the New York *Evening Hawk* (Are you in trouble? Do you need advice? Write to Miss Lonelyhearts and she will help you) decided to walk from the Hawk Building across the park to Dele-hanty's speakeasy.	The Miss Lonelyhearts of the New York Herald *Post-Dispatch* (Are-you-in-trouble?-Do-you-need-advice?-write-to-Miss-Lonelyhearts-and-she-will-help-you) sat at his desk and stared at a piece of white cardboard.

Not only has the actual name for Miss Lonelyhearts been removed, but the name of the newspaper has also been changed for the sake of greater realism; and the lines lead directly to the blasphemous prayer Shrike has had printed, bringing the reader immediately to the heart of the conflict within the hero. Elsewhere, in the first-person draft, the hero attempts to explain himself to the reader: "Don't misunderstand me. My Christ has nothing to do with love. Even before I became Miss Lonelyhearts, my world was moribund. I lived on a deserted stairway of ornate machinery. I wrote my first love letters on a typewriter.... I turned to Christ as the most familiar and natural of excitants. I wanted him to destroy this hypnosis. He alone could make the rock of sensation bleed and the stick of thought flower." This explanatory passage was deleted in revision, allowing the reader more dramatically to grasp Miss Lonelyhearts's mental state through understatement.

The revisions also show West confronting and overcoming problems of diffuseness. In the early draft of the opening chapter Miss Lonelyhearts prepares to go to Delehanty's, and on the way pauses to rest for a moment on a bench in the small park. But here he decides against going to the speakeasy after all, returns home, goes to bed, and reads Father Zosima's sermon in *The Brothers Karamazov*, after which he falls asleep and has a dream in which he and two other college friends, on a drinking spree, decide to sacrifice a lamb in a quasi-religious ceremony, a botched attempt that turns into sordid cruelty. In revision, Miss Lonelyhearts, in his office, is reading the letters from Sick-of-it-all and Desperate when Shrike appears, and their first confrontation concludes the chapter dramatically. In the second chapter he not only prepares to go but does go to Delehanty's, where he meets Shrike and Miss Farkis, a strikingly self-contained "scene." Only in the next chapter does Miss Lonelyhearts return home to read the Father Zosima passage and have the dream. With far greater concentration of effect, West finds the proper place for the lamb incident, which dominates the chapter in which it appears.

Other revisions reveal West's attention to nuance. In the early part, for example, the mirror on the wall of Miss Lonelyhearts's room, an emblem of his introspection, is removed. The sacrifice of the lamb scene is bathed in blood in the early draft ("A thick stream of blood pumped over their heads and clothes"), but is muted in the later one. A dream in which he appears as a child in a flannel nightgown, with his head bent in prayer on the knees of the mother he innocently "loved," a scene which precedes his later rage over the loss of love, is removed as being too explicit. In the early draft, the letter from Broad Shoulders contains more pedestrian details and is less powerful than the letter as it appears in the final version, an indication of how carefully West weighed every word, how he built up effects in revision as well as toned them down.

All the magazine-draft chapters contain lines and passages that were refined upon in the book version. In certain cases names were changed. Fay Doyle's husband was named Martin before becoming Peter, and her daughter Lucy was at first named Mary. In some instances, gross touches were softened. The "clean old man" at the comfort station is said to turn away "to wipe himself with some paper from the roll beside the seat," but in the book version he turns away "to wipe his mouth." In the seduction scene, Fay Doyle "caught [Miss Lonelyhearts's] head and put her tongue into his mouth"—which in the book version becomes, "and kissed him on the mouth." The revisions include scores of minor alterations, all of which contribute to the polish of the final draft. In general, West's tendency is to abbreviate, foreshorten, and to avoid direct statement or explanation; and in this way the novel becomes not only more certain in its tone but also more cryptic and mysterious.

If the revisions reveal West's refinement upon his conception, they do not, of course, explain the conception. West himself has commented on the composition of *Miss Lonelyhearts* in "Some Notes on Miss L.," published in *Contempo* magazine in 1933;[3] but it is difficult to know how seriously to take what he says. He explains that *Miss Lonelyhearts* "became the portrait of a priest of our time who has a religious experience. His case is classical and is built on all the cases in James' *Varieties of Religious Experience* and Starbuck's *Psychology of Religion*. The psychology is theirs not mine. The imagery is mine." He also remarks that while writing the novel, he conceived of it as a comic strip:

> The chapters to be squares in which many things happen through one action. The speeches contained in conventional balloons. I abandoned this idea, but retained some of the comic strip technique: Each chapter instead of going forward in time, also goes backward, forward, up and down in space like a picture. Violent images are used to illustrate commonplace events. Violent acts are left almost bald.[4]

Miss Lonelyhearts does have something of the nature of a comic strip or cartoon. Each chapter is dramatically focused by a single event or brief sequence of events, comparable to the series of pictorial frames of a comic strip. Like the figures in a cartoon, West's characters are stripped down to the sharp outline of a few traits. Pete Doyle is a cripple, his wife is sexually devouring, Betty is simple and unworldly, Shrike is a mocker. They have also been strongly visualized (Miss Lonelyhearts's long, bony "biblical" face, and Pete Doyle's built-up shoe which he drags after him), and West makes frequent use of the tableau. The endings of the chapters, particularly, often use framing tableaux that bring the chapters to visual climaxes. The novel's denouement also has the graphic, pictorial quality of a comic strip ending— Miss Lonelyhearts's fall on the staircase a visual analogue of his fall from the grace he had just imagined.

But if *Miss Lonelyhearts* is a comic strip, it is a distinctly sinister one. A death theme runs through it, evoking a dead world that cannot be brought to life, and the novel ends with death. One of the prominent features of *Miss*

Lonelyhearts, as compared to *Balso Snell*, is the manner in which West moves from an indeterminate interior landscape that can be located nowhere in time and space to a concrete social setting of the thirties. Its setting, with the exception of a brief visit to the Connecticut countryside, is New York, which has been created with a harsh stylization that could be compared to the hard-boiled detective fiction of Dashiell Hammett. Hammett, in fact, was West's guest at the Sutton Hotel when *Miss Lonelyhearts* was being written, and he read the novel in an early draft. West, in turn, had read Hammett's detective novels, as well as many of the issues of *Black Mask*, the great magazine forum for hard-boiled detective fiction of the thirties. When *Miss Lonelyhearts* was published, Josephine Herbst called it a "moral detective story"—and it does give the impression of a raw world in which values have disappeared, and in which violence is sudden and frequent. As in Hammett's fiction; the quester figure is alone in what is essentially an irrational world; and curiously, in the early draft, but later removed, Miss Lonelyhearts is even compared to a detective. As he waits in the park for Mrs. Doyle to appear, he examines the sky "like a stupid detective who is searching for a clue to his own exhaustion." A few minutes later, "the detective saw a big woman enter the park and start in his direction." Miss Lonelyhearts is evoked here as a man who searches for clues to the mystery of an absent God, and in his later wanderings he attempts but fails to unravel the mystery.

The hard-boiled aspect of *Miss Lonelyhearts* can be noticed in chapter 5, which begins in Delehanty's speakeasy as a group of nameless, dimensionless men assault women verbally, particularly women writers who pretend to one aesthetic ideal or another. One of the men tells of a woman writer who was hurt "by beauty," and is taken "into the lots" one night by eight men and gang raped, presumably as a curative for her illusions. Another man relates a story about a female writer who cultivated "hard-boiled stuff," and is assaulted and sexually abused for three days by a group of hardened, low-life men who resent her glamorization of the primitive and physical. Not only is violence recounted by these men in the accents of a calloused dehumanization, it also erupts in fact. Miss Lonelyhearts is struck suddenly in the face at one point, and by the end of the chapter, in another speakeasy, he is hit over the head with a chair. The chapter ends with his loss of consciousness. West's characters, in fact, show very little consciousness of any kind, whether social, aesthetic, or political.

Although *Miss Lonelyhearts* is not a political novel, a criticism of capitalism does enter into it. In *Miss Lonelyhearts*, unlike *Balso Snell*, West is unusually conscious of the life of the masses, of a suffering that he has related to society's complicity in the dehumanization of its members, its trashing of their very dreams. Miss Lonelyhearts's girl friend Betty, who represents the status quo and does not question it, wants him to go to work for an advertising agency, where he will be a manipulator of dreams for commercial ends. As it is, as a newspaper columnist, he offers mere palliatives for suffering, all that his spiritually deadened society can provide its members.

About the role of society in the manipulation of dreams, West is quite explicit. "Men have always," he, writes, "fought their misery with dreams. Although dreams were once powerful, they have been made puerile by the movies, radio and newspapers. Among many betrayals this one is the worst." Miss Lonelyhearts often seems, powerlessly, like a man in a cage. His solitary room and office at the newspaper are like boxes; and in an earlier draft the street upon which he looks from his office window is "walled at both ends." In his office he meditates on life as a desert, a place of inertia, animality, and violence, which are part of everyday life. His petitioners for help seem to him to live in little enclosed spaces, surrounded by commercial billboards that serve as reminders of violated values. In such a meaningless world, violence is a logical outcome.

Elsewhere, in a dream sequence, Miss Lonelyhearts is in the window of a pawnshop, where he attempts to create order out of the paraphernalia around him. He tries to assemble stable shapes from the musical instruments, umbrellas, and derby hats, and eventually forms a large cross. When the cross becomes too large for the pawnshop, he moves it, in his imagination, to the shore of the ocean. But here each wave throws up more debris, adding to the stock of the cross faster than he can extend its arms, and he becomes a kind of Sisyphus struggling with an impossible task. The sequence implies the impossibility of Miss Lonelyhearts's effort to create order out of chaos; but the pawnshop image is particularly interesting, since it evokes the discarding or destruction of dreams in a commercial society. When West refers to "the business of dreams," he implies that human dreams are an industry for capitalist exploitation. In an early section, Shrike produces' a newspaper clipping about a religious sect that will hold a "goat and adding machine ritual" for a man about to be executed in a Colorado prison. The clipping is of course a parody of American religious sects that have become "worldly" and incoherent. But it also suggests that the prisoner, who slew another man in an argument over a small amount of money, is a "goat," or scapegoat of the society, in which spiritual reality is no more meaningful than the figures in an adding-machine tally.

Although West does not refer specifically to the Depression, it is an unnamed presence in the novel.[5] When Miss Lonelyhearts returns from his escape vacation in the country, the first thing he notices as he drives into the city are the Bronx slums. It is at this point that he recognizes the hopelessness of his "mission." People wander the streets with "broken hands" and "torn mouths." A man on the verge of death staggers into a movie theater showing a film called *Blonde Beauty*, an escapist sexual fantasy; and a ragged woman with "an enormous goiter" gleefully picks a love-story magazine out of a garbage can. These are the betrayed ones, betrayed by their culture—the spiritually beggared.

West's portrait of Miss Lonelyhearts, however, is less a social than a psychological study, one which is indebted particularly to Dostoyevsky.[6] Dostoyevsky's "underground man" supplies the model for Miss Lonelyhearts's self-division and psychological suffering; and Raskolnikov[7] in *Crime and Punishment* especially prepares for him—in his impulse to play a heroic role for which he is not necessarily qualified, his fevered dreams, isolation within an oppressive society, and obsession. As if to make the Russian analogy unmistakable, West has Goldsmith, an underling of Shrike's, address Miss Lonelyhearts by asking "How now, Dostoievsky?" Dostoyevsky is referred to again when Miss Lonelyhearts withdraws to his room to read *The Brothers Karamazov*, and Father Zosima's sermon is quoted: "Love the animals, love the plants, love everything. If you love everything, you will perceive the divine mystery in things. Once you perceive it, you will begin to comprehend it better every day. And you will come at last to love the whole world with an all-embracing love." It is this vision of an all-embracing love that torments Miss Lonelyhearts with its unattainability, and is part of his "Christ complex."

Miss Lonelyhearts is also similar in a number of essentials to Prince Myshkin, in *The Idiot*, who yearns for a community of Christian love and brotherhood in a society that would seem to deny its possibility absolutely. Alone, in a deeply disillusioning world, Prince Myshkin finds that he can only be misunderstood, and becomes increasingly estranged. In the end his retirement to the Swiss sanitarium indicates the futility of his quest. Like Myshkin, Miss Lonelyhearts is set apart from others by his spiritual aspiration that is out of key with the materialistic world in which he lives, so that he is regarded as a freak and suffers the torment of the misfit. To his friend John Sanford, West boasted that he could rewrite Dostoyevsky "with a pair of shears"; and remarkably he has done just that, reproducing Dostoyevsky in miniature in an American Depression setting.

Miss Lonelyhearts's dreams are inner psychological dramas, like the dreams in Dostoyevsky, but they have also been influenced by Freud and the surrealists. Freudian symbolism is apparent, for example, in the scene in which Miss Lonelyhearts meditates in the little park near a Mexican War obelisk. "He sat staring at [the obelisk] without knowing why," West comments, "until he noticed that it was lengthening in rapid jerks, not as shadows usually lengthen. He grew frightened and looked up quickly at the monument. It seemed red and swollen in the dying sun, as though it were about to spout a load of granite seed." A moment later, his thoughts turn to the desire for sex that he has been suppressing. The scene is not actually a dream but it is something like a dream state, and another dream state occurs when Miss Lonelyhearts drives through the Bronx slums, where "crowds of people moved through the street, with a dream-like violence," an image that might have come from a surrealist canvas. In an actual dream late in the novel, West's imagery is oddly reminiscent of a Salvador Dali painting: "A train rolled into a station, where [Miss Lonelyhearts] was a reclining statue holding a stopped clock, a coach rumbled into the yard of an inn where he was sitting over a guitar, cap in hand, shedding the rain with his hump."

Miss Lonelyhearts takes much of its life from West's striking and haunting imagery. It is difficult to say how West learned to use imagery to such effect, but he may well have been influenced by the poetry of the period—by the Imagists, Ezra Pound, and William Carlos Williams, in whose verse the image takes on a luminous life of its own. He was undoubtedly influenced by T.S. Eliot, since the symbolism of *The Waste Land* is apparent in the novel. *The Waste Land* theme is particularly evident in West's depiction of the small, barren park, which ought to be a spiritual oasis in the city but is instead a miniature wasteland—a setting of desiccation and blight. Describing the little park, West writes: "The decay that covered the surface of the mottled ground was not the kind in which life generates. Last year, he remembered, May had failed to quicken these soiled fields. It had taken all the brutality of July to torture a few green spikes through the exhausted dirt." In this wasteland park, Miss Lonelyhearts waits for a spring that does not come—until the end, when it brings only death.[8]

Although hardly noted in the past, Fitzgerald's *The Great Gatsby* is also a decided influence on West's novel.[9] Both are classic works of miniaturization that are tragic and comic at once, and end with the death of the heroes, who have been obsessed with an illusion of spiritual transcendence, If *Miss Lonelyhearts* has a cartoon quality, its characters limned in sinister caricature, so does *The Great Gatsby*. Myrtle Wilson, in *The Great Gatsby*, establishes the type of the cheap, sexual woman, preposterous in her vulgarity, who is reimagined exuberantly by West in Fay Doyle. Fay has, in fact, the name of another character in Fitzgerald's novel, Daisy Fay, whose beguiling sexuality proves to be sterile illusion; and this instance of common naming is given increased importance by its appearance again in *The Day of the Locust*, in which Faye Greener is a vacant Venus.

Myrtle Wilson, like Fay Doyle, is married to a pathetic failure of a man. Wilson pumps gas, and Pete Doyle reads gas meters, but neither is fueled with any vitality or has any sense of direction in his life. Wilson, according to

Myrtle, "doesn't even know he's alive," and Doyle, as his wife says, "is all dried up." Their sexually starved wives cheat on them, and then, in the grotesque endings the husband-failure insanely shoots the hero. The absurdist climax of *The Great Gatsby* becomes the ultimate absurdist joke of *Miss Lonelyhearts*. A death theme is pervasive in *The Great Gatsby*, as it is again in *Miss Lonelyhearts*, not only because the heroes must die but also because the cultures themselves are dead, and any attempt to transcend them is doomed to failure.

V.S. Pritchett has described *Miss Lonelyhearts* as an "American fable," and it is as a fable, with an intricate miniaturization of effect, that frequently calls *The Great Gatsby* to mind. Quite apart from the similarity of at least two of the principal characters and of the endings, the novels group together as very artful works belonging to a special, very limited tradition in modern American fiction. The fable dimension of the novels derives in part from their quest themes and quester heroes whose failures reveal the most elemental truths of their cultures. But it is insinuated, too, in the dream forms of the works, the "magical" realism they employ. The real worlds they explore seem distorted, so that the meanness of life becomes almost incredibly mean, menacing, evil—although comic too. Meyer Wolfsheim, with his cuff buttons made of human molars, becomes a plausible figure in the bizarre world in which he appears. The sexually devouring Fay Doyle, whose arm is like a "thigh," can be credited in *Miss Lonelyhearts*, with its vision of radical dislocation. In each novel a limited number of characters drawn in caricature interact in a morally charged atmosphere. Good and evil are constantly involved in the tensions of the works, in which values have become inverted. Both "fables" have a quality of lightness and grace, yet have been intensely and powerfully focused, and are modern moralities.

Miss Lonelyhearts can be compared to *The Great Gatsby* in still other ways.[10] Both are strongly visualized and imagistic, and are structured dramatically, developing in a series of distinct scenes, with many chapters dominated by a single episode. Both are elegantly satirical, and show special finesse in their reproduction of vulgar people and their banal speech. Scenes in *The Great Gatsby* are comic and horrible at once, as in the scene at the Washington Heights apartment; and this dual quality informs *Miss Lonelyhearts*—in the letters written to Miss Lonelyhearts, for example, and in Miss Lonelyhearts's seduction by Fay Doyle. The sterility of women in *The Great Gatsby* is striking, and it is again in *Miss Lonelyhearts*, in which, as in Fitzgerald, sexuality is linked with death. In all of these respects Fitzgerald is a presence in the background of *Miss Lonelyhearts*, which, remarkably original as it is, yet does have a context in the American literature that immediately precedes it.

West's modernist vision of alienation in *Miss Lonelyhearts* is focused by its hero, "Miss L," and by New York, which has been captured with a foreshortened intensity. The job at which Miss Lonelyhearts works gives him what little personal identity he has but, ironically, it is essentially merely a purveying of illusion. His advice-giving is offered to the unhappy in lieu of real religious sureties, which have long since disappeared. The earlier Protestant faith that once bolstered the nation has by the opening of the novel become an anachronism. In its place spurious religious cults flourish in the West, like the "Liberal Church of America," which intimates the breakdown of religious authority. The burden of finding spiritual guidance has fallen upon the isolated individual, and the individual alone is helpless in a chaotic world.

Miss Lonelyhearts himself has been provided with a religious background, is the son of a Baptist minister, and has "an Old Testament look." His high, narrow forehead and long, fleshless nose give him the aspect of "the New England puritan." A curious feature of Miss Lonelyhearts, however, is that his Baptist father seems unreal. So, for that matter, does the younger sister he remembers briefly in one episode. He seems so remote from a real family that one has an impression that he never had any. As for New England, he appears unacquainted with it, is so urban in his conception that when he sets foot in the Connecticut countryside, it seems a wholly new world to him. Ordinarily a character having a religious background that seems merely putative would not be credible. Yet Miss Lonelyhearts can somehow be accepted, for it is as if his urbanization has wiped out his background, made it intangible, and obliterated it. He is now essentially without connections, either to the pastor to the present—a modern "stranger," like Camus's Meursault.

Miss Lonelyhearts's removal from family and tradition is shared by the other characters in the novel. His girl friend Betty is depicted as a kind of "average" girl, but what is peculiar about her is that she gives no sense of having a family; she lives alone in the city, and seems to know no one other than Miss Lonelyhearts. Two "families" are shown in the work, the Shrikes and the Doyles, but they are nightmare versions of wedded life. Between husband and wife there is no communication. There is, indeed, a horrifying hostility in their relations. Fay Doyle feels no affection for her husband, is contemptuous of him as "a shrimp of a cripple," and betrays him sexually. Shrike and his wife despise each other, and live together in a state of sexual warfare. These marital partners are as much cut off from others as those who live by themselves, like the "clean old man." They are all devastatingly alone.

The letters Miss Lonelyhearts receives all center upon the isolation and helplessness of those who write them. Sick-of-it-all has been made pregnant yet again by her husband, a "religious" Catholic who will not permit her to have an abortion, although she has been advised by her doctor that she will die in giving birth again, and her kidneys ache agonizingly. A letter from Harold S., fifteen, informs Miss Lonelyhearts that his sister, thirteen, a deaf mute, has been sexually abused on the roof of their building by a stranger, but is "afraid to tell mother on account of her being liable to beat Gracie up." On a previous occasion, when little Gracie tore her dress, her parents had locked her in a closet for two days. Furthermore, if the boys on the block hear that she has been molested "they will say dirty things like they did on Pee Wee Conors' sister the time she got caught in the lots." These letters suggest an almost insane lack of caring or of compassion toward those who have every right to look for understanding.

The most horrendous of the letters is from Broad Shoulders, married to a man who, at different times, has deserted her and refused to support her and their children. While living with her he hides under the bed all day, lying in his own "dirt," waiting to frighten her to death when, cleaning under the bed, she comes upon him. She is so "frighted" by him that she becomes temporarily paralyzed from the waist down. At the end of the letter she reveals that a male boarder she has taken in so that she will be able to meet the rent "tries to make me bad and as there is nobody in the house when he comes home drunk on Saturday night I don't know what to do." In the letters of Broad Shoulder's and the others, one finds only a failure of communication between people—between husbands and wives, children and parents, children and their peers.

Miss Lonelyhearts is in the same situation as those who apply to him for help. He is alone, feels his own helplessness, and is gripped by fear. When the novel opens, this fear has already taken hold of him; he is obsessional, and committed to what he himself calls a "Christ complex." *Miss Lonelyhearts* is, in part, a study of a neurotic personality. Even within his own mind, Miss Lonelyhearts doubts himself, the role he is steadily impelled to assume. In the complicated character doubling of the novel, Shrike, the mocker, is a projection of a part of himself. Shrike is a "satyr," while Miss Lonelyhearts has a chin like a "cloven hoof"; and no more than Shrike can he will away his animal nature, his frustration, the inner violence he feels.

West's linking of Miss Lonelyhearts and Shrike occurs early in the novel in the course of two parallel scenes that follow one another. In the first, Miss Lonelyhearts goes to Delehanty's speakeasy, where he meets Shrike. Before long Miss Farkis, Shrike's latest girl friend, appears and Shrike, who has already described her chief attributes for Miss Lonelyhearts by drawing a pair of breasts in the air, reduces her further upon introduction, "making her bow as a ventriloquist does his doll." They begin to talk, but when Miss

Farkis attempts to join in the discussion, Shrike raises his fist "as though to strike her." He delivers a blasphemous "sermon" while caressing her body, at the conclusion of which, in an extraordinary image, he buries "his triangular face like the blade of a hatchet in her neck." He first reduces her to a sexual object, and then vents his anger and violence upon her. In a scene that appears soon after this one, Miss Lonelyhearts goes to visit Betty, hoping that she may help to restore his troubled spirit. But once with her, he seems to taunt her for her sexuality, and with sadistic cruelty reaches under her robe and gives a sharp tug to her breast. He delivers a kind of "sermon" on his Christ complex as he touches her shoulder "threateningly," and she raises her arm "as though to ward off a blow." In these scenes Miss Lonelyhearts and Shrike appear as figures in parallel, in threatening relationship to the women to whom they turn for solace.

Throughout the novel Miss Lonelyhearts and Shrike are played off against one another as would-be "believer" and as "denier." Miss Lonelyhearts, as a spiritual counselor to suffering humanity, has already begun to put himself in the place of Christ, and Shrike has adopted the role of Antichrist. The two are brought into tense, dramatic conjunction in the opening paragraph, as Miss Lonelyhearts stares at a piece of white cardboard on which Shrike has had printed an ironic prayer to "Miss L":

> Soul of Miss L, glorify me.
> Body of Miss L, nourish me.
> Blood of Miss L, intoxicate me.
> Tears of Miss L, wash me.
> Oh good Miss L, excuse my plea,
> And hide me in your heart,
> And defend me from mine enemies,
> Help me, Miss L, help me, help me.
> In saecula saeculorum. Amen.

Shrike's prayer is a parody of the "Anima Christi," or "Soul of Christ," from Ignatius Loyola's *Spiritual Exercise*; and it identifies Miss Lonelyhearts as a saint, after the pattern of Loyola. Loyola, who founded the Society of Jesus (the Jesuit order), zealously served the cause of Christ, and through discipline and desire for sacrifice made himself a master of the spiritual life. Miss Lonelyhearts, too, is a defender of Christ, and desires to serve the spiritually needy.

After reading the prayer card, and the letters to him from a number of desperate people in the city, Miss Lonelyhearts goes out to Delehanty's, stopping on the way to meditate in the little park. The condition of life seems

to him like that of a "desert" as he enters the park at the "North Gate"[11]—
an allusion to Ezra Pound's "Lament of the Frontier Guard," a vision of
isolation in a ruined world that begins "By the North Gate, the wind blows
full of sand." This saint in a modern urban desert is beset by doubt, yet clings
to the idea of attaining spiritual enlightenment. As he enters the park,
however, "the shadow of a lamppost that lay on the path ... pierced him like
a spear," which implies that this enlightenment may only be a lonely
martyrdom. In Delehanty's he is again confronted by Shrike, and another
saint is mentioned, St. Thomas Aquinas, who sought to bridge the gap
between spirit and body. Almost immediately, in another of his deflating
parodies, Shrike declares that he is himself a saint ("I walk on my own
water"), and he delivers a sermon discrediting religion, while he fondles Miss
Farkis.

This early antithetical linking of Miss Lonelyhearts and Shrike
continues on thereafter through the rest of the novel. Miss Lonelyhearts
leaves Delehanty's for his bare room that is like a monk's cell. It has no
furnishings, except for an effigy of Christ at the foot of his bed, and is "as full
of shadows as an old steel engraving," or religious etching. It is in this room
that Miss Lonelyhearts has hallucinatory dreams and fever, and chants
"Christ, Christ, Jesus Christ" while looking at the "image that hung on the
wall." Shrike enters Miss Lonelyhearts's room twice in the course of the
novel, each time with disturbing effect. On the first occasion, Miss
Lonelyhearts has suffered a breakdown and is nursed by Betty, who attempts
to restore him with her own version of order. At this point Shrike bursts in
drunkenly and, after Betty leaves, delivers a harangue, citing the possible
avenues of escape available to him, while denying the efficacy of each in turn.
The Church, he declares, is the only hope, and he dictates an imaginary,
cynical letter to Christ, calling for help for Miss Lonelyhearts. He thus
pushes Miss Lonelyhearts ever closer to despair.

Shrike appears in the room a second time late in the novel, again drunk,
with a group of others. He rushes Miss Lonelyhearts off to his apartment to
take part in a game that he has devised called "Everyman his own Miss
Lonelyhearts," in which he will produce letters from the newspaper file,
written by the most wretched, and ask Miss Lonelyhearts to provide "an
absolute value and *raison d'être*." It is worth noting that when Shrike bursts
into the room, Miss Lonelyhearts is caught naked, since in the scene that
follows he is, in effect, stripped naked by Shrike, challenged in public in an
entertainment which implies that his column of solace to the bereft is itself
only a parlor game. What is more, he asks the delayed question of how it is
possible to love humanity. One of the letters is from an elderly woman who
has just lost her sole source of support, wears heavy boots on her torn,

bleeding feet, and has rheum in her eyes. "Have you room in your heart for her?" Shrike asks devastatingly. He accidentally reveals a letter, furthermore, that has just come from Pete Doyle, threatening to blow Miss Lonelyhearts's brains out. Doyle is the very image of suffering humanity that Miss Lonelyhearts has attempted to succor, but cannot be loved because he is an incoherent monstrosity.

The scene ends with "the gospel according to Shrike," his Antichrist version of what life really consists of. In the "gospel," Shrike envisions Miss Lonelyhearts's passage through life as a sordid ordeal, a struggle to realize a high ideal that is based on illusion. In the final pages of the novel, in fever, Miss Lonelyhearts believes that a miracle has occurred and that, Christlike, he can minister to the abject with his love. With outstretched arms, he approaches Pete Doyle, then making his way awkwardly up the stairway, and is shot to death by him. In this final scene Miss Lonelyhearts's outstretched arms have the iconography of Christ on the cross.

R.W.B. Lewis, in *Trials of the Word*, has commented on Shrike as the novel's Antichrist, and his observations warrant quoting at length:

> The novella moves unfalteringly between nightmare and actuality, its tone between horror and jesting, which is West's exemplary way of apprehending *our* world as under the dominion of a contemporary Antichrist ... It is Shrike who rules over and preys upon an urban scene composed of the heartless, the violent, and the wretched. And it is Shrike who pits himself against the would-be imitator of Christ, the hopeless columnist we know only by his pen name Miss Lonelyhearts, and whom Shrike torments in particular by spoken parodies of the Eucharist—that holy *communion* after which Miss Lonelyhearts so yearns.... In a ludicrously ill-timed and feverish effort to embrace and hence to redeem by love at least one individual human victim—a crippled homosexual named Peter Doyle—Miss Lonelyhearts is accidentally shot and killed, and in the abrasively ironic eschatology of this novella, the field is left to the further machinations of the Antichrist. But Shrike, consummate satirist though he is, is at the same time an object of satire—and the field of his triumph is no more than a frozen chaos.[12]

Lewis presents his case for Shrike as the Antichrist of the novel extremely well, but he does not quite grasp Shrike's role. Shrike does bear a likeness to the Antichrist, but it is part of West's larger intention that he is not the Antichrist himself, any more than Miss Lonelyhearts is the Nazarene. An

Antichrist, or devil, does claim the world of *Miss Lonelyhearts* as his dominion, but Shrike is as much his victim as "Miss L." Shrike suffers from the same exacerbated rawness of nerves as Miss Lonelyhearts, and the very shrillness of his refusal of belief (his name could almost read "shriek") indicates that he is gripped by a similar hysteria. Nor does he triumph, however emptily, in the novel. Shrike preaches a cynical gospel of pure sensation, but what is striking about him is that his reduction of life to the sexual, or purely physical, brings him no plea sure. He is gnawed by torment in each of his appearances in the novel, and in one revealing moment, when he speaks of his life with his wife, his masklike "dead pan" breaks, and "pain actually crept into his voice." Rather than being the Antichrist of the novel, as Lewis mistakenly assumes, he is Miss Lonelyhearts's fellow sufferer.

Although he never appears, an Antichrist does rule in the work. He is the lord of disorder, and he possesses terrifying, even absolute, power. This "devil" is implied in Miss Lonelyhearts's reveries of his childhood, in which "something had stirred within him" when he shouted Christ's name, and he is tempted to bring it to life. But what this "something" is that stirs in him is made to seem fearful, as if the revelation he awaits may be wholly unlike that which he dimly imagines. Shifting forward to the present in his reverie, Miss Lonelyhearts reflects that "he knew now what this thing was—hysteria, a snake whose scales are tiny mirrors in which the dead world takes on a semblance of life. And how dead the world is.... He wondered if hysteria were really too steep a price to pay for bringing it to life." West's imagery evokes a world of the living dead, beyond reclaiming, and in the possession of a demon-snake whose mirror-scales flash illusion. In his room, when Miss Lonelyhearts begins to chant Christ's name, "the snake started to uncoil in his brain, he became frightened and closed his eyes." In the final chapter, a shout of "Christ, Christ" echoes through his brain, as his room is transformed into a vision of grace and he talks to God, telling him that he now "accepts" life. A moment later he walks out of the room to confront chaos and violence. Just before this scene Shrike had announced to the group at his apartment: "This is only one more attempt against him by the devil. He has spent his life struggling with the arch fiend for our sakes, and he shall triumph. I mean Miss Lonelyhearts, not the devil." But it is the devil, of course, who presides at Miss Lonelyhearts's undoing, who punishes his presumption, his attempt to quicken the dead world into life.

Miss Lonelyhearts's Christ delusion is implied throughout the work, and it is often dramatized on the level of sexual fear. In an early chapter, Miss Lonelyhearts, as a college student, discusses the existence of God with two other young men in a dormitory room, after which, on a drinking spree, they go out at dawn to sacrifice a lamb in a religious ritual. The sacrifice of the lamb takes places in the spring, and is a rite of purification. But they cannot believe as much in the innocence of the lamb as they would like, and drink heavily to work up a delusionary excitement. Not surprisingly, the sacrifice of the lamb is botched, becoming a brutal killing, an early undermining of Miss Lonelyhearts's yearning for transcendence. But what should be noted about the scene, too, is its sexual undercurrent. On the way to the ritual, the young men sing an obscene version of "Mary Had a Little Lamb," which presumably substitutes for "lamb," a four-letter epithet for the female sexual organ. In the nursery rhyme, Mary and her "innocent" lamb are identified (one always accompanies the other), and there is some suggestion that it is the female herself whom Miss Lonelyhearts seeks to restore to innocence, to purge of sexuality—an effort that is doomed to failure and drives him into a violent state of rage.

Miss Lonelyhearts's yearning for innocence and the violence associated with it are also seen in the later chapter entitled "Miss Lonelyhearts and the Clean Old Man." The chapter begins at Delehanty's, where male patrons take obvious pleasure in relating how women writers, claiming to have aesthetic ideals, are sexually assaulted and brutally demeaned. This brutalization is a form of revenge by men for the painful loss of their own earlier ideals—a demand that those claiming to ideals be made to confront the sordid emptiness and horror at the basis of life. At one point in the scene Miss Lonelyhearts himself has a reverie of his young sister as she dances to the music of Mozart, a brief vision of innocence and grace that is shattered when he is struck in the face by another man—an act of senseless, anonymous urban anger.

After Miss Lonelyhearts leaves the speakeasy with his friend Gates, he directs his own anger at an old homosexual in a comfort station. First at the comfort station and then at an Italian speakeasy where they take him, they taunt him and demand to know the story of his unhappy life. The old man, who carries a cane and dresses as if he had some claims to respectability, is not forthcoming with a confession, and Miss Lonelyhearts becomes virtually hysterical, twisting the old man's arm until the man screams. Miss Lonelyhearts here continues a pattern begun early in the chapter. He attempts to strip the old man of his genteel pretensions and make him confess to the loneliness, degradation, and suffering of his life.

But why, when he is balked in this attempt, should Miss Lonelyhearts lose his self-control so totally? His response to the old man, it should be noted, is complicated by the pity he wishes to feel for him, a pity mingled with evident disgust. He seeks to enter into his degradation, to establish a spiritual union with him. His spiritual failure quickly turns into rage and physical assault. Surely his rage is due to the "doubling" that is intimated to exist between them. The homosexuality to which the old man will not admit also seems present, at least latently, in Miss Lonelyhearts, whose spiritual protestations are comparable, in a way, to the old man's genteel clothes. In this context, Miss Lonelyhearts's rage against the old man's refusal to confess is an attack upon himself, upon his own duplicity.

The old man in the comfort station will not allow Miss Lonelyhearts to "love" him, but later he finds an ideal candidate for his spiritual embrace, Pete Doyle. Doyle is undisguisedly wretched, a cripple with a cane and a built-up shoe, which he drags behind him, making "many waste motions, like those of a partially destroyed insect." He is unsuccessful with women, and called "a queer guy" by his wife, who disdains and mistreats him. Although repelled by Fay Doyle, even though he allows her to seduce him, Miss Lonelyhearts is much attracted to her husband, the very image of human infirmity. To "love" Pete Doyle, the least and most lowly placed of humanity, is, in the context of Father Zosima's sermon, to "see God."

The courtship of Miss Lonelyhearts and Pete Doyle is grotesquely comic, perhaps the most grotesque courtship in American literature. In a late scene set at Delehanty's, Miss Lonelyhearts meets Doyle for the first time, and Doyle produces a letter he has written to him and now lets him read. The letter, which begins "I am a cripple 41 years of age which I have been all my life," recounts the various indignities he has suffered, and asks "but what I want to no is what is the whole stinking business for." Even if inarticulately, Doyle asks the big questions: What is life all about? Why, if there is a just God, do human beings suffer meaninglessly? Miss Lonelyhearts experiences an identification with him as his double, a physical cripple as he is a spiritual one. Hence their first embrace. "When Miss Lonelyhearts was puzzling out the crabbed writing," West comments,

> Doyle's damp hand accidentally touched his under the table. He jerked away, but then drove his hand back and forced it to clasp the cripple's. After finishing the letter, he did not let go, but pressed it firmly with all the love he could manage. At first the cripple covered his embarrassment by disguising the meaning of the clasp with a handshake, but soon he gave in to it and they sat silently, hand in hand.

The courtship is continued at the Doyle house, where the two go after leaving Delehanty's. Mrs. Doyle makes aggressive advances to Miss Lonelyhearts, who fends her off, and when she leaves the room for a moment he smiles "beatifically" at the cripple. Doyle extends his hand, and Miss

Lonelyhearts clasps it, smiling. They are still holding hands when Mrs. Doyle reenters the room and comments: "What a sweet pair of fairies you guys are." At this point, Miss Lonelyhearts delivers a sermon to the effect that "Christ is love," which makes the Doyles feel embarrassed. He is already overwrought, at the evident failure of the Christlike part he has attempted to play, when Doyle is sent out to buy a bottle of whiskey, and in Doyle's absence he is set upon sexually by Mrs. Doyle, whom he beats in a blind rage and then flees from their house. His rage is triggered by his obvious failure to establish a spiritual union with the Doyles. His "love" message is mocked by sexuality: Mrs. Doyle's rapacious heterosexuality and the latent homosexuality hinted at in his handholding with her husband. His attempt to intervene in the lives of the Doyles leads not to love but to his own frenzied beating of Mrs. Doyle, and to Doyle's crazed response (his belief that he had come to their house to rape his wife, was not the redeemer he claimed to be) that sends him to Miss Lonelyhearts's door with gun in hand. At the top of the stairs, in his final delusion, Miss Lonelyhearts reaches out to embrace the cripple, just as Betty appears, and confusion follows. In a way he is killed not even by Doyle but by the accidental discharge of the gun, a meaningless, impersonal act suggesting the irrational nature of life that Miss Lonelyhearts has attempted to order with "love."

Miss Lonelyhearts's "Christ complex" has inevitably invited Freudian interpretations, beginning with Stanley Edgar Hyman's influential discussion of the final scene:

> It is of course a homosexual tableau—the men locked in embrace while the woman stands helplessly by—and behind his other miseries Miss Lonelyhearts has a powerful latent homosexuality.... We could, if we so chose, write Miss Lonelyhearts' case history before the novel begins. Terrified of his stern religious father, identifying with his soft loving mother, the boy renounces his phallicism out of castration anxiety—a classic Oedipus complex. In these terms the Shrikes are Miss Lonelyhearts' Oedipal parents, abstracted as the father's loud voice and the mother's tantalizing breast. The scene at the end of Miss Lonelyhearts' date with Mary Shrike is horrifying and superb. Standing outside her apartment door, suddenly overcome with passion, he strips her naked under her fur coat while she keeps talking mindlessly of her mother's death, mumbling and repeating herself, so that Shrike will not hear the sudden silence and come out. Finally Mary agrees to let Miss Lonelyhearts in if Shrike is not home, goes inside, and soon Shrike peers out the

door, wearing only the tops of his pajamas. It is the child's Oedipal vision perfectly realized.[13]

One would not even have to endorse Hyman's Oedipal reading of the scene between Miss Lonelyhearts and the Shrikes to be aware of how devastatingly it comments on Miss Lonelyhearts's sexuality. As he hears footsteps approaching the door, Miss Lonelyhearts "limps" behind the projection of an elevator shaft. The shaft itself is phallic, Shrike's phallicism is startlingly evident in his sudden appearance wearing only his pajama tops, and Miss Lonelyhearts cowers in the shadows of the shaft like a guilty child. Clearly this final moment of the chapter reveals Miss Lonelyhearts as sexually maimed.

West's concerns in *Miss Lonelyhearts*, including problematic identity and violence, can be noticed in the pervasive imagery of the novel. In the opening prayer, which introduces the theme of the work, a key word is "heart": "hide me in your heart / And defend me from mine enemies." The name Miss Lonelyhearts itself, even if ironic, makes one continually conscious of the heart, the seat of compassion and love. At one point in the work, Miss Lonelyhearts "killed his great understanding heart by laughing," and in a dream sequence, he attempts to shape the paraphernalia in a pawnshop window into the shape of a heart. But an imagery running counter to it is that of stone or rock, implying an inability to feel—an extension of what West, in *Balso Snell*, had called the "Mundane Millstone." At the beginning Miss Lonelyhearts, discouraged, remembers Shrike's comment that he should give his readers "stones." "Give us this day our daily stone" becomes a parodic version of the Lord's Prayer. All that Miss Lonelyhearts can feel as he enters the little park is "the stone that had formed in his gut."

The menacing buildings that surround the park are the work of a civilization of "stone breakers," and it is implied that nature has retaliated upon this culture of "forced rock and tortured steel," in which the natural, the ability to feel spontaneously and purely, has become distorted and is transmuted into hardness and inhumanity. Fay Doyle's legs are like boulders, enormous grindstones, and late in the work Miss Lonelyhearts imagines that he has come into possession of a faith that will protect him from the brutalization that is everywhere about him, a faith analogous to the rock of faith on which the Church was built. But the rock he possesses within himself merely deadens him to external reality, to the catastrophe awaiting him at the stairway landing.

Breasts appear with extraordinary frequency, but rather than suggesting natural innocence or tender maternity, they have a purely sexual connotation. Fay Doyle, a voluptuary, has breasts of mammoth size. Miss

Farkis means no more to Shrike than a pair of breasts, and Mary Shrike uses her breasts as a form of sexual enticement (an enticement made grotesque by the fact that her mother had died of cancer of the breast). Miss Lonelyhearts sadistically twists Betty's nipple, as if to pluck it violently from her body, and elsewhere parts of the human anatomy are wrenched from the whole, or made to resemble other, disparate parts of the anatomy. Betty's upraised arms pull her breasts up "until they were like pink-tipped thumbs," and other allusions to breasts take strangely nonorganic forms, as in the oddly memorable reference to the naked girl in the mineral water poster whose nipples are "like tiny red hats."

Religious imagery and allusions abound in the novel, but they all suggest an inaccessible tradition, twisted into sterile modern forms. Beginning with the opening paragraph, in which Miss Lonelyhearts reads Shrike's prayer card addressed to a secular Christ, the newsroom of the New York *Post-Dispatch* is evoked as a modern temple of faith, to which the wretched send their letters that are like prayers for deliverance. That the newsroom, the New Church, cannot aid them is implied immediately in the image of the newspaper that is blown in the wind over the park "like a kite with a broken spine." The newspaper's broken spine introduces the crippling theme, and by the end the newspaper is associated with outbursts of violence. Fay Doyle uses a rolled-up newspaper as a club with which to beat her husband, and he, in turn, goes to Miss Lonelyhearts's room with a gun concealed under a newspaper.

A number of religiously connotative names appear in the novel, but those who bear them imply merely a religious ideal that has become incoherent. Mary and Joseph are present in the childless, frigid Mary Shrike, and in Joseph Zemp (alluded to in a newspaper clipping) who is slain in an argument over a trifling amount of money. Doyle has the same name as Peter, who founded the Christian church on the rock of faith. Miss Lonelyhearts's friend Gates has a name with religious associations, but he merely accompanies Miss Lonelyhearts to a comfort station where they torment the "clean old man," hoping to wring a sordid story from him as the real "truth" of his life. The life of the city, as it is imagined in *Miss Lonelyhearts*, is cramped and claustrophobic. There are no real homes in it, only apartments and rooms that seem hardly lived in, or that have hostile or horrifying associations. Delehanty's speakeasy is the single social center shown in the novel, and it is "illegitimate," entered through an "armored door" with a small aperture that, on the other side, reveals a glowingly red, bloodshot eye. In the color symbolism of *Miss Lonelyhearts*, nature has a gray, oppressive shading. "The gray sky" looks "as if it had been rubbed with a soiled eraser," obliterating any meaning that might be found in it. At the same time, the color red appears frequently, and has been associated with sex and violence.

In a variety of images West employs, innocence ends inevitably in disillusionment and animality. No vegetation grows in the little park, and if flowers were to spring up, watered by the "tears" of the city's inhabitants, they would smell of "feet." The imagery of the rose, that reminder of Christ's perfect love, appears early when Miss Lonelyhearts, thinking of what he will say to the despondent letter writers, reflects that "his heart was a rose and in his skull another rose bloomed." Yet later he twists Betty's breast as a rose that he will pluck, and wear in his buttonhole as if it were no more than an artificial decoration. In the final scene, Miss Lonelyhearts's room seems full of grace, "as clean as the innersides of the inner petals of a newly forced rosebud," but the vision proves delusionary and is quickly followed by his death.

Shrike remarks that somewhere in the jungle of entrails within man's body "lives a bird called the soul," yet Shrike's own name is taken from the "butcher bird," which impales its victims on thorns before tearing them apart with its hooked beak. Shrike bears the insignia of the trinity in his triangularly shaped head, but his face is, in fact, "a dead, gray triangle." In one of his many parodies, Shrike describes God as "Father, Son, and Silver Wire-haired Terrier"; and at times West plays with the idea of the dog as God spelled backwards, an anagram of man's condition. When Miss Lonelyhearts tells Betty hysterically that he is a "humanity lover," he is said to "bark" out the words; and later, in one of the novel's most harrowing scenes, Pete Doyle is beaten by his wife with a rolled-up newspaper, which he seizes in his teeth while rolling on the floor like a dog.

Sadistic violence and cruelty are everywhere present in West's tropes of weapons and sharp blades and knives. Miss Lonelyhearts is pierced by a shadow "spear." Shrike's face is like the blade of a hatchet. The husband of Broad Shoulders leaves hammers and knives under his pillow to "fright" her. In the pawnshop window, in Miss Lonelyhearts's dream, "a tortured high light twisted on the blade of a gift knife." He drives the effigy of Christ into the wall of his room with a "spike," hoping to see it writhe. Shrike tells Miss Lonelyhearts that sleeping with his wife "is like sleeping with a knife in one's groin," an obvious image of castration.

Those who write to Miss Lonelyhearts are women who have been oppressed and mistreated by men, yet other women in the novel are men's victimizers. They seem sexually damaged in one respect or another, and use their sexuality in a way that prohibits any exchange of genuine feeling or intimacy. Miss Farkis has a name that suggests "far-kiss," or a remoteness from feeling. She appears only briefly and hardly speaks at all, but there is nevertheless a mannishness about her that is striking. She has "thick ankles, big hands, a powerful body, a man's haircut," and she acknowledges her introduction to Miss Lonelyhearts "with a masculine handshake." She is not necessarily implied to be a lesbian (although she could be), but she is clearly sexually ambivalent. Mary Shrike is even less at ease with her sexuality. Although she dresses in a way that coquettishly calls attention to her breasts, she is actually frigid, and does not know how to be natural. She wears a sexy garment, "a tight, shiny dress," yet it resembles "glass-covered steel." Lacking spontaneity and on the deepest level hating sex, Mary Shrike is as sterile as the world that made her and that she reflects. Fay Doyle is not repressed, like Mary Shrike, but rather deranged in her femininity, a sexual warrior who destroys her husband and fills Miss Lonelyhearts with fear.

In *The Bostonians*, Henry James dramatized a cultural breakdown in late nineteenth-century America through a derangement in the relation of the sexes, with masculinized women and effeminized men who cannot come together with any ease or naturalness. *Miss Lonelyhearts* carries this analogy between cultural breakdown and sexual dislocation even further, envisioning a world in which embitterment over the loss of faith and ideals produces a warlike relationship of the sexes, the maiming of both men and women alike.

West's characters are all stunted half persons or non-persons who grope for an identity or sense of wholeness that they cannot find. The protagonist has no name except the pen name he uses in his column, one with a gender that would seem to cancel out his manhood. Implying her incompleteness, Betty has no last name; and Shrike has no first name, only a last one that limits his identity by likening him to a nonhuman creature, a ferociously assaultive bird. The people who write to Miss Lonelyhearts have no real names, only generic labels, like Sick-of-it-all. Miss Farkis has no first name, and is reduced to nonentity by Shrike's use of her as a ventriloquist's doll. Mary Shrike, Fay, and Pete Doyle have names, but they do not know who or what they are. The features of Pete's face are incoherent. His eyes fail to balance, and his mouth is not under his nose; his forehead is shaped like a chin and his chin is like a diminutive forehead. When he talks his speech makes no sense. "He was giving birth," West remarks, "to groups of words that lived inside of him as things, a jumble of retorts he had meant to make when insulted and the private curses against fate that experience had taught him to swallow."

These characters have more in common with the characters in *Balso Snell* than one might think since, like the characters in the earlier novel, they are unable to become "real," to enter intelligibly into life. Mary Shrike is a good example of this. Miss Lonelyhearts joins her in an excursion to a nightclub called the El Gaucho, where an orchestra plays a Cuban rhumba, and waiters are dressed as South American cowboys. The nightclub is like a theater, which offers romantic illusion as reality. Its guitars, bright shawls, exotic foods, and outlandish costumes are, as West remarks, "part of the business of dreams," a form of escape for people from the emptiness of their lives. In this atmosphere, Mary offers herself to Miss Lonelyhearts "in a series of formal, impersonal gestures," a "pantomime" of real emotion. Miss Lonelyhearts has been intrigued by a medal she wears on a chain around her neck, and at the El Gaucho, in a fine touch, is at last able to glimpse the medal, which turns out to be a high-school athletic award for first place in the one-hundred-yard dash. It is preposterous that this medal lying in the cleavage between her breasts should be an athletic award. Presumably it would be something of a religious or at least personal nature that would involve tenderness or sentiment.

Mary Shrike's romantic daydream at the El Gaucho is followed by a horrifying scene in front of her apartment door, where she is literally stripped naked by Miss Lonelyhearts. Not wanting to let her husband know, through a long awkward silence that she is being seduced by Miss Lonelyhearts, she mumbles in a kind of chant: "My mother died of cancer of the breast.... She died leaning over a table. My father was a portrait painter. He led a gay life. He mistreated my mother. She had cancer of the breast...." Her recall of her "interesting" parents is a romanticization of a life that is wholly without meaning. The reality of her situation is that she has just been stripped by one man, and will soon be "raped" by another, waiting at the other side of the door.

If Mary Shrike has no real existence at all, Betty has hardly more. Her neatness or orderliness precludes any consciousness of suffering or of the irrational in life. She wishes to "adjust" Miss Lonelyhearts to her own painfully limited vision. When he experiences a spiritual collapse, she appears at his room and spoon-feeds him chicken soup as if he had a cold. Her stunting is implied when Miss Lonelyhearts turns on her viciously, denouncing her "wide-eyed little mother act." It is an act, insofar as it is a confining role she plays that keeps her from having to confront the madness of life.

When Miss Lonelyhearts accompanies her for a weekend in the country, Betty is depicted as an unfallen Eve, set against an Edenic landscape. It is, however, an Eden in decay. The hamlet not far from the retreat is named Monkstown, but it has already been corrupted by the secular. Miss Lonelyhearts goes there to pick up newspapers, a reminder of the encroachment of devitalized dreams. He stops at the Aw-Kum-On Garage, which suggests a leering overture to quick sex; and the comments of the garage man about "Yids" implies an ugly division among men, a loss of the ideal of brotherhood. The retreat itself is shadowed menacingly by "deep shade" and silence that is like "a funereal hush." The new green leaves on the trees shine in the sun "like an army of little metal shields," and the sound of a thrush singing is "like that of a flute choked with saliva." Nature seems contaminated, its innocence at the verge of being lost. The chapter ends with Miss Lonelyhearts's sexual act with Betty, which brings about the "fall" of this Adam and Eve. Once their relationship becomes overtly sexual, there is no longer an Eden to which they can return.

Before long, Betty realizes' that she is pregnant, and she adopts another role, like that of Janey Davenport in *Balso Snell*, playing the part of the girl in trouble, derived in type from romance magazines. She breaks the news to Miss Lonelyhearts at a soda fountain where they go on a date, drinking strawberry sodas through straws—a parody of "adolescent love." Her "light blue" dress, at the same time, intimates that she is a version of the Virgin Mary, removed from sexuality "immaculately." As Virgin Mary and "adolescent girl," Betty will marry Miss Lonelyhearts, and they will have a happy future in Connecticut, like a couple in a romance magazine story. In this projective escape, Betty is reduced to the dimensionless status of her decorative "party dress." Miss Lonelyhearts, West remarks sardonically, "begged the party dress to marry him, saying all the things it expected to hear, all the things that went with strawberry sodas and farms in Connecticut."

But the most dimensionless of the female characters is Fay Doyle, who derives from Mary McGeeney, at the end of *Balso Snell*, when she surrenders to the urgings of sex, muttering "yes, yes" to its biological dictates. A motif that prepares for her appearance is that of nature as it continually tends toward decay and formlessness, the "entropy" West refers to that is a more powerful and relentless process than man's ability to create order. Comically, when she seduces Miss Lonelyhearts, she is captured as an embodiment of the mindless, instinctual drives of entropic nature. Her call to him to hurry is a "sea moan," and when she lies beside him she heaves, "tidal, moon-driven." When Miss Lonelyhearts leaves the bed after their sexual experience, he is "like an exhausted swimmer, leaving the surf."

What is striking about her sexuality is that it is without intelligence or form, and is a gruesome distortion of the "feminine." When she first appears in the little park, she is dressed in a strangely mismatching outfit that includes a plaid skirt and Tam O'Shanter, as if she were a member of a Scottish marching regiment, and she is said to resemble "a police captain." Although Miss Lonelyhearts engages in sex with her, it is she who makes the aggressive advances and who overpowers *him*. Her mindlessness is revealed in her account to Miss Lonelyhearts of her life with her husband. She tells of having been given a child out of wedlock by a certain Tony Benelli, a "dirty dago" she thought was a "gent." Doyle marries her, providing her with a husband and her daughter Lucy with a father; yet rather than feeling gratitude, she demeans her husband through a need to assert herself.

She even takes little Lucy to Benelli's home, where she stages a scene, shouting "he's the father of my child" in front of Benelli and his wife, before the Benellis threaten to call the police and she "beats it." Later, at home, she tells the child that she should remember that "her real papa" was a man named Tony Benelli and that he had wronged her, a story inspired by "too many movies." Her playing the aggrieved woman such as she has seen in films merely blinds her to her injury of her child and husband, whose fondness for the child she resents. She destroys his last sustaining illusion, that he is a father and adequate man, and in the "theatrical" scene that ensues the Doyles strike each other. When Doyle attempts to hit his wife with his cane he misses, falls onto the floor, and begins to cry pathetically. "The kid was on the floor crying too," she says, "and that set me off because the next thing I knew I was on the floor bawling too." In this scene of utter squalor and confusion, her sentimentality is again a means of dramatizing herself, so that she does not have to examine her own vacancy.

Perhaps the single most important line in *Miss Lonelyhearts* is spoken by one of the anonymous voices at Delehanty's. Miss Lonelyhearts is being discussed, and various opinions of his Christ fixation are put forward. One voice, however, stands out from the others in the insight it affords. "The trouble with him," the voice says, "the trouble with all of us, is that we have no outer life, only an inner one, and that by necessity." In the barrenness of their world, West's isolated characters are driven inward upon themselves, forced to embrace illusion, and living through illusion as they do they cannot establish contact with others. They are all participants in a Theater of the Absurd, acting out illusionary parts.

The principal theatrical roles have been assumed by Miss Lonelyhearts and Shrike, the two most sentient characters. They might be said to stand, respectively, for heart and head: Miss Lonelyhearts would come to terms with life through sympathy and compassion, Shrike attempts to deal with it through his hardened intelligence. One is a humanity lover, the other a God-hater. In each case, in the extremity of their attitudes, they become isolated characters confined within, stunted by, the theatrical roles they assume. Even early in the work Miss Lonelyhearts is identified as an actor. Shadows "curtain" the arch that leads into the little park where he goes to meditate on modern sainthood. In the ritual of the lamb's sacrifice he plays the part ostentatiously of the priest, and in his column he is an ersatz Christ. In each case, he pretends to an identity he cannot justify in his actual experience.

Referring to his column, Miss Lonelyhearts refers to "the Christ business," and as such it is merely another of the many commercialized dreams of escape from an irreducible emptiness.

What one notices about Miss Lonelyhearts is that he constantly drives himself to feel more than he can. In the early scene in which he removes the effigy of Christ from its backing and drives it into the wall with a spike, he hopes to see it writhe, and is disturbed that Christ's expression remains "decoratively placid." He himself would wish to feel with great intensity, but can never feel enough, so that he is conscious of his own spuriousness. When he attempts to explain himself to Betty as a "humanity lover," he begins to shout at her, "accompanying his shouts with gestures that were too appropriate, like those of an old-fashioned actor." By the end of the scene, in fact, he turns on her angrily and cries: "What's the matter, sweetheart? ... Didn't you like the performance?" When he attempts to enunciate his gospel of love to the Doyles at their home, he forces his voice to shrillness, until it becomes a "stage scream." This theatrical imagery continually reminds the reader that Miss Lonelyhearts is attempting a heroic role that eludes him.

Shrike, too, is highly theatrical. As a Christ-mocker, he strikes attitudes, and is characteristically captured in theatrical tableaux. He twice raises his fist to Miss Farkis, a gesture that seems "frozen" like a camera still, and buries his hatchetlike head in her neck in a "frozen" moment that ends the chapter. A passage in the original version of this chapter, but removed in revision, reads: "Shrike and his stage, the speakeasy, made [Miss Lonelyhearts] feel that he was wandering, lost without hope of escape, among the scenery and costumes in the cellar of an ancient theatre."[14] Shrike is locked into his role just as Miss Lonelyhearts is locked into his. His illusion is that he can compensate for the loss of God and of spiritual values through a defiant hedonism. But hedonism is merely another escape dream, as he himself, at one point, notes, and for Shrike it is singularly and bitterly pleasureless. Shrike's shrillness is an attempt to kill the nerve of feeling, which mocks his attempt to find self-mastery through hardened intelligence alone. Inwardly divided, caught between a spirituality that is dead and a sexuality that is malignant, Miss Lonelyhearts and Shrike are "performers" unable to achieve an authentic sense of self.

West's conception of his characters as grotesque performers is at times accompanied by a vaudeville motif. Miss Lonelyhearts dreams that he is a magician juggling doorknobs, on the stage of a crowded theater. At his command, they bleed, flower, and speak—a clownish parody of his role as a modern-day Christ. He attempts to create shapes out of pawnshop paraphernalia, performing in its window that is like a stage for onlookers. Although he makes spiritual claims, he is at various times the butt of low-comedy humor, particularly when he attempts to assert his manhood, a measure of his ability to control the world around him. His sex scene with Fay Doyle might have been put on the stage, its broad humor of gigantic woman versus small, inadequate man would draw the laughter of the crowd.

Shrike, too, has vaudeville associations. "He practiced a trick," West writes, "used much by moving-picture comedians—the dead pan"; regardless of his gestures, his face is always blank. He is an absurd clown with an inanimate face and a dead soul, a satirist whose ungodly jests are turned ultimately upon himself. Finally, Pete Doyle is a comic performer, however unwillingly. When he returns home, for instance, he is grabbed comically by his wife, who "shakes the breath out of him." In the end, he can only burlesque himself. When he brings Miss Lonelyhearts home, Mrs. Doyle makes sexual advances to his friend, and Pete "groans," exclaiming: "Ain't I the pimp, to bring a guy home for my wife?" He drops to his knees and does an imitation of a dog; and when Miss Lonelyhearts bends over to help him, Doyle tears open Miss Lonelyhearts's fly, rolling "over on his back, laughing wildly." His burlesque of himself as a pitiful cuckold is only too accurate a rendering of the disparity between the characters' yearning for a sense of meaning and the actual meaninglessness of their lives.

One would wonder what, in West's own experience and psychic makeup, could have produced such a bleak vision of life. One might speculate that its origins lay in West's own sense of exclusion from life and of sexual inadequacy. West's treatment of women is particularly revealing since, whether frigid or sexually devouring, they all seem threatening. Homosexuality also enters importantly into the work, and one would surmise that Miss Lonelyhearts's problem of latent homosexuality was also West's. Miss Lonelyhearts's passive-hysteric nature, certainly, carries the suggestion of some innermost hysteric tendency in the man who created him so powerfully. The very power of *Miss Lonelyhearts* attests to its having been written from tremulous nerves and acute inner anxieties. *Miss Lonelyhearts* has the quality of a waking dream, a truly and magnificently haunting one that is, in some ways, a sexual dream.

V.S. Pritchett has called *Miss Lonelyhearts* "very nearly faultless,"[15] but one could quibble with a few things. Betty finds that she is pregnant rather too quickly after she has sex with Miss Lonelyhearts, and the business of Pete Doyle's threatening letter, accidentally picked up with other mail and read by Shrike at the party, is perhaps too "managed." Doyle's appearance at Miss Lonelyhearts's building at the end, with gun in hand, is just possible, given his derangement and sense of betrayal, but because he is so passive, so hopelessly crushed, one wonders if he would be capable of this final outburst. More generally, the final three chapters have a sped-up hysteria that is slightly out of key with the earlier chapters of the novel. But these quibbles mean little compared to the deep impression of life the novel conveys. An astonishing performance, *Miss Lonelyhearts* is a work that an author, if he is exceptionally gifted and unusually fortunate, might write once in a lifetime.

Miss Lonelyhearts is a luminous and deeply compelling work that has great character conceptions, from "Miss L" himself to Shrike and the Doyles. The preposterous Fay Doyle is so inspired a conception that no other female character of a similar banality can compare with her in the whole range of twentieth-century American writing. Not since *The Great Gatsby* has a novel created its age with such merciless satire. Its craftsmanship and vivid style belong to the twenties, but its mood is distinctively part of the thirties. It is the most "original" novel to come out of the Depression, a "religious" work of macabre humor that searches into the dark places of modern loneliness. Its quality, finally, is its ambiguousness, its odd mixture of comedy and horror; its mingling of realism and fantasy; its exposure of Miss Lonelyhearts's illusion, yet its compassion for the "lost" and certitude of good cause for the sorrowing heart of Miss Lonelyhearts.

NOTES

1. The "Susan Chester" letters, kept by West and later made available to Martin, are discussed in *Nathanael West: The Art of His Life*, pp. 110, 187. Curiously, certain details in the letters to Miss Lonelyhearts that give the impression of having been invented by West have some basis in the letters themselves. One woman wrote that she was "stooping to put the broom under the bed to get the lint and dust ... lo-behold I saw a face which resembled the mask of a devil—only the whites of his eyes and hands clenched ready to choke anyone." The woman signed herself "Broad Shoulders," adding, "Susan, don't think I am broad shouldered. But that is just the way I feel about life and me." Her name, "Broad Shoulders," and the incident of the man under the bed, were incorporated by West into the longest and most disturbing letter Miss Lonelyhearts receives. West's method, generally, was to make the letters more illiterate, increasing the effect of the writers' helplessness, and to make their contents more unsettling. A sixteen-year-old girl, for example, had written to "Susan Chester" of her weak knee that made her walk with a slight limp; but in the letter in the novel, the girl, more disturbingly, has no nose.

2. The chapters are: "Miss Lonelyhearts and the Lamb," *Contact*, 1 (February 1932): 80–85; "Miss Lonelyhearts and the Dean Pan," *Contact*, 1 (May 1932): 13–21; "Miss Lonelyhearts and the Clean Old Man," *Contact*, 1 (May 1932): 22–27; "Miss Lonelyhearts in the Dismal Swamp," *Contempo*, 2 (July 5, 1932): 1–2; "Miss Lonelyhearts on a Field Trip," *Contact*, 1 (October 1932): 50–57. The serial chapters are reprinted in William White, *Nathanael West: A Comprehensive Bibliography* (Kent, Ohio: Kent State University Press, 1975), pp. 132–62. Critical articles on West's revisions are: Carter A. Daniel, "West's Revision of *Miss Lonelyhearts*," *Studies in Bibliography*, 16 (1963): 232–43; reprinted in Jay Martin, ed., *Nathanael West: A Collection of Critical Essays* (Englewood Cliffs, New Jersey: Prentice–Hall, 1971), pp. 52–65; and Robert I. Edenbaum, "To Kill God and Build a Church: Nathanael West's *Miss Lonelyhearts*," *CEA Critic*, 29 (June 1967), 5–7, 11;

reprinted in Thomas H. Jackson, ed., *Twentieth Century Interpretations of Miss Lonelyhearts: A Collection of Critical Essays* (Englewood Cliffs, New Jersey: Prentice–Hall, 1971), pp. 61–66.

3. Nathanael West, "Some Notes on Miss L.," *Contempo*, 3 (May 15, 1933): 1–2; reprinted in William White, *Nathaniel West: A Comprehensive Bibliography*, pp. 165–66; and in Jay Martin; ed., *Nathaniel West: A Collection of Critical Essays*, pp. 66–67.

4. Nathanael West, "Some Notes on Miss L.," in Martin, ed., *Nathaniel West: A Collection of Critical Essays*, p. 66.

5. John O'Hara's *Appointment in Samarra* (1934) was published only a year after *Miss Lonelyhearts*, and it, too, belongs distinctively to the American Depression period. Different as they are, the novels have certain features in common, since they are tautly written, brilliantly controlled anatomies of particular American locales of the early thirties. Each is concerned with misery, loneliness, and the loss of identity in a society in which meaning can no longer be located, and where all things end in a trauma of sexuality. *Appointment in Samarra* takes place during the three days of the Christmas holiday, and an absent Christ broods over its scene of violence and despair; and in *Miss Lonelyhearts*, Christ is called upon and petitioned, but only a sordid confusion is revealed. Death is a common theme, and both heroes become increasingly disoriented in the course of the works, losing their lives at the end. Both novels are symptomatic of what Josephine Herbst called "a Great Distress."

6. In the early 1930s, West met frequently with a group of young Jewish intellectuals to discuss music, literature, and politics at the apartment of George Brounoff on Central Park West. According to Martin, Dostoyevsky "inevitably provided the major ideals for the group. They read all his works in translation and were especially influenced by *The Brothers Karamazov*, but also by *A Raw Youth*, *The Idiot*, *The Possessed*, and *Crime and Punishment*.... The kind of Christ figure or secular saint which they found in Prince Myshkin appealed strongly to them as the highest development, along certain lines, of their own ideals" (Martin, p. 114). West, however, mocked the sentimental idealism of the group before his Village friends, and insisted that people were victims, who used ideal figures such as Christ to conceal their condition from themselves. Dostoyevsky, nevertheless, remained one of West's major literary interests, and he read his novels over and over during the course of his life. The dramatic and strongly scenic construction of Dostoyevsky's novels, and his preoccupation with intense inner states of conflict, influenced West significantly.

7. Randall Reid, in *The Fiction of Nathanael West*, pp. 50–52, has compared Miss Lonelyhearts to Raskolnikov in some detail. He comments: "Both Raskolnikov and Miss Lonelyhearts are, when we meet them, already launched on an obsessive idea whose genesis is only hinted at. In both, the obsession ambiguously reflects a personal illness and a real external problem—it is simultaneously true that Miss Lonelyhearts is driven by 'hysteria' and that he is driven by a clear perception of the misery of others. In both cases, the external problem is the fact of apparently hopeless suffering. And in both casts, the resulting obsession focuses on the necessity of an heroic action—Raskolnikov imitates Napoleon; Miss Lonelyhearts imitates Christ. The heroic action raises a series of questions: Is the action desirable? Is the hero capable of it? Are his apparent motives real? Raskolnikov and Miss Lonelyhearts' alternately doubt the action itself and their own worthiness to attempt it.... Both are ... poised between mocking antagonists and loving but incomprehending girls."

8. West's incorporation of *The Waste Land* into *Miss Lonelyhearts* has been noted in the past by Edmond L. Volpe, "The Waste Land of Nathanael West," *Renascence*, 13

(1961), 69–77, 112; reprinted in Thomas H. Jackson, ed., *Twentieth Century Interpretations of Miss Lonelyhearts*, pp. 81–92; and by Victor Comerchero, *Nathanael West: The Ironic Prophet* (Syracuse, New York: Syracuse University Press, 1964), 86–88. Volpe regards *Miss Lonelyhearts* as a more negative version of *The Waste Land*, since at the end of his poem Eliot offers qualified hope, while West denies that any is possible. Comerchero focuses upon the Grail quest theme, viewing Miss Lonelyhearts as a searcher who hopes to renew the blighted land.

9. The only critic in the past to have commented on *The Great Gatsby* and *Miss Lonelyhearts* is Randall Reid, pp. 98–99. Reid remarks: "The triad of Doyle, Mrs. Doyle, and Miss Lonelyhearts recalls the similar grouping of Wilson, Myrtle Wilson, and Gatsby in *The Great Gatsby*. In both novels, a crippled or devitalized cuckold is married to a vulgar but vital woman, and in both novels the cuckold mistakenly kills the 'spiritual' hero in revenge for his wife's betrayal.... Even the styles of Fitzgerald and West are related. Both write with an acute ear for vulgar speech, with an instinct for poetry and comedy. I think West learned from Fitzgerald, and I think the grotesque fate of Miss Lonelyhearts was a conscious echo of Gatsby's grotesque end."

10. There are even very specific moments in *Miss Lonelyhearts* that are reminiscent of Fitzgerald's novel. Pete Doyle's physical gestures are not synchronized with his speech, and his features do not compose to form any coherent whole, so that his face is "like one of those composite photographs used by screen magazines in guessing contests." His facial incoherence is similar to that of Myrtle Wilson's sister Catherine in *The Great Gatsby*, since her face, too, has a blurred and incoherent quality. The descriptions occur at the beginning of scenes of radical confusion and squalor. In another passage, Miss Lonelyhearts "was conscious of two rhythms that were slowly becoming one. When they became one, his identification with God was complete." The lines recall the passage in *The Great Gatsby* in which Gatsby confuses Daisy with God, and at their lips' touch "the incarnation was complete."

11. Pound's translation of Li Po's "Lament of the Frontier Guard" is a "wasteland" poem that focuses upon desolation and a sorrow from which there is no escape. The "gracious spring" of the poem has turned into an autumn of suffering and isolation, making it apt in connection with the little park, where Miss Lonelyhearts meditates in the spring that cannot arrive, and where his burden cannot be lightened.

12. R.W.B. Lewis, *Trials of the Word: Essays in American Literature and the Humanistic Tradition* (New Haven: Yale University Press, 1965), pp. 213–14.

13. Stanley Edgar Hyman, *Nathanael West* (Minneapolis: University of Minnesota Press, 1965), p. 23.

14. Nathanael West, "Miss Lonelyhearts and the Lamb," *Contact*, February 1932; reprinted in William White, *Nathanael West: A Comprehensive Bibliography*, p. 133.

15. V.S. Pritchett, *The Living Novel & Later Appreciations* (New York: Random House, 1964), p. 279.

JOHN KEYES

"Inarticulate Expressions of Genuine Suffering?": A Reply to the Correspondence *in* Miss Lonelyhearts

Miss Lonelyhearts begins with the writer at work; or not at work. Sitting at his desk, staring at a mock prayer, a parody of the *Anima Christi* printed on a piece of white cardboard by his feature editor, Shrike, Miss Lonelyhearts is "still working on his leader," a rhythm of clichés: "Life is worth while, for it is full of dreams and peace, gentleness and ecstasy, and faith that burns like a clear white flame on a grim dark altar."[1] A writer with writer's block, with only one thesis, and no language, no will to convey his message, he is the artist who cannot act, for writing is an act. He has been paralyzed by the collective misery of the world. He cannot write, he feels, because the letters he receives are unanswerable, because the one relevant reply, the power of Christ, is a "business" that will make him "sick" (p. 68). To him, the letters are "no longer funny.... All of them [are] alike, stamped from the dough of suffering with a heart-shaped cookie knife" (p. 66). In a distant rather formal speech, he explains the situation to his girl friend, Betty, impersonalizing himself in the process:

> Perhaps I can make you understand. Let's start from the beginning. A man is hired to give advice to the readers of a newspaper. The job is a circulation stunt and the whole staff considers it a joke. He welcomes the job, for it might lead to a

From *The University of Windsor Review*, vol. 20, no. 1 (Fall–Winter 1987). © 1987 The University of Windsor Review.

gossip column, and anyway he's tired of being a leg man. He too
considers the job a joke, but after several months at it, the joke
begins to escape him. He sees that the majority of the letters are
profoundly humble pleas for moral and spiritual advice, that they
are inarticulate expressions of genuine suffering. He also
discovers that his correspondents take him seriously. For the first
time in his life, he is forced to examine the values by which he
lives. This examination shows him that he is the victim of the joke
and not its perpetrator (p. 106).

To him, the conclusion is evident. Sentimental, illiterate, unintentionally
comic, the correspondence is nonetheless the inescapable, unanswerable
evidence of universal evil.

But writers are readers too, the acts are complementary, and the failure
of the one may have its sources in the failure of the other. Why should we
assume the letters are the same as he describes them? Yet this is what the
criticism has done. Throughout the seven books on West, the three dozen or
so articles on *Miss Lonelyhearts*, the correspondence itself has received no
sustained analysis. The critics have reacted to it, but with much the same
moral sobriety and anguish as has Miss Lonelyhearts; the unstable
protagonist's flawed perceptions have become the norm of response. In the
earliest book, James Light saw the correspondence arising from "desperate
and helpless people who have no other place to turn."[2] Victor Comerchero
said it "captures the essence of a pervasive, inexplicable human suffering that
afflicts guilty and innocent, pious and impious alike ... there is little irony in
the letters."[3] Randall Reid felt the letters may be "trite, illiterate, and
sentimental, but the misery which they reveal cannot be doubted, nor does
anyone in the novel seriously doubt it"; as a result, he said, "in a world where
evil and unrelieved suffering are everywhere, redemption is an absolute need.
There is no other answer to the cry for help."[4] Kingsley Widmer's view was
more balanced. The letters, although "self-parodying," reveal a world of
"hardly   remediable   human   suffering....   The   problems   given   are
predominantly female and sexual, around physical and psychological
crippling, in a context of the moralistically punitive. Such miseries cannot be
readily ameliorated, often not genuinely assuaged, and traditionally call for a
religious answer"; they suggest an "unredeemable disorder in the moral
universe."[5] Having said this, they were then free to skirt the correspondence,
letting their emphasis fall upon other aspects: the search for Christ, whether
genuine or ironic or both; literary technique, background, and sources;
biography.

Some correspondence this must be, to so inflict itself on consciousness and conscience, to have such an overwhelming mass power to silence all reply. Surely it must evoke, if not our startled awe, at least our deepest sympathy. William Carlos Williams felt this in his review in 1933:

> The letters-to-the-papers which West uses freely and at length must be authentic. I can't believe anything else. The unsuspected world they reveal is beyond ordinary thought. They are a terrific commentary on our daily lack of depth in thought of others. Should such lives as these letters reveal never have been brought to light? Should such people, like the worst of our war wounded, best be kept in hiding?[6]

Apparently West felt the same way too, at least of the originals upon which his own were based. His biographer, Jay Martin, tells us that

> West was deeply affected when he first read the letters; later, reading them aloud to the Brounoff circle, he betrayed considerable—to his friends, surprising—emotion in his voice and manner. He had obviously been, as one of his audience on that occasion says, "terribly ... hurt by them." But he did not surrender to them; from them he made a novel that included this emotion but also the hard calculations of fictive technique.[7]

West skilfully altered the originals:

> The skills with which West heightened the effect of reality in the original letters is demonstrated by his alterations in them, his deliberate cutting of all stylistic pretenses in order clearly and boldly to stress the pain of the writer, and his heightening of the shy, genteel attempts to conceal the pain evident just beneath a reasoned surface.[8]

The proof of this is given in a comparison of Desperate's letter with its archetype:

> The repetitions, the calculated intensification of pain, and the pitiable, conscious reiteration of clichéd phrase and pattern all hint at a kind of torment far deeper and more significant than that suggested by the language of the original letter.[9]

"A sad letter" has thus been "transform[ed] into a tragic one."'[10]

It is doubtful, however, that the alterations have increased much pain or torment in this or any of the others, or that there was much of either in the originals. If Martin is correct, then West has misread the originals; certainly Martin and the others have misread West's. If West was hurt by the letters that he read, his sympathy was surely misplaced.[11] His art was not. If anything, it often isolates and satirizes the typicality of complaint, heightens the internal confusions, increases the likelihood of unintentional self-exposure, turns the archetype into a comic cliché. However gruesome the content, the letters, as everyone admits, are comic. Self-exposure is one function of comedy. Since these authors constantly betray themselves in their prose,[12] they cannot be accepted at their own estimation. The failure to see this suggests the commentary on the correspondence has, for some time now, been marked by emotional, certainly not intellectual, illiteracy.[13]

How can we speak favorably of correspondents who write, less for advice than to continue as they are, to someone who has nothing to offer? The criticism surely misses the mark. It is untrue that the correspondents "have no other place to turn" (Miss Lonelyhearts and his ilk are among the last people from whom any sensible person should seek help). The letters are unintentionally ironic. The correspondents' sufferings are explicable, not mysterious; they have a recognizably human frame of reference. One can doubt the misery expressed. There are other answers to practical, human problems than religious redemption; indeed, it is spiritually smug to assume, or imply, that someone else's need for such redemption is greater than one's own. The distinction between "hardly remediable human suffering" and "unredeemable disorder" is not marginal. The correspondents, moreover, take Miss Lonelyhearts a good deal less seriously than either he or they think they do. Their pleas are not always "humble": Peter Doyle's letter partly bullies Miss Lonelyhearts; Fay Doyle's is seductive; while Sick-of-it-all and Broad Shoulders are veteran complainers (one suspects the latter is a nag). To view the correspondence, then, as Miss Lonelyhearts views it, is to magnify the suffering it expresses and to ignore the ironies inherent in the correspondent–columnist nexus.

These letters would entrap us, just as Miss Lonelyhearts is trapped, consciously, I believe, by the one he receives from Fay Doyle. But give them the close readings they deserve and they will reveal themselves as a reservoir of false emotions, a dumping ground or junkyard for them; they are Miss Lonelyhearts' Sargasso Sea.[14] They fill us with spurious feelings, or would try to, just as Miss Lonelyhearts, during his confrontation with the Doyles, understandably felt, in a brilliant image of sexual reversal, "like an empty bottle that is being filled with warm, dirty water" (p. 130). They are, in a sense, pornographic, provoking excess, encouraging us to wallow in a sentimentality of response.[15] That Miss Lonelyhearts should misread them and overreact to his misreading is what we should expect. His responses are as flawed as his perceptions. His column progresses from smarm (p. 66) to justified suffering (p. 116); he construes marital love as a relation between a Magna Mater and a child (p. 129). He is thus a failure in his chosen role of intercessory artist to the masses; he can read neither the emotions (nor the media) correctly. The letters, as Martin has told us, were based on those to Susan Chester or to others of her kind;[16] a similar one to one of her descendants exemplifies both the permanence of mass complaints and the emotional confusions they evoke. It can function as typical.

"To Put It Bluntly, I'm Ugly"

Dear Ann Landers: I am not a scatter-brained teenager, so please rule out that possibility. I'm a young woman, 23, who is finding life intolerable because—to put it bluntly—I am ugly.

I'm beginning to hate myself. All my life people have made cruel remarks because of my looks. I've tried to rise above the insults and tell myself these people are ignorant or they wouldn't say such hurtful things. It doesn't help.

In my entire life I have had only six dates. I know now these fellows took me out only because they felt sorry for me. I'm not just plain-looking, Ann. My features are grotesque. I look like a freak.

I've been brooding about the hopelessness of my situation for what seems like an eternity and have even considered suicide. Can you help?

— Ugly

Ann says: If looks were the magic key to happiness, all beautiful people would be happy people. And you and I both know tortured souls who have fallen flat on their lovely faces and made a shamble of their lives.

Your low opinion of yourself dates back to early childhood. Therapy may help. I hope you'll give it a try.

Des Moines *Sunday-Register*
Nov. 25, 1962
Home-Family Section

Is it insensitive not to be "terribly hurt" by this? The letter, a defensive, evasive, and contradictory exhibition of self-pity and self-loathing, inadvertently denies the esteem the writer claims for herself and exposes her propensities to reject either the sympathy or the attentive interest she seeks;

Ann, unlike Miss Lonelyhearts, avoids the trap inherent in this sort of request—the emotional blackmail (help me, or else)—and she gives the "right" advice, but her ready-made clichés, the echo of Shrike's, shun personal contact, cancel expressive identity, and repudiate the remedy they offer, thereby diminishing the likelihood of its acceptance. Indeed, one is more angered by the reply than injured by the letter; in her gently scolding lecture, Ann reduces her correspondent to a child, who, then, the ironies are manifold, could not possibly be concerned with the problems she expresses so much better than Ann. The correspondence is thus a paradigm of mutual inauthenticity, but it is an inauthenticity which a complacent and self-gratulatory press compounds and heaps upon its readers. The writer's audience is a fiction, Walter Ong has said;[17] the fiction of it here is as the Sunday family, pious and domestic, serene in the illusion of an emotional communion between itself and the syndicated column, a communion which, if accepted, controverts the emotional sensitivity of the family that accepts it. To write to such a source is, then, to express a desire not to seek an answer: it is the espousal of wish, free vanity publishing, the self-indulgent sufferer asserting, with a public confessional and a nom de plume, the artist's role if not his compensations; thus, neither Ann nor Miss Lonelyhearts can provide a solution because they, and the media, are a part of the problem. Ann's insensitivity saves her; immune to writer's block, she will rise to write another day. But Miss Lonelyhearts, lacking her self-saving virtues and defects, can resolve his intercessory predicament only when he "submit[s] drafts of his column to God and God approve[s] them" (p. 139), a resolution transmuting the Deity into his senior editor, and ultimately, transforming the columnist into Christ, the answer to all the letters. Mercifully, Miss Lonelyhearts will be freed from language. He will not need to give a reply. He will become the reply.

Ann, at least, will not play Christ. Moreover, there is nothing in the letter from "Ugly" to suggest that Christ is the answer to it. The distinction can be grasped in Shrike's parodic letter to Christ, to the "Miss Lonelyhearts of Miss Lonelyhearts" (p. 110). With its parodic plea, "How can I believe, how can I have faith in this day and age?", it translates Miss Lonelyhearts, the columnist, into the correspondent now writing to the ultimate Columnist, Christ, but about an issue different from the issues contained in the letters he receives. In essence, the critics have assumed that Shrike's plea is unanswerable, and since that is so, a double assumption, that the correspondence is too. Within Miss Lonelyhearts' polarized sensibility, it seems to be Christ or nothing. But Miss Lonelyhearts' problem is not one shared by his correspondents. The issue satirized here, a crisis of faith, is not the substance of any of his letters. Neither they, nor "Ugly," are concerned with religious faith or doubt, but with action, with how to live in this world. Some even wonder "what to do" (pp. 66, 67, 68, 116, 120). It is Miss Lonelyhearts' mistake, not Ann's, to assume that they are, to assume that "Christ was the answer" (p. 68), to affirm the value of suffering (p. 116) and to justify it, and in so doing to project his fervent obsession upon his correspondents. It is an assumption presented as a Truth, resting apparently on its self-evidential nature. What West has exposed and satirized in this "New England puritan" with a "bony chin ... shaped and cleft like a hoof", who, with an "Old-Testament look," appears "like the son of a Baptist minister" (p. 69), is the choplogic mentality of the fundamentalist world of evangelical revivalism in which Christ becomes the answer to every letter, to every human problem, from migraines to bankruptcy. Obviously, when the answers are always the same, the questions have not been answered, because the questions are not always the same. Christ, it is clear, is not the answer, because Christ was never the question. Christ has become a manoeuvre to escape from the issues of the letters.

Fortunately, the answers can be inferred from an analysis of them, for the answers are implicit in the problems. Six are presented directly in the novel, two more are referred to by Shrike, and part of one is read by him when Miss Lonelyhearts is absent. Of the six, half are by women, two are by adolescents (one girl, one boy), and one is by a man. The letters from the women, "Sick-of-it-all," "Broad Shoulders", Fay Doyle, are easy to dispose of.

"Sick-of-it-all" (pp. 66–67), with "7 children in 12 yrs," is "sick and scared," in pain, pregnant again, and perhaps in danger of death. Her situation is acute, but her letter, with its insistent, complaining tone, evokes irritation rather than sympathy.[18] Her remark that her husband "promised no more children on the doctors advice as he said I might die but when I got back from the hospital he broke his promise and now I am going to have a baby," puts the burden for her predicament, and for prevention, and the means of it, solely upon her spouse. She is a too common female type, passive and victimized, or seeing herself as such, the blameless instrument of Church and husband, institution and male. In her eyes, her husband is responsible and she is innocent. But "it dont pay to be inocent." The unintended irony between innocent as sexually ignorant and innocent as guiltless is quite apparent. She was the first, she is not the second. There are other ironies as well. She contemplates suicide but "cant have an abortion on account of being a catholic." Her litany of hurts—"sometimes I think I will kill myself my kidneys hurt so much," "I dont think I can stand it my kidneys hurt so much," "I cry all the time it hurts so much,"—progressively hint at a decline in intensity of reaction, as though the *act* of writing is itself giving solace to her. But she chooses to cry rather than to act, and ends her letter, saying, "I dont know what to do." Obviously, she must do more than write, which is for her a form of temporizing. She will have to choose between pain and the risk of death, on the one hand and religious faith, on the other. The choice may not be easy, but the choice is there, to be made, lived through, lived with. To fail to act is to increase the agony, intensify the complaint, for she is also suffering from the pain of indecision. Unfortunately, this sort of woman is not the sort who decides. Should she survive her eighth child, she would more likely have a ninth, out of sheer passivity, than a hysterectomy. And compose yet another letter.

The letter by the voluble "Broad Shoulders" (pp. 116–121), a woman who can't stop talking, is by far the longest in the novel. Its content— manifest—is the sorrow of marriage, her marriage, a squalid, neurotic disorder of debt, wife beating, venereal disease, sexual hysteria and paralysis, and threats of homicide. Her woes are not the fault of God or governments or nature or the way things are; they are man-made woes, for which she is partially to blame. She shirks responsibility for getting married: "During the war I was told if I wanted to do my bit I should marry the man I was engaged to as he was going away to help Uncle Sam and to make a long story short I was married to him" (p. 116). She blames her husband entirely for their economic plight; she is the steady worker, he is not. Nonetheless, she has a child, which puts her out of the work force, lays the burden of support upon a "lazy" man (p. 117), and, with financial difficulties increasing, two years later has a second. She does this while in poor health from the first. She sees herself as a mother, but, with her husband disintegrating, becoming dangerously unstable, she, through her passivity, continues to expose her children to a violent relationship. She is also ambivalent toward the sexual advances of her boarder: "He tries to make me be bad and as there is nobody in the house when he comes home drunk on Saturday night I dont know what to do but so far I didn't let him" (p. 120). As is consistent with the passive view, she sees things happening to herself, as though she is not an agent: "if I ever write all the things which happened to me living with him it would fill a book" (p. 120).

She has, however, already written too much. The childlike, gossipy tone, affirmed by the subtle, slight reiteration of the interjection, "well," the breathless, run-on sentences, the repetitiveness, lead the reader to ask, with some impatience, despite the mounting interest of her husband's metamorphosis, what does the woman want?—and to find her questions at the end incredibly anticlimactic: "Shall I take my husband back? How can I support my children?" (p. 121). The answer to the first is obvious. It is better not to live with a psychopath. Even she knows this. She has left him four times before. And how can she take him back when she doesn't know where he is? The answer to the second is only a touch more demanding, even given depression America. She had been working, supporting her children because of the failure of her husband. She can continue to do this, with her mother, or a new boarder, to watch mutually over the children. There is more than one boarder in the world. With replies at least so simple in this case, replies she really knows, why, then, does she write? To talk, one must assume, and in so doing, to justify herself. Which means, unconsciously, she must sense the need. Brilliantly, West terminates the chapter with the letter, leaving the reader to supply his own emotion, to measure the distance between his response and the one he imagines was Miss Lonelyhearts'. The distance should be great.[19]

Fay Doyle is a grotesque, but aggressive, incarnation of these complaining women. Her letter (pp. 97–98), with its request for "a talk," is a seduction, and Miss Lonelyhearts knows it. He sits, "trying to discover a moral reason for not calling" her (p. 99). Whether moral reasons exist or not, there are at least professional ones. In acceding, he violates the distance between correspondent and columnist, confuses advice with personal involvement, ultimately compounds the issue by becoming a part of the problem, and is destroyed because of it. The immediate result, after the adultery, is a letter made vocal, "a gigantic, living Miss Lonelyhearts letter in the shape of a paper weight ... placed on his brain." Spoken in a voice "as hypnotic as a tom-tom, and as monotonous," it cancels feelings, dulls emotions. "Already his mind and body were half asleep" (p. 102). He must have heard it before: a history of marital grievance, an illegitimate child, a father unwilling to admit paternity, a foster parent offering selfless but sexless love, a wife refusing to accept responsibility for her marriage. It is not true that "it was on account of Lucy that [Fay] had to marry her husband" (p. 102). She didn't have to marry anyone. "Nudged ... into speech with her elbow" (p. 103), Miss Lonelyhearts replies—"Your husband probably loves you and the kid" (p. 103)—a reply the audience rejects with the question: "What girl wants to spend her life with a shrimp of a cripple?" (p. 104). If she doesn't, and if that is the issue, the purpose of the talk, she has the freedom and the power to leave. But one suspects the purpose is to make Miss Lonelyhearts the husband, to force him to become the solution. Ironically, it is a solution which Miss Lonelyhearts accepts when he becomes, not Fay's husband, but Christ, the universal spouse to the afflicted.

The letters from "Desperate" (p. 67) and "Harold S." (p. 68) are the most difficult to answer because they represent the sort of gross evil, the abuse of children, that led Ivan Karamazov and Jean Tarrou to repudiate God's universe.[20] And since they are from juveniles, they can make a legitimate claim upon the adult world. Desperate, given her grotesque physical deformity—she was born without a nose—her age, so sensitive to sexual longing and rejection, her artless search for reasons based on misguided religious guilt, her polite question of suicide, is, on one level, extremely touching. She has not only been abused by nature, she has been cruelly neglected by others. The question, first of all, is not what she should do, but what should have been done, or initiated, at the moment she was born. What is most shocking here is that neither the family, nor the State, nor the medical profession, has made, in the sixteen years of her life, any attempt to remedy through reconstructive surgery, the indifferent cruelty of nature.[21] If the technology is unavailable, however, we are faced with the problem of reconstructing her perception. We should be faced with this in any case. Desperate will have to be told, and made to see by being shown, the normality of handicaps, the relativism of beauty, the possibilities of physical love for those the mainstream rejects. Because, regardless of the surgery, that is where the issue lies. Unfortunately, given her awareness that beauty if what counts—she has a "nice shape" and "pretty clothes"—it is likely that she would reject a boy who looks the way she does; that she doesn't desire just a normal boyfriend, she desires a handsome one. Her problem, then, is twofold: her appearance and her perception. The problem with the first beclouds the problem with the second. Despite our sympathies,[22] Desperate is no more than an adolescent version of her complaining female counterparts, Sick-of-it-all, Broad Shoulders, and Fay Doyle. One could not expect her values to transcend contemporary standards—and they don't.[23] She wishes, in essence, to be pretty, much like Fay Doyle, who had been "a pretty girl and could of had [her] pick (p. 104). Her capacity to feel is also questionable. She laments the absence of boyfriends as much as the absence of a nose.[24] Indeed, she wants the latter, not to live a complete life in the mainstream of society, but merely to acquire the former; given such a motive, one can doubt her happiness with the former if, or when, she should acquire the latter. The trap within her sad letters is that, unintentionally, it encourages us to idealize the one with the deformity. The adult Desperate, if a victim, will, like the others, be self-victimized.

Of all the letters, the one from Harold S. makes the greatest demand upon us, because, by contrast, it exposes our deficiencies as adults. Not only is the writer an adolescent, he does not write for himself, but for his younger sister. She is thirteen, deaf and dumb, "not very smart on account of being deaf and dumb," and has been raped on the roof of their tenement house. The letter is as much a revelation of Harold's fears for her as it is of Gracie's plight. He is afraid Gracie may be pregnant, afraid of his mother's violence if she should find out, worried "the boys on the blok ... will say dirty things" about her. He wonders what to do. Ironically, the letter, the only selfless one, the only one without personal complaint, contains its own reply and exemplifies it. Harold is taking a first step, however incorrect, in helping someone else, assuming responsibility for his sister while the adult correspondents do not assume responsibility for themselves. His words, however artless, at times bear a quiet dignity, and suggest, since he would not do to Gracie what has been done to her by others, a potential remedy. "I am the only one who loves her," he says. If the love that Harold feels is not transferable to the adult world of the mother or the society of "the boys on the blok", and one fears that it is not (the adult correspondence suggests egocentricity as causative), then he will have to love and protect her all the more. In this case, Christ is the answer if Christ is a metaphor for a secular caritas, the love that protects till one no longer needs protection, which is not limited to the religious of any religion, or excluded to the unreligious. Ironically, as though it is a message from child to parent, adolescent to adult, only the letters from the children, Desperate and Harold S., contain the word, love; the adults are preoccupied with sexual failure. Miss Lonelyhearts' reluctance to reply demonstrates his failure, not sexually, not as a priest (*his* egocentricity), but as a parent.

Peter Doyle's letter (pp. 125–126), with its rage and hatred; its American working class hostility and suspicion toward Communism, the bosses, the press, women; its sense of economic deprivation and of immediate physical pain;—nonetheless represents the culmination of the others. It probes beneath the temporal toward finality. Doyle is not searching for solutions—economic, political, domestic—he is asking Miss Lonelyhearts "what is the whole stinking business for." The focus is existential. He demands *the* reply: the unified spiritual field theory masked behind phenomena. Angrily, he is claiming the *right* to know. Now, this is a fairly heady assignment, even for a journalist, and the journalist might, understandably, balk at having such a responsibility, the purpose of existence, gratuitously thrust upon him. But the relationship between correspondent and columnist, however inauthentic, justifies a response of some kind. Whether "the whole stinking business" demands a religious solution is at least open to debate. Doyle has no religious consciousness and would tend to assume that it doesn't. His question springs from marital discord and physical pain, not from a philosophical or religious quest; solve his problems and you eliminate his question. The question is thus for him a symptom, not a goal. The reply Miss Lonelyhearts gives is a handclasp of Christian love blurred with homoeroticism. A more positive one, to this audience, would have been an admission that the claim is false, we have no right to know; an acknowledgement of ignorance fused with personal acceptance, of a willingness to continue despite our lack of knowledge of ultimate purposiveness or cause, and regardless of conditions, a stubborn but conscious fidelity to life since that is what we have. A slippery answer, obviously, to one in physical pain. Without an anodyne, it is possible to reason, be driven, from toothache to suicide. But the only response is to cheat, which is what Miss Lonelyhearts does, and which is why he fails. He *forces* his hand "to clasp the cripple's" (p. 126). He forces himself to love.[25]

Taken as a whole, then, the correspondence does not attest to irremediable evil, but to problems created and compounded by several aspects of human frailty and meanness—folly and selfishness, occasional brutality, egocentricity, vanity, reluctance, the unwillingness to take responsibility for one's life—a litany of moral and psychological weaknesses which the correspondents, perversely, would prefer to live in rather than to change. It is a secular manifestation of the unpardonable sin, turning one's heart, not from God's free grace, but from the possibilities of human growth. These writers are not in love with anything so much as with their problems. Although they often wonder "what to do", they do not wish to act. At best, they merely wish. But wish contains its own inversion: since it incorporates no effort, the wish to be changed is no different from the wish to remain as one is. Under these conditions, they can be left only with *Weltschmerz*, a sentimental pessimism, sorrow felt as life's necessary portion, and this they would twist for self-advantage. If writing creates its audience, these writers have most surely created theirs. Seeing themselves as victims, they have cast Miss Lonelyhearts as their saviour. It is a role he wanted to play, in any case. He is, thus, less a desperate last chance for them, the last person to turn to, than the first person to whom they have turned, and his responses define himself as one of them. The relationship between the two is, then, mutually destructive. In attempting to cope with a problem they have merely extended its dimensions, for each has sought a relationship in which neither has anything to contribute; the correspondents seek only to receive, while Miss Lonelyhearts fictionalizes himself as their redeemer. A more productive attitude to suffering would negate Miss Lonelyhearts as audience and artist: a discomforting "cure" for both columnist and correspondents since it would nullify his chosen role of saviour as much as theirs of being saved. But each side needs the other to continue to remain as it is, to obscure the heart of true feelings, the deep sense of aggrievement, the conviction that life owes them something: a normal body, a blissful marriage, a *Weltanschauung*.

A solution to a problem, however, is not a reply to the correspondence. The letters, with their illiteracy, their unintentional humour, their at times pornographic luxuriance of complaint, involve us in what is now called the problem of language, the trustworthiness of words as signs, their current (in)capacity to represent a reality beyond themselves. The novel, with its clichés, set speeches, jokes, with its comic protagonist who moves from a pseudonym to a metaphor,[26] dramatizes this theme at its heart, the authenticity of words, all words, of the letters, of the column, of the press, of this essay, of the novel itself. The verdict on the novel is in; it is an aesthetically satisfying linguistic construction, a work of art, but fiction has the freedom to be self-enclosed, to create its own reality rather than reflect the reality of the outside world, assuming one exists.[27] The essay must assume a referent behind the word and hope the two have made at least a nodding acquaintance. The letters, as do the column and the press, fluctuate in an unstable middle ground between essay and novel. Their words simultaneously entrap both the reader and their authors. The assumed referents are fact and emotion. They represent the fact inconsistently and consistently misrepresent the emotion. Since the correspondence and the column are published in the press, another false letter to the world, one victimizing both correspondent and columnist, it is obvious the problem lies with the user and not with language per se.

West's focus in *Miss Lonelyhearts* is not with evil or with "human pain and suffering,"[28] as has so often been thought, but with the responses they evoke. His concern is sensibility, expression and reaction, the inadequacy of the one, the absence of the other. The novel leads us to play, quite seriously, Shrike's cynical game, "Everyman his own Miss Lonelyhearts" (p. 132), as I have been playing it here, and to unmask ourselves as we play it. The response West dramatizes is not revolution, rebellion, self-help, but the victim–saviour nexus; institutionalized by the press, given sham permanence, it sustains and exacerbates the conditions it was, hypothetically, intended to correct. The correspondents, capitulating to their woes, have projected their burdens onto another, equally infirm, encouraging him to adopt the grotesquely comic masquerade of scapegoat and saviour, a role he needed only their stimulus to encourage him to play. It is for them an exit, a way out; with Miss Lonelyhearts on stage, they need confront nothing, not even their own nothingness. Their self-indulgent prose masks paralysis of will.

The approach outlined in this essay casts the audience in the role of moral agent. It is a role the correspondents would reject. They will not fictionalize themselves in this way. Their reactions to Miss Lonelyhearts' clichés ought to tell us this: "Being an admirer of your column because you give such good advice to people in trouble," writes Broad Shoulders (p. 116); and Peter Doyle: "I thought I would write to you after reading your answer to Disillusioned" (p. 125). Such responses tell us that they are satisfied with replies Miss Lonelyhearts must have found inadequate; that they do not take him seriously, or that they do when he does not; that they want consolation, not the pain and risk of change. Could he pen a genuine message of Christ, convey the notion that Christian redemption is not a free ticket to retire from choice or conflict, they would reject that too, in words that would indicate a bland acceptance of it. If Miss Lonelyhearts knows this, it is another reason he cannot write. The correspondents are the writer's nemesis, another block, the audience that will not listen. They condemn the writer to silence. They defeat the word. And the Word.

NOTES

1. *The Complete Works of Nathanael West*, New York, Farrar, Straus and Cudahy, 1957, p. 66. All subsequent references to the novel are drawn from this edition and are cited in the body of the text.

2. James F. Light, *Nathanael West: An Interpretative Study*, Northwestern University Press, 1961, p. 75.

3. Victor Comerchero, *Nathanael West: The Ironic Prophet*, Syracuse, N.Y., Syracuse University Press, 1964, p.77.

4. Randall Reid, *The Fiction of Nathanael West: No Redeemer, No Promised Land*, Chicago, University of Chicago Press, 1967, pp. 41–42, 49–50.

5. Kingsley Widmer, *Nathanael West*, Boston, Twayne Publishers, 1982, pp. 27, 31, 33.

6. "Sordid? Good God!", *Contempo*, July 25, 1933, p. 8. Williams, though, did remark in the same review that "no serious advice can be given to despairing people who would patronize and even rely on such a newspaper office.... the newspaper by this means capitalizes misfortune to make sales ... Imagine a sensitive man running such a column, a man of imagination who realizes what he is doing and the plot is wound up" (p. 5). Although he seemed willing to accept the correspondents at their own estimation, Williams did perceive correctly that both they and the column are a part of the problem.

7. Jay Martin, *Nathanael West: The Art of His Life*, New York, Farrar, Straus and Giroux, 1970, p. 186.

8. *Ibid.*, p. 187.

9. *Ibid.*, p. 187.

10. *Ibid.*, p. 187.

11. We do not have access to the originals except for what is quoted in Martin. An astonishing, but typical, analysis can be found on p. 110:

> The letters were, to be sure, romantic and shot through with fantasy thinking; but there was no pretension in them, only unbearable pathos. One, signed "Broad Shoulders," began: dear Susan:
>
> I have always enjoyed reading your column, and have benefited by your expert advice. Now I must ask you for advice for myself. I have been married for twenty years. I have a girl 19 and a boy of 17. From the very beginning I realized that I had made a mistake in marrying my husband. But the children came soon after, and I was obliged for their dear sakes to stand through thick and thin, bitter and sweet. And also for decency sake.

We do not see the direction the letter takes, since no more is quoted in the text, but even this fragment reveals itself not as a sample of "unbearable pathos," but of unintentional self-exposure. "Broad Shoulders" is defending herself against her husband and using her children as the defence. *From the very beginning*, she had realized the mistake of her marriage; yet two years later she brought a second child into a bad relationship. She justifies her action on the basis of "decency" and duty. The sweet, polite, almost simpering tone is manipulative, intended to manoeuvre us into "pathos"; she *wants* us to feel sorry for herself, even though,—in a letter that contains "no pretension",—she paints herself as heroic. But the absence of a third child is suggestive. West's treatment of the letters in the novel indicates he neither succumbed to the originals nor was hurt by them, but that he saw through them at once.

12. "The writers seem sublimely unaware that their words, like double agents, constantly betray them" (Jeffrey L. Duncan, "The Problem of Language in *Miss Lonelyhearts*," *The Iowa Review*, Winter, 1977, p. 119). Although his focus is upon language in the novel and not upon the correspondence itself, Duncan is nonetheless the only writer to take a negative view of the letters: "They reveal a reality, unarguably, but it is hardly one of genuine suffering, much less of profound humility. Instead they betray mere attitudes struck, postures assumed, poses wantonly displayed, a comic pornography of suffering and trouble. If they express anything authentic—though it is doubtful that these women give a fig about authenticity—it is a desire for suffering.... And if they are to be pitied, it is because they do not, perhaps cannot, suffer" (p. 117).

13. The ability to read or to sense an emotion is not a requirement of the profession.

14. The image is drawn from *The Day of the Locust*. "He thought of Janvier's 'Sargasso Sea'. Just as that imaginary body of water was a history of civilization in the form of a marine junkyard, the studio lot was one in the form of a dream dump" (p. 353).

15. D.H. Lawrence's well-known remark in "Pornography and Obscenity" that "sentimentality is a sure sign of pornography" comes to mind here.

16. Martin, pp. 109, 186.

17. "What do we mean by saying the audience is a fiction? Two things at least. First, that the writer must construct in his imagination, clearly or vaguely, an audience cast in some sort of a role ... Second, we mean that the audience must correspondingly fictionalize itself. A reader has to play the role in which the author has cast him, which seldom coincides with his role in the rest of actual life" (Walter J. Ong, S.J., "The Writer's Audience Is Always a Fiction," *PMLA*, January, 1975, p. 12).

18. Yet Light can speak of "the pathos of Sick-of-it-all" (p. 77).

19. A negative appraisal of the wife does not, of course, constitute a defence of the husband. If the portrait of him is accurate, he may well be lethal. Institutionalization or incarceration would appear to lie in his future. Whether these are liberal solutions or not, they are certainly self-preservatory.

20. This is an evil implicit in Broad Shoulders' letter—her son has inherited venereal disease (p. 118)—but it is totally blurred by her chattering egocentricity.

21. There are economic and political extensions to the matter. Desperate could be granted the surgery were the egalitarian United States, an extraordinarily expensive country in which to be ill, less hysterical about dispensing free or low-cost medicine to the masses on a socialistic basis. Or, to acknowledge a solution from the opposite wing, were the large corporations, such as the *New York Post-Dispatch*, willing, if not to provide the money, which would be a tax write-off in any case, then to sponsor a fund, and call for contributions. Or if the medical profession were willing to work without compensation.

22. And our sympathies, we must acknowledge this, may be a mask for the reverse, our unadmitted revulsion toward her physical condition.

23. "The letter's words spell our a troublesome truth, that this girl, however

unfortunate, has tacky values. She would give a great deal to be Homecoming Queen" (Duncan, p. 126).

24. "The tragedy of the girl born without a nose is not only that she is deformed but that she dreams of a handsome boyfriend to take her out on Saturday nights" (Robert I. Edenbaum, "To Kill God and Build a Church: Nathanael West's *Miss Lonelyhearts*," *The CEA Critic*, June, 1967, p.7).

25. There are also two letters referred to in Shrike's game, "Everyman his own Miss Lonelyhearts" (pp. 133–134). The first, from a seventy year old woman whose son has died and who sells pencils for a living, does not tell us what she wants. The second, from a paralytic boy who wants a violin, may seem heartrending, but is, in a way, in its amusing, ironic sadness, an emblem of all of us, who have to discover how to live in a creative tension between yearning for the impossible and being content with what we can do. Miss Lonelyhearts is not present to hear the third, an angry warning from Peter Doyle.

26. Duncan, p. 121.

27. One could argue that West has done just this, that his characters, living only in the self-enclosed world of the novel, have no objective existence, that all solutions have been deftly precluded, that he has set up conundrums, emotional and moral ones, solutions to which the novel will not permit a reply. Certainly there is no character within the novel with emotional sanity or awareness, no norm. But the aesthetic order of the novel is a metaphor for the possibility of order and sanity.

28. "The obsessive theme of *Miss Lonelyhearts* is human pain and suffering, but it is represented almost entirely as female suffering" (Stanley Edgar Hyman, *Nathanael West*, Minneapolis, University of Minnesota Press, 1962, p. 19).

ROBERT WEXELBLATT

Miss Lonelyhearts *and* the Rhetoric of Disintegration

I. *MISS LONELYHEARTS* AND THE ORDER OF DISORDER

It is just as bad to write a disorderly book about disorder as a boring one about boredom. Still, if a writer believes things are falling apart, where can he find an order in which to write about it? What form would be credible? Modernist writers, who were in this situation, lay extraordinary stress on order just because they did not believe in the existing forms, artistic or cultural. They invented their own in which to express this lack of belief. They made forms which would not betray their sense of disintegration.

The most common modernist solution to the formal problem of a work devoted to the theme of disintegration is simply to make artistic order of the breakdown of all other orders, finding a solution in the failure of solutions. West's *Miss Lonelyhearts* illustrates this tactic as a caricature does a face. What is more, the book's central episode, "Miss Lonelyhearts in the Dismal Swamp," is a caricature of this caricature. By means of cliché and parody, by dint of an attitude made possible by cultural decadence, Shrike here declaims a sermon on the inadequacy of all answers to and escapes from the problem of suffering; he expresses the failure of spiritual order to withstand spiritual entropy. Shrike's rhetoric mocks each of his seven deadly escapes, while the remainder of the novel dramatizes the same thing.

The paradoxical fact is that works about disintegration, such as *Miss*

From *College Literature*, vol. 16, no. 3, 1989. © 1989 by West Chester University.

Lonelyhearts, bring form itself into question but are themselves rigorously composed. *Miss Lonelyhearts* suggests three ways of stating the special formal character of these works. First, they can succeed only to the extent that they present disorder in an orderly fashion. Second, they are essentially dispositions of elements rather than organic wholes, unified by some internal principle. Finally, they are dependent for their own forms on failed solutions and broken orders. West uses parody so intensively in *Miss Lonelyhearts* because he is a modernist jokester who wants to demonstrate the failure of these solutions, and parody is the most concentrated and, so to speak, elegant literary tool by which characteristic styles, beliefs, and attitudes can be made to look ridiculous. The episodic pattern of *Miss Lonelyhearts* does not merely parody comic-strips and the Stations of the Cross; the episodes also burlesque the patterns of reversed quest, failed conversion, approach/avoidance anxiety neurosis, desperate escapism. In its surrealistically electrified, intermittently violent style, *Miss Lonelyhearts* demonstrates how the disease of disintegration may be said to provide the language of its own diagnosis.

II. *Miss Lonelyhearts* Makes Fun of Where It Comes From

West's parodies are a "peculiar kind of joking," which is what he called his entire oeuvre. His parodies are also proof of the lengths to which he took the rhetoric of disintegration. Understood merely as a technique parody is barely adequate to cover all he does. West casts a cold eye on all kinds of books, writers, styles, ideas—particularly on those which most attract him— so that, for him, parody amounts virtually to a cultural attitude. For instance, it is not ordinary parody when West writes a take-off on a serious work which he regards with seriousness and even admiration but nonetheless burlesques. This is the case with the uses to which he puts *Crime and Punishment* in his first two novels, for example, or "The Waste Land" in his second.[1] Nor is parody an entirely satisfying classification for what he does in *Miss Lonelyhearts* with William James' *Varieties of Religious Experience* or Freud's Oedipal case-studies, both of which he acknowledged as sources in the essay "Some Notes on *Miss Lonelyhearts*." Parody complicates West's relations with his sources and influences, but a few things can be done to sort out these vexed relations. First, a distinction—convenient even if *ad hoc*—can be drawn between sources and influences; second, one can examine the original way in which West treats each; finally, one can try to elucidate the effect of West's attitude toward these sources and influences and his extraordinary way of proclaiming them.

For the sake of the present discussion, a *source* is something affecting the novel's content and an *influence* something affecting the author's style. The distinction is useful though, in a sense, arbitrary because West's manner and matter are equally permeated by parody. Here, for example, is a typical instance of what might be called stylistic influence: *Miss Lonelyhearts* is full of arresting pictorial images which derive from West's interests in surrealistic art, Christian imagery, and the crude graphics of the comics. All these influences are to be found in the following passage:

> Suddenly tired, he sat down on a bench.... If he could only throw the stone. He searched the sky for a target. But the gray sky looked as if it had been rubbed with a soiled eraser. It held no angels, flaming crosses, olive-bearing doves, wheels within wheels. Only a newspaper struggling in the air like a kite with a broken spine.[2]

The parody of Counter-Reformation imagery is obvious enough, but the parody extends also to the soiled sky and all, the recurrent surrealist images in the book where natural events are likened to artificial effects. West's use of comic-strip graphics is nearly a species of "serious" parody; it is like the 17th-century devotional poets' adaptation of Petrarchan conventions to religious themes. The struggling newspaper which is like a kite with a broken spine is a complex comic-strip image with multiple meanings. It suggests that mass culture, in which Miss Lonelyhearts is professionally complicit, is a broken and weightless thing; it confirms the omnipresence of violence, and suggests that flights of the spirit, like Miss Lonelyhearts', are impossible or doomed. West's fondness for ending an episode with a sharply violent image is also a parody of the drawing in comic-strips, confirming the violence he strove for in describing non-violent events, as when he depicts Shrike with the mannish Miss Farkis:

> His caresses kept pace with the sermon. When he had reached the end, he buried his triangular face like the blade of a hatchet in her neck. (74)

West's manipulation of such stylistic influences is distinctive enough, but just as interesting is the way he parodies his sources. There are several good examples. In the opening episode itself West has Shrike perform a nasty take-off on the prayer, *Anima Christi*, perhaps because it is customarily printed at the head of Ignatius Loyola's *Spiritual Exercises*, of which *Miss Lonelyhearts* is also a sort of parody. West's college dalliance with Christian mysticism gave him similar sources which infuse the whole novel:

In *Miss Lonelyhearts* the *Anima Christi* parody is but one of the allusions throughout the novel to aspects of hagiography or biblical events....[3]

A still more significant example of West's peculiar method is the use he makes of Freud's Oedipal case-studies. In his article on *Miss Lonelyhearts* West wrote boldly:

Psychology has nothing to do with reality nor should it be used as motivation. The novelist is no longer a psychologist. Psychology can become something much more important. The great body of case histories can be used in the way ancient writers used their myths. Freud is your Bulfinch; you cannot learn from him.[4]

This blunt declaration means more than it is usually taken to, which is simply that West expects his readers to pick up Miss Lonelyhearts' Oedipus complex with a minimum of clues. In fact, if "psychology has nothing to do with reality" and cannot be used to establish "motivation," then it will not do to *believe in* the Oedipus complex itself in the usual way. Even Freud's order, a modernist staple, is not credible to West. Rather, he sees Freud as a sort of Ovid, a compiler of myths, his theories only as another set of orderly fragments to shore against the cultural ruins. Freud provides West with a uniquely effective way of presenting what, in the case of his hero's psyche, is quite literally an ordered disintegration. When one ignores what West says in his article and what it implies about the way in which Freud is being parodied (along with the Grail legend, Dostoyevsky, William James, and the other sources of *Miss Lonelyhearts'* content), one gets an analysis like the famous one by Stanley Edgar Hyman—insightful and accurate in most details, but entirely missing West's tone:

Terrified of his stern religious father, identifying with his soft loving mother, the boy renounces his phallicism out of castration anxiety—a classic Oedipus complex. In these terms the Shrikes are Miss Lonelyhearts' Oedipal parents, abstracted as the father's loud voice and the mother's tantalizing breast. The scene at the end of Miss Lonelyhearts' date with Mary Shrike is horrifying and superb. Standing outside her apartment door, suddenly overcome with passion, he strips her naked under her fur coat while she keeps talking mindlessly of her mother's death, mumbling and repeating herself, so that Shrike will not hear their sudden silence and come out. Finally Mary agrees to let Miss Lonelyhearts in if Shrike is not home, goes inside, and soon Shrike peers out the door, wearing only the top of his pajamas. It is the child's Oedipal vision perfectly dramatized; he can clutch at his mother's body but loses her each time to his more potent rival.[5]

Psychology has nothing to do with *reality*. If the reality of this work is disintegration, then Freud's theories are too pat to reflect reality. Not credible, but still useful. Freud provides an abbreviated *method* of characterization for West, not an *explanation* of character. Hyman's analysis only reveals that Miss Lonelyhearts is a classic Oedipal case, that West has, as he says, "perfectly dramatized" Freud; but West has also made his protagonist a classic case of hysteria and a classic instance of conversion psychology, as well as a classic Grail-quester. And these are all of *equal* value; it is not as if the Freudian level provides the real truth about Miss Lonelyhearts while all the others are merely so many metaphoric ornaments. In fact, they are all parodies. That is why they are so perfect, so classic. As soon as West's parody is acknowledged, the idea of *levels* itself dissolves. For instance, it is just as possible to compare Miss Lonelyhearts to the original Oedipus as to Freud's little boy: both are trying to remove a plague from their subjects, to discover their own identities, to rejuvenate a dead land. Both become scapegoats.[6]

The sources for *Miss Lonelyhearts* are not obscure. As Eliot did in his footnotes to "The Waste Land," West tells us what they are. But it has not always been recognized that West entertains toward these sources the attitude of a parodist. Why parody? Parody becomes possible—for West, necessary—when a work of art, a doctrine, a stance loses authority and authenticity, when its qualities, explanations, or consolations are perceived to be stylized and unrealistic. West used parody to make artistic sense out of images or theories which could no longer make sense of the world or provide their wonted solace. His parody of his own sources is therefore inextricable from *Miss Lonelyhearts'* theme of disintegration. Parody is the method by which he fuses form to content. This unity is all the firmer because West's sources are themselves patterns of disintegration. At the heart of the vegetation rite, the Grail legend, the Oedipus story is the effort to resuscitate a dead land; at the core of Raskolnikov's fate, the hysteric's responses, the mystic stages of conversion are the same anxiety, the same threat of despair. The final event of the novella can be viewed as the death of a scapegoat, the failure of a religion, a homosexual tableau, a wry commentary on mass culture, a take-off on *The Great Gatsby*, or a sordid and pathetic event. The fragments of order qualify one another. Each line of significance is, in effect, reinforced and diminished by the others. All enter into the final effect. The mystic conversion is turned upside down by hysteria, Zossima is shouted down by the Grand Inquisitor, the world is the fish and Christ the fly, *caritas* is soiled by homosexuality, the graceful Sonia becomes an ineffectual and pregnant Betty. All the orders are there, but in their plurality, as in their parody, none works.

III. *MISS LONELYHEARTS* AND THE POETRY OF CLICHÉ

Cliché is the first immediacy of *Miss Lonelyhearts'* style. It is West's mastery of cliché that earns him a title as a poet of mass culture. The manufacturing of clichés, the transmogrification of any idea into a slogan, any attitude into a posture, any belief into a convention, and any dream into a business distinguishes mass culture. In certain respects, cliché serves as the specific agent of disintegration in all the novels of West; just as, in a more general sense, W.H. Auden found what he dubbed "West's disease" to be endemic to a "democratic and mechanized society like our own."[7] One can pinpoint the cultural ailment in each of West's books by looking at the sources of the clichés in each: in *The Dream Life of Balso Snell*, bad and good art; in *A Cool Million*, popular notions of American political, economic, and social life; in *The Day of the Locust*, the movies. In *Miss Lonelyhearts*, the source of clichés is the whole range of responses to the problems of human suffering and cosmic disorder, from Christianity to alcohol.

Miss Lonelyhearts' attempts to answer the letters of the sufferers are clichéd. Doyle's complaints are clichés. Every moment of peace or order—to which Miss Lonelyhearts is abnormally, even Euclideanly, sensitive—is at once undercut by violence, just to show it is only an illusion, just another cliché. In the following passage, for example, it is nearly as if West were anticipatorily parodying J.D. Salinger:

> As Miss Lonelyhearts stood at the bar, swaying slightly to the remembered music, he thought of children dancing. Square replacing oblong and being replaced by circle. Every child, everywhere; in the whole world there was not one child who was not gravely, sweetly dancing.
>   He stepped away from the bar and accidentally collided with a man holding a glass of beer. When he turned to beg the man's pardon, he received a punch in the mouth. (84–85)

The power of West's writing to inflict pain has much to do with this disconcerting ability to submerge himself in vulgarity while simultaneously transcending it and then denying even the possibility of transcendence. The pain comes from the realization that West uses clichés which, after all, people believe in and live by. Even West's revision of the original Susan Chester letters makes them appear more clichéd and repetitive.[8]

Since it is both cause and consequence, cliché bears a double relation to the theme of cultural disintegration. Cliché is a cause in that to use a cliché makes human response derivative, vulgar, and insincere. Cliché is an effect because, in the cultural situation of *Miss Lonelyhearts*, any response that is proposed is instantly transformed into a cliché; after all, it has all been *done before*. The first French stockbroker to leave his family to paint in Tahiti is Gauguin, but what of the second?

Other writers have used cliché to depict cultural decay, but West goes further by proposing a falsification of feeling as well as thinking. The notion that feelings can be as derivative and untrue as ideas is one that people resist mightily. The Romantic faith in the genuineness of feeling runs deep with us—back to Rousseau and Wordsworth, forward through Kierkegaard to Sartre. Nevertheless, to show emotions as clichéd is essential to West's method. When other writers satirize clichéd human responses they almost always are aiming at intellectual affectation; they favor the implication that authenticity has only been suppressed and thus is possible. Indeed, they insist on it by using a *genuine* character as a foil for the cynic. But in West the plain sense is that Shrike can only mock, Betty can only give idiotic pep-talks, journalists only joke, and Mary, Faye, and Doyle can only react in the pitiful ways they do. This sense of personal limitation, or *automation*, builds up the theme of falseness having infected the whole of humankind. West's idealist is not authentic; Miss Lonelyhearts himself is aware of the clichés he writes.

In rigidly disciplined works exceptions confirm rules. West derives immense power from the sheer pervasiveness of cliché and can create a striking effect by violating this expectation, much as a poet writing strict heroic couplets can shock with one alexandrine. Of all the characters in *Miss Lonelyhearts*, Shrike is the most self-possessed, the one whose self-control expresses itself most consistently in his deliberate use of clichés for purposes of rhetorical aggression. This consistency lulls the reader into forgetting that he or she is not reading a comic-strip at all, that even Shrike may have another dimension, an actual suffering self behind the "dead triangle" of his face. One almost overlooks the most basic truth about brilliant mockers like Shrike, whose name invokes the butcher bird impaling its prey on thorns as Shrike punctures feelings, answers, escapes, faiths, and ideals on the long darts of his mockery. So when for one moment the mask is lowered, the effect is remarkable:

"My good friend, your accusation hurts me to the quick. You spiritual lovers think that you alone suffer. But you are mistaken. Although my love is of the flesh flashy, I too suffer. It's suffering that drives me into the arms of the Miss Farkises of this world. Yes, I suffer."

Here the dead pan broke and pain actually crept into his voice. "She's selfish. She's a damned selfish bitch. She was a virgin when I married her and has been fighting ever since to remain one. Sleeping with her is like sleeping with a knife in one's groin." (92)

This passage provides another reason for the prevalence of cliché in the book. For Shrike, the burlesquing of all sincere attitudes is a psychological defense expressed rhetorically. He is a verbal bully. Any response other than cynicism shows that one is vulnerable, a potential sucker. In an atmosphere of disintegration, vulnerability, even in one's language, is a psychological threat:

It was Miss Lonelyhearts' turn to laugh. He put his face close to Shrike's and laughed as hard as he could.

Shrike tried to ignore him by finishing as though the whole thing were a joke. (92)

As Hemingway's code was to the twenties, West's friend Dashiell Hammett's was to the thirties. Even Shrike complains about it: "Everybody is so hard-boiled," he whines smirkingly. West sheltered Hammett during his stint as night manager of the Sutton Hotel in New York. In his recent book, R.E. Long points out that the connection was literary as well as personal:

West ... had read Hammett's detective novels, as well as many of the issues of *Black Mask*, the great magazine forum for hard-boiled detective fiction of the thirties ... curiously, in the early draft ... Miss Lonelyhearts is even compared to a detective. (48)

The chief virtue of the hard-boiled egg is that it is not easily cracked. Hammett's pose is as ripe for parody as any other. In *Miss Lonelyhearts*, then, cliché dominates for two reasons: first, as a consequence of the disintegrating state of the culture; second, because people either choose, like Doyle, to live by clichés or, like Sam Spade, to hide behind them emotionally.

IV. *MISS LONELYHEARTS* DEEP DOWN IN THE DISMAL SWAMP

In West, cliché is a sub-species of parody. Shrike's central sermon is built on the paralyzing rehearsal of parodied escapes and poses, but it is through cliché that the speech's overall rhetorical effect is achieved, a parasitic effect. This anti-sermon is a distillation not only of West's considerable powers of parody but also of his reading and interests, as in this sardonic admixture of Huysmans and Hammett:

> ... soon you must die. You keep a stiff upper lip and decide to give a last party. You invite all your old mistresses, trainers, artists and boon companions. The guests are dressed in black, the waiters are coons, the table is a coffin carved for you by Eric Gill. You serve caviar and coffee without cream. After the dancing girls have finished, you get to your feet and call for silence in order to explain your philosophy of life. "Life," you say, "is a club where they won't stand for squawks, where they deal you only one hand and you must sit in ... remember, when you throw box cars, take the curtain like a dead game sport, don't squawk...." (108–109)

West places Shrike's sermon in the "Dismal Swamp" episode, the eighth of the fifteen in the book. This episode is a pause at the center of *Miss Lonelyhearts* which clarifies all that has and has yet to happen. The action stops to make space for meditation and nightmare:

> ... Miss Lonelyhearts became physically sick and was unable to leave his room. The first two days of his illness were blotted out by sleep, but on the third day, his imagination began again to work. (104)

Miss Lonelyhearts' imagination is febrile and hallucinatory. He finds himself in a pawn-shop window amidst "the paraphernalia of suffering"—a surrealistically detailed vision of stuff and fragments. This chaotic dream leads logically to the central thematic statement of the book:

> Man has a tropism for order.... The physical world has a tropism for disorder, entropy. (104)

This battle of human and natural tropisms—which are even deeper and blinder than instincts—sums up the issue for both Miss Lonelyhearts and *Miss Lonelyhearts*. The character's nightmare shows us what the book itself is doing: "First he formed a phallus of old watches and rubber boots, then a heart of umbrellas and trout flies...." Here is the work of the artist of disintegration. "These fragments I have shored against my ruins" is how Eliot put it. West must make order to have a book, and Miss Lonelyhearts needs order to answer the letters. The obsession with order runs even deeper. Randall Reid observes that Miss Lonelyhearts' "almost insane sensitiveness to order" is also "a classic symptom of preconversion psychology ..." (103).

Betty arrives suddenly, complete with chicken soup. It is ironic that her custom is to set the room "in order." Before leaving, she has a conversation with Miss Lonelyhearts which includes an extended statement of the *donnée* of the work. This is an awkward passage; it reads like a note West might have written himself after his first glimpse of the Susan Chester letters which inspired the novella. Possibly the passage is an unrevised leftover from an earlier stage of composition, before West divided the original hero Thomas Matlock into Miss Lonelyhearts and Shrike, idealist and cynic:

> ... Let's start from the beginning. A man is hired to give advice to the readers of a newspaper. The job is a circulation stunt and the whole staff considers it a joke. He welcomes the job, for it might lead to a gossip column, and anyway he's tired of being a leg man. He too considers the job a joke, but after several months at it, the joke begins to escape him. He sees that the majority of the letters are profoundly humble pleas for moral and spiritual advice, that they are inarticulate expressions of genuine suffering. He also discovers that his correspondents take him seriously. For the first time in his life, he is forced to examine the values by which he lives. The examination shows him that he is the victim of the joke and not its perpetrator. (106)

Artistically, this may be the most unsuccessful passage in the book; and yet it is most useful in seeing where West's distinctive success lies.

The definitive triumph of the book, its rhetorical pyrotechnics, is to be found perfectly exemplified in the remainder of this same episode, in Shrike's oration on the seven deadly escapes. The sources of Shrike's speech are well known; in fact, the point is that they are known too well. Travelogues, bestsellers, Victorian poetry, Huysmans' *À Rebours*, Dashiell Hammett's tough detective stories—all are reduced to the same level of vulgar insincerity by what West must have striven for most in his many revisions. This is the *tone* in which Shrike explodes the Return to Nature, the South Seas, Hedonism, Art, Suicide, Drugs, and God ("Preventer of Decay").

The rhetorical structure of the sermon is the same as the structure of *Miss Lonelyhearts* as a whole. Both move from topic to topic. As Shrike does in his sermon, so the novella takes up escape after alternative, alternative after solution, solution after way out. In both cases everything fails. Sex with

Faye Doyle shows the oceanic life-force perverted to marine refuse: "She made sea sounds; something flapped like a sail; there was the creak of ropes; then he heard the wave-against-a-wharf smack of rubber on flesh" (101). The return to the country with Betty is no good either; death, decay, and anti-semitism lurk in the undergrowth. Betty's bovine healthy-mindedness is also a no-go; Miss Lonelyhearts' disorder strikes even him as "more significant than her order." The novella creates mystery only to increase disillusion. Between Mary Shrike's forbidden Jocastan breasts there is only a high school track medal. Drinking leads Miss Lonelyhearts down a blind alley and will not slake his thirst; joking resolves nothing, while actually trying to *be* Christ is simply suicidal.

Rhetorically, every striking image in the book points to the dismal swamp, from the polysemous pun of Shrike's "dead pan" and the park where it "had taken all the brutality of July to torture a few green spikes through the exhausted dirt," to the "multiple chaos" of pedestrians and traffic, or the "canvas-colored and ill-stretched" sky in which Miss Lonelyhearts searches "for a clue to his own exhaustion." Occasionally West's highly worked language will directly divulge this topical structure, for the novella is self-similar throughout, its overall structure reproduced in individual episodes. For instance, toward the beginning of "Miss Lonelyhearts and Mrs. Shrike" West writes:

> When he had regained the street, he started to laugh. Although he had tried hot water, whisky, coffee, exercise, he had completely forgotten sex. (89)

V. *Miss Lonelyhearts* Meets Susan Chester and William James

Miss Lonelyhearts is a pinwheel of which the mainpin is the letters, a circle of which the letters are the dead-center. Coffee, exercise, sex—each excursion, escape, and speculation turns Miss Lonelyhearts back again upon the letters' urgency and horror. For him, personal salvation is no more acceptable than personal escape, so that sickness and disorder come to seem preferable to order and health. All of Miss Lonelyhearts' gyrations return him to the same point, the same role, the same problem: to answer the letters. There are escapes, but no escape.[9]

West's work always displays a great deal of motion but scarcely any advance. It is the stasis of his situations that provokes his peculiar sort of poetry, a still poetry of picture and design, essentially a decadent poetry. Miss Lonelyhearts cannot really be said to *come to* his "religious experience." The final event in the book is only a singularly climactic way of viewing the first episode. Through all the parodies and clichés, jokes and mock-sermons, there has been an unrelenting reference to the world of Sick-of-it-All, Harold S., Broad Shoulders, and Desperate. The suffering revealed in the letters is undeniable. Randall Reid cites William Carlos Williams' 1933 review defending the book against a charge of sordidness:

> The letters which West uses freely and at length must be authentic. I can't believe anything else. The unsuspected world they reveal is beyond ordinary thought.... Should such lives as these letters reveal never have been brought to light? Should such people, like the worst of our war wounded, best be kept in hiding? (49)

No doubt *Miss Lonelyhearts* is a terrible book. And no doubt it is always our wish somehow to turn hate into love, pessimism into optimism, death into immortality, suffering into wisdom. West has written deliberately, even rather gaily, against the grain of this wish by a discipline that kept him close to the letters and the problems—artistic, social, philosophical—they crystallized for him. According to Jay Martin, West's biographer, it was unquestionably the Susan Chester letters that inspired him to write *Miss Lonelyhearts* (109). The title of West's first episode derives from a passage in William James, a passage of which he must have remained mindful as he reworked his story:

> How irrelevantly remote seem all our usual refined optimisms and intellectual and moral consolations in the presence of a need of help like this! Here is the real core of the religious problem: Help! Help! No prophet can claim to bring a final message unless he says things that will have a sound of reality in the ears of victims such as these.[10]

West's rhetorical strategies in *Miss Lonelyhearts* are the consequence of the title character's inability to say such things to such victims.

NOTES

1. West's use of these sources has been thoroughly examined by his major critics. Consider the following, for example, in R.E. Long's *Nathanael West* (New York: Ungar, 1985) 52. "Dostoyevsky's 'underground man' supplies the model for Miss Lonelyhearts' self-division and psychological suffering; and Raskolnikov in *Crime and Punishment* especially prepares for him—in his impulse to play a heroic role for which he is not

necessarily qualified, his fevered dreams, isolation within an oppressive society, and obsession."

2. *The Collected Works of Nathanael West* (New York: Farrar, Straus, and Cudahy, 1957) 71.

3. D.R. Mayer, "West's Parody of the *Anima Christi* in *Miss Lonelyhearts*," *The Explicator*, 34.2 (1975): item 11.

4. Cited by Randall Reid, *The Fiction of Nathanael West: No Redeemer, No Promised Land* (Chicago: University of Chicago Press, 1967) 72–73.

5. Stanley Edgar Hyman, *Nathanael West* (University of Minnesota Pamphlets on American Writers, No. 21, 1962) 23–24. For a careful yet thoroughgoing Freudian interpretation of the book see James L. Hickey, "Freudian Criticism and *Miss Lonelyhearts*," in *Nathanael West: The Cheaters and the Cheated*, ed. David Madden (Deland, Florida: Everett/Edwards, 1973) 111–149.

6. See Victor Comerchero, *Nathanael West: The Ironic Prophet* (Syracuse: Syracuse University Press, 1964) 84–85.

7. W.H. Auden, "Interlude: West's Disease" in *The Dyer's Hand and Other Essays* (New York: Random House, 1956) 245.

8. Jay Martin, *Nathanael West: The Art of His Life* (New York: Farrar, Straus, and Giroux, 1970) 187.

9. The ambivalence of West's work, or at least of those who read it, continues to prompt differences of opinion. For examples, see M. Tropp, "West and the Persistence of Hope," *Renascence* 31 (1979): 205–214, and A. Klug, "Nathanael West: Prophet of Failure," *College Literature* 14 (1987): 17–31.

10. William James, *The Varieties of Religious Experience* (New York: Longmans, Green, 1925) 162. It is noteworthy that this passage comes from the end of James' third lecture, "The Sick Soul," and in a section considering the "inescapable problem of evil." An examination of West's use of Jamesian psychology can be found in Carroll Schoenewolf, "Jamesian Psychology and Nathanael West's *Miss Lonelyhearts*," *San Jose Studies* 7.3 (1981): 80–86.

BEVERLY J. JONES

Shrike as the Modernist Anti-Hero in Nathanael West's Miss Lonelyhearts

In a discussion of Nathanael West's *Miss Lonelyhearts* in *American Apocalypses*, Douglas Robinson challenges the conventional alignment of Miss Lonelyhearts with Christ and Shrike with Satan, pointing out that such a thematic reduction overlooks the evidence that West more often aligns his antagonists the other way by presenting Lonelyhearts as a restless Satan wandering through chaos and Shrike as the Christ figure whose rhetoric becomes "his image of order, his rock, which guarantees his invulnerability throughout the novel" (126). Although Robinson does not elaborate on this concept, a close textual study of the novella will show that his reversal of traditional roles is viable, especially in the character of Shrike, who exposes the hypocrisy and irrationality of Lonelyhearts' religious mania with an unrelenting nihilism that identifies hill as the modernist antihero.

A general note on the nature of heroism in modern fiction seems appropriate here. In Radical Innocence Ihab Hassan asserts that, because part of the make-up of the hero in American fiction of the past was his ability to mediate between the Self and the World, the restlessness and rebellion in the heroic soul remained quiescent, and the hero's struggles affirmed the harmony of the inner life of man and the external world of God, nature, and society. Today, however, that harmony is rapidly disappearing:

From *Modern Fiction Studies*, vol. 36, no. 2 (Summer 1990). © 1990 by the Purdue Research Foundation.

The World, in our time, seems to have either vanished or become a rigid and intractable mass. The anarchy of nihilism and the terror of statism delimit the extremes between which there seems to be no viable mean. Mediation between Self and World appears no longer possible—there is only surrender or recoil. In his modern recoil, the hero has become an anti-hero. (327)

In West's novella, one of Lonelyhearts' newspaper associates alludes to this breakdown of mediation between Self and World: "The trouble with him, the trouble with all of us, is that we have no outer life, only an inner one, and that by necessity" (15). Man's inner life, or Self, has become so alienated from society that his outer life, or World, no longer exists in any meaningful way. In Hassan's view, however, the estranged antihero reacts to the modernist dilemma by recoiling from nihilism, whereas in *Lonelyhearts*, Shrike embraces it as his system of order.

Lonelyhearts' response to the modernist predicament is the fever of religious hysteria, and because it leads not to redemption through Christian love but to Violence and death, he fails in his messianic role and ironically becomes the agent of chaos. On the other hand, Shrike's impious modernist response, because it enables him to function and thrive in a world where the good, the true, and the beautiful do not exist, becomes the source of a virtually unassailable stability. An unabashed voluptuary, a debauchee, and a dead-pan but otherwise very lively satyr, Shrike resolutely refuses to allow his pagan pleasures to be displaced by Lonelyhearts' dreary Christian asceticism. To that end, he undertakes his own mock apologia in Delehanty's bar, prefacing his drunken declamation by disclosing that he can walk on his own water and inquiring whether his audience has heard of "Shrike's Passion in the Luncheonette or the Agony in the Soda Fountain" (7). What follows could be referred to as his Sermon in the Speakeasy:

Under the skin of men is a wondrous jungle where veins like lush tropical growths hang along over-ripe organs and weed-like entrails writhe in squirming tangles of red and yellow. In this jungle ... lives a bird called the soul. The Catholic hunts this bird with bread and wine, the Hebrew with a golden ruler, the Protestant on leaden feet with leaden words, the Buddhist with gestures, the Negro with blood. I spit on them all. Phooh! And I call upon you to spit. Phooh! (7–8)

Shrike does not intend his discourse to be spiritually uplifting but sexually titillating, because it is engendered by his lechery for his latest conquest, Miss Farkis. His grandiloquent utterance is punctuated by periodic nuzzling and rump patting designed to result not in faith but fornication: "His caresses kept pace with the sermon. When he had reached the end, he buried his triangular face like the blade of a hatchet in her neck" (8).

Lawrence DiStasi writes that Shrike applies the deflated concept of Christianity to sexual seduction in a parody of the tradition of courtly love: "Where the latter moved toward non-violence and gentilesse, however, this parody illustrates the counter movement in the modern world. This simultaneous demystification of religion and love results in the unbinding of the aggressive component in each of them, leaving only violence in their place" (87).

In a modernist society where carnality and the appetites of the flesh have consigned courtly love to the scrap heap, Shrike rules with supreme authority. He encourages his frigid wife Mary to see other men, as she points out, "To save money. He knows that I let them neck me and when I get home all hot and bothered, he climbs into my bed and begs for it. The cheap bastard!" (22). Yet the marriage remains intact. Shrike freely admits that his love is "of the flesh flashy" (21) and that if he suffers, it is only because he must endure the indignity of having to wait while Lonelyhearts arouses his wife for him. After a date featuring many long, wet kisses, Mary disappears into the apartment, and Shrike emerges momentarily to inspect the corridor, wearing only the top of his pajamas. Following the transubstantiation, by proxy, of body and blood into lust, Shrike the modernist priest, clad in his pajama-top chasuble, prepares for the sacrament of predatory sex. In an alarming reduction of Christian anthropomorphism to pagan atavism, Shrike's apotheosis of the libido is figured forth in the iconography of the Mexican War obelisk, an enormous phallus of stone, perpetually rigid, "lengthening in rapid jerks ... red and swollen in the dying sun, as though it were about to spout a load of granite seed" (19).

As the modernist antihero, Shrike has his own system of order to shore against ruin, an uncompromising cynicism made all the more impenetrable by the fact that there is nothing arcane about its major tenet. There is no meaning in anything, especially suffering, and there is no escape from it in this or any other life. With the gleam of polished parody, Shrike blocks every conceivable retreat from pain, including the pastoral: "You buy a farm and walk behind your horse's moist behind.... To this rhythm you sow and weep and chivy your kine between the pregnant rows of corn and taters"; the South Seas à la Gauguin: "The tourists envy you your breech clout and carefree laugh and little brown bride and fingers instead of forks"; the pleasure dome: "You fornicate under pictures by Matisse and Picasso, you drink from Renaissance glassware and often you spend an evening beside the fireplace with Proust and an apple"; and the sanctuary of tuneless Art: "You know that your shoes are broken and therefore pimples on your face, yes, and that you have buck teeth and a club foot, but you don't care, for tomorrow they are playing Beethoven's last quartets in Carnegie Hall and at home you have Shakespeare's plays in one volume" (34–35). Shrike's flamboyant oratory delineates a modernist epistemology proclaiming tire wisdom of a chilling contempt which mocks Camus's pronouncement that "There is no fate that cannot be surmounted by scorn" (90). I sneer, therefore I am.

The main thrust of Shrike's messianic mission as the modernist antihero is to expose the hypocrisy of Lonelyhearts' Christianity, with its neurotic. fixation on the Clark mysteries of blood and martyrdom. Removing the ivory figure from its cross, Lonelyhearts essays the recrucifixion of Christ by nailing him to the wall with spikes, but "Instead of writhing, the Christ remained calmly decorative" (8). Lonelyhearts' vision of the disastrous attempt to kill a lamb, emblematic of Christ, complete with ritual butcher knife and incantation over an alter strewn with buttercups and daisies, reveals his preoccupation with blood sacrifice and his horror at being unable to consummate it properly. The knife snaps, and the mutilated lamb crawls away into the bushes, where Lonelyhearts later returns to crush its head with a stone, "leaving the carcass to the flies that swarmed around the bloody altar flowers" (10). Lonelyhearts' bungled sacrifice, it turns out, is made ironically not to God but to Beelzebub, Lord of the Flies. It is characteristic of Shrike's acuity that he perceives this attraction to sadism and violence beneath Lonelyhearts' mask of piety, and he calls upon Lonelyhearts to stop wearing the hair shirt and pondering the Passion: "You're morbid, my friend, morbid. Forget the crucifixion, remember the Renaissance. There were no brooders then. I give you the Borgias. What a period! What pageantry! Drunken popes ... Beautiful courtesans ... Illegitimate children ..." (5–6, ellipses West's).

Shrike also sees through the pretense of Lonelyhearts' crusade to alleviate human suffering, and so does Lonelyhearts, who knows very well that his humble Father Zossima posturing is all in the name of greed: "His column would be syndicated and the whole world would learn to love. The Kingdom of Heaven would arrive. He would sit on the right hand of the Lamb" (8), in the glorious fulfillment of the Puritan American Dream updated to the twentieth-century. To Shrike, the concept of fame and fortune as a syndicated columnist is rational enough, because self-aggrandizement is after all the sole motive of man's endeavor, but he objects to Lonelyhearts' sanctimonious, breast-beating altruism as the avowed driving force of his ambition. With a pragmatism that is totally incorruptible, Shrike refuses to compromise the purity of his self-interest by disguising it as anything else.

He advises Lonelyhearts to avoid recommending suicide to the column, not because life is worth living or because his readers should give a damn about anything but because, as Shrike puts it, "your job is to increase the circulation of the paper. Suicide, it is only reasonable to think, would defeat this purpose" (18). In the same spirit, Goldsmith, one of Shrike's disciples, suggests that Lonelyhearts should satisfy the sexual needs of one of his frustrated correspondents in order to "get the lady with child and increase the potential circulation of the paper" (26).

Shrike also decries Lonelyhearts' self-righteous obsession with providing spiritual sustenance to the wretched soul in pain, and to that end he manages to debunk the profundities of the Lord's Prayer, the French aristocracy, and the Eucharist all in one fell spoof: "I advise you to give your readers stones. When they ask for bread don't give them crackers as does the Church and don't, like the State, tell them to eat cake. Explain that man cannot live by bread alone and give them stones. Teach them to pray each morning: 'Give us this day our daily stone'" (5). Gerald Nelson explains that Shrike's shrill insistence is based on his messianic mission to reveal the truth, foul as it is: "He is not a black priest; there is no perversion in him. He does not try to cover up or delude his parishioners. He preaches with a beautifully pristine, deliberate ruthelessness. It is not his fault if he drives his flock mad" (82).

In order to ensure the triumph of his own gospel of negativism, Shrike also demolishes the reality of suffering, not only of Lonelyhearts but also of the letter writers, and he burlesques their imbecilic utterances to reduce them to the level of absurdity:

> This one is a jim-dandy. A young boy wants a violin. It looks simple; all you have to do is get the kid one. But then you discover that he dictated the letter to his little sister. He is paralyzed and can't even feed himself. He has a toy violin and hugs it to his chest, imitating the sound of playing with his mouth. How pathetic. However, one can learn much from this parable. Label the boy Labor, the violin Capital and so on.... (53)

Shrike is able to handle the letters and the banality of Lonelyhearts' response to them with equally derisive facility because, as Jeffrey Duncan notes, both bear the same message: "the human race is a poet that writes the eccentric propositions of its fate, and propositions, fate, the race itself amount only to so much noisy breath, hot air, flatulence" (118).

In the modernist world, which Jonathan Raban describes as "the urban industrial environment of pulp media and cheapjack commodities" (222),

Shrike reigns supreme as the Primum Mobile, the first mover, for neither
Lonelyhearts nor his correspondents has any existence outside the artificial
framework of clichés created by Shrike and the newspaper to define them.
Once set in motion, his mechanical media universe can only operate
according to the linguistic laws he has set down.

Shrike's crowning achievement is his unmasking of Lonelyhearts as a
vengeful, Calvinistic Jonathan Edwards for the mass media, eager to preach
his hellfire and brimstone sermon, perhaps edited to "Sinners in the Hands
of an Angry Columnist," and featuring such highlights as "Suffer, you
wretched bunch of freaks. Neither God nor I can stand to have you in our
sight because you are uglier than you can imagine in your wildest
nightmares" (116–127). Gerald Nelson points out that Lonelyhearts, whose
Christianity is actually closet voyeurism, enjoys the suffering of his letter
writers and offers to supply a spiritual dimension that will heighten rather
than alleviate their physical and mental pain: "Instead of merely moaning, he
wants them to really face the agony of emptiness, and die. So that he can
watch" (87). As the chief agent and overseer of this abyss of misery,
Lonelyhearts emerges as the modernist Satan.

Shrike, on the other hand, has no desire to feed the repulsive little
spiders into the flames of perdition; instead, he would offer his readers the
insipid tripe they want to hear, the kind of bromide he dictates with relish to
Lonelyhearts and which Lonelyhearts can only mimic later:

> Do not let life overwhelm you. When the old paths are choked
> with the debris of failure, look for newer and fresher paths. Art is
> just such a path. Art is distilled from suffering. Art is One of Life's
> Richest Offerings. For those who have not the talent to create,
> there is appreciation. For those.... Go on froth there. (4)

Shrike's glib rhetoric becomes the Logos; his irony is transmitted as the
modernist Word. The Antichrist is the monomaniacal Lonelyhearts,
described by Shrike as the "still more swollen Mussolini of the soul" (52),
bloated by a surfeit of pseudo-divinity, corruption incarnate.

The clash between the modernist responses of Shrike and Lonelyhearts
is a fight to the finish, and the introduction of Fay and Peter Doyle into the
fray signals the onset of the apocalyptic showdown. Shrike immediately
acknowledges the truth that the Doyles are living the reality of an American
nightmare from which it is impossible to awaken them. When he asks Doyle,
whom West describes as a "partially destroyed insect" (44), to speak for
humanity from the vantage point of a gas meter reader, Doyle replies with a
leer that his profession has replaced the defunct iceman in the stories about

sexual dalliance in the suburbs. Vastly amused, Shrike roars, "What? I can see you are not the man for us. You know nothing about humanity; you are humanity. I leave you to Lonelyhearts" (45). Shrike knows that the diabolical, death-ridden heretic, whose bony chin is "cleft like a hoof" (4), is waiting in a vengeful delirium to claim both Doyle and his wife,

Merging the motif of the loathsome insect suspended over the fire with his blood sacrifice, fixation, Lonelyhearts postulates a dialectic of transfiguration through pain: "Christ died for you. He died nailed to a tree for you. His gift to you is suffering and it is only through suffering that you can know him" (39). Lonelyhearts renounces the Christian doctrine of deliverance through the redemptive love of the Son of God, whom he describes as the "black fruit that hangs on the crosstree" (49) and touts a cheapened mimicry of the savior's transcendent agony and death as a nostrum for the torments of his correspondents' souls. In a "stage scream," Lonelyhearts then hysterically invokes the serpent of temptation in the Garden: "Man was lost by eating of the forbidden fruit. He shall be saved by eating of the forbidden fruit. The black Christ-fruit, the love fruit" (49). The apostasy of Lonelyhearts' exhortation to corrupt divine grace with dimestore carnality does not inspire the hoped-for regeneration but a lewd ritual of seduction, as the lickerish Mrs. Doyle "waved her behind at him like a flag" and "after doing a few obscene steps in front of him ... opened the neck of her dress and tried to force his head between her breasts" (50). With the Christian compassion twisted into a fury of sadistic violence, Lonelyhearts can only respond by inflicting pain: "He struck out blindly and hit her in the face. She screamed and he hit her again and again. He kept hitting her until she stopped trying to hold him, then he ran out of the house" (50).

Shrike is much more Christ-like in his understanding that, in twentieth-century America, the downtrodden want ways to hang onto life and enjoy their puerile amusements, not ways to suffer and die. The sixteen-year-old girl who writes Lonelyhearts about her misfortune of being born without a nose only wants the nose she never had, or failing that, the illusion of a nose and a few nights out on the town, riot plastic surgery of the soul that leaves her with the same hole in her face where a nose should be. And Lonelyhearts, blinded by his delusion, fails to see that he is involved not in a miraculous revelation of his power to heal but in the oldest, tackiest story in the dirty joke book, the adulterous triangle with Doyle as the gun-toting cuckold threatening murder and mayhem. He has no real desire to kill Lonelyhearts; he just wants to be talked out of it and go on home where he can bark like a dog at his wife, tear open the fly of whatever man happens to be in the apartment at the time, roll over on his back, and howl to be scratched. Then dragging his club foot up and down cellar stairs to read meters won't seem so bad after all. In a world where faith is dead, West seems to suggest, what Doyle wants to do is what most of the rest of us really want to do in order to survive. Mark Conroy writes:

> The stories we tell ourselves, like the stories we tell others, are as necessary as they are fraudulent; and the more irrelevant they become, the more necessary they may well seem. The narrative of *Miss Lonelyhearts* in the story of this cruel calculus. It is a tale where Shrike has the last laugh, because he has already written the first line. (124)

The confidence and strength of Shrike's laughter is the measure of his successful demystification of man's spiritual longing to merge with the absolute. Miles D. Orvell explains Shrike's victory over Lonelyhearts' attempts to restore the suffering world around him:

> Walt Whitman had tried—in his own time, and with a precedent conception of the relatedness of the physical and the spiritual lives—to move from the inner vision to the world, and with a hard, underlying view of the speedy progress America was making toward a muscle-bound, impoverishing materialism; but for Whitman the move had been chiefly imaginative, a matter of poetry and prophecy, and so buoyed by a resurgent optimism. West was heir to Whitman's insight that in our modern industrial society, spiritual, sexual and institutional energies are bound together; but it was West's twentieth-century view that regeneration is an agony, and, it would seem, a deception. (167)

Perhaps, then, it is time to leave Whitman behind and to listen to the word of a later prophet, Yeats, who heralded the second coming of a savior more suited to our times. And so, its hour come round at last, the rough beast slouches not toward Bethlehem but toward twentieth-century America, where he is born in *Miss Lonelyhearts* and is named Shrike, after the bird that mercilessly impales its prey on thorns.

If we doubt that Shrike is the true modernist Christ, who the prophet tells us has a "gaze blank and pitiless as the sun," we have only to look into his face: "Although his gestures were elaborate, his face was blank. No matter how fantastic or excited his speech, he never changed his expression. Under the shining white globe of his brow, his features huddled together in a dead, gray triangle" (6).

ics, and anglo-catholic in religion" (vii), and insisting that he had "no
being modern," he rejected the role of vanguard and offered his own
"civilization" as an "alternative to modernity." Moreover, because
pressed doubts "whether civilization [could] endure without religion,
ion without a church" (155), he concluded by conjoining civilization
tianity.

tements like these must have struck West with considerable force.
criticized writers like Galsworthy, Bennett, and Wharton for their
lism and admired the Modernists, especially Eliot, for working
n Anglo-American avant-garde. Eliot's ideas, even in the
ion of For Lancelot Andrewes, indicated clearly that his early
efforts to "make it new" were turning a corner back toward
ve traditions. West, having repudiated his own Judaism and having
nsively in the philosophy and history of religion, from De
History and Literature of Christianity to Abelson's Jewish Mysticism
's From Ritual to Romance (Martin 58), did not wish to promote
m of religion or to see Modernism moving toward an intellectual
th the Church. His treatment in Miss Lonelyhearts of Eliot's
thus largely critical and often parodic as West takes issue with
presses his fear that ritual, modernized and commodified, would
e a powerful form of seduction. At its most extreme, it would
and legitimate the basest instincts of a culture's inhabitants.
ding The Waste Land within Miss Lonelyhearts, West parodies
nts of the poem in order to dramatize the dangers of authority
self. He rewrites the death/life tensions of the poem into utter
d critically examines the role of the quester/savior—merging it
Tiresian figure. But critics who have studied Miss Lonelyhearts
of Eliot's work have emphasized the derivative elements o
rather than the critical stance that West takes in relation t
d L. Volpe, for instance, cites numerous parallels to sugges
have culled The Waste Land for serviceable motifs and that i
liot and sharing his concerns, he created a central quester wi
would sympathize. According to Volpe, if Lonelyhear
with the paradigmatic quest, his failure is not of his ov
it is caused by the inability of others to accept his sincere
ge.

ment cannot account for the fact that Miss Lonelyhearts,
ers, luxuriates in a series of narcissistic and destruc
ecause Volpe believes that West wants readers to sympatl
nist right to the end, Volpe is compelled to explicate
g chapters as a loss of narrative control on West's part.

WORKS CITED

Camus, Albert. *The Myth of Sisyphus*. New York: Vintage, 1955.

Conroy, Mark. "Letters and Spirit in *Miss Lonelyhearts*." *Nathanael West's "Miss Lonelyhearts": Modern Critical Interpretations*. Ed. Harold Bloom. New York: Chelsea, 1987. 111–124.

DiStasi, Lawrence. "Aggression in *Miss Lonelyhearts*: Nowhere to Throw the Stone." *Nathanael West: The Cheaters and the Cheated*. Ed. David Madden. Deland: Everett/Edwards, 1973. 83–101.

Duncan, Jeffrey L. "The Problem of Language in *Miss Lonelyhearts*." *Iowa Review* 8 (1977): 116–127.

Hassan, Ihab. *Radical Innocence: Studies in the Contemporary Novel*. Princeton: Princeton UP, 1973.

Nelson, Gerald B. *"Lonelyhearts." Ten Versions of America*. New York: Knopf, 1972. 79–90.

Orvell, Miles D. "The Messianic Sexuality of *Miss Lonelyhearts*." *Studies in Short Fiction* 10.2 (1973): 159–167.

Raban, Jonathan. "A Surfeit of Commodities: The Novels of Nathanael West." *The American Novel and the Nineteen Twenties*. Ed. Malcolm Bradbury and David Palmer. New York: Arnold, 1971. 215–231.

Robinson, Douglas. "The Ritual Icon." *American Apocalypses: The Image of the End of the World in American Literature*. Baltimore: Johns Hopkins UP, 1985. 198–232.

West, Nathanael. *Miss Lonelyhearts*. New York: New Directions, 1969.

MIRIAM FUC

Nathanael West's Miss
The Waste Land

Nathanael West had studied T.S. E
1928 volume, *For Lancelot Andrewes: Es*
drafting his manuscript of *Miss Lonely*
Pound, Crane, and Stevens, West had s
of the Modernist poets and written hi
the Cities."[1] He had traveled to Paris
circles and briefly met Eliot. When h
The Dream Life of Balso Snell and beg
in particular, makes explicit use o
Adventurer," its protagonist daydr
Perilous, a wounded king, a desert
story as recounted by Jessie Westo
Eliot in *The Waste Land* (Martin, *N*
completed "The Adventurer," b
materials interestingly appear in
1929—*Miss Lonelyhearts*.

Initially drawn to the bold
starting to look cautiously at E
ideological conservatism. Eliot
henceforth his general point of

in poli
claim t
idea of
Eliot ex
and reli
to Chris
St
He had
tradition
toward
Introduc
Modernis
conservat
read exte
Labrialle's
to Weston
another fo
alliance w
materials is
Eliot and ex
ultimately
camouflage

Embe
crucial elem
outside of th
barrenness a
with his own
in the conte
West's novel
Eliot. Edmon
that West mu
deference to E
whom readers
wreaks havoc
making. Rathe
imperfect mess

This argu
the final chapt
hallucinations.
with his protag
novel's concludi

From *Studies in Short Fiction*, vol. 29,

more likely, however, given West's tendency toward satire and parody—and his explicit use of these techniques in his earlier *The Dream Life of Balso Snell* (1931)—that in *Miss Lonelyhearts* he *does* maintain narrative control and fully intends to expose Miss Lonelyhearts as a bogus, obsessive savior who, under the pretext of enacting a program for salvation, deforms the salvation dream into a sadomasochistic fantasy of empowerment.

West establishes a *Waste Land* context by writing into the first few pages of *Miss Lonelyhearts* a landscape that obviously draws upon the poem. However, he twists well known elements of "The Burial of the Dead" into violent and surreal permutations in order to deride Eliot's tentative projections of hope. The arid landscape in both works has the potential to rejuvenate, but in *Miss Lonelyhearts* it takes on a repugnant surreality through crude phallic symbolism. In the poem, April's efforts to breed life into the dead land and to instigate the seasonal cycle is persistent but gentle, achieved gradually by "stirring," "mixing," and "breeding." The poem's dichotomy between winter and spring, sterility and fertility operates in *Miss Lonelyhearts*, but the transition from winter to spring is a violent struggle between warring elements. Miss Lonelyhearts crosses a small city park:

> He walked into the shadow of a lamp-post that lay on the path like a spear. It pierced him like a spear. As far as he could discover, there were no signs of spring. The decay that covered the surface of the mottled ground was not the kind in which life generates. Last year, he remembered, May had failed to quicken these soiled fields. It had taken all the brutality of July to torture a few green spikes through the exhausted dirt. (4–5)

The ground is so desiccated that spring growth wrenched from the dirt is a violation of a landscape better left dead. In addition, West adds an unpleasant sexual twist to the scene. The grass consists of phallic spikes, the feminine earth is "dirt," and fertilization is tantamount to torture, caused by the brutal penetration of July. Leaning on a stone obelisk, Lonelyhearts finds that it offers no relief but erotically comes to life: "The stone shaft ... was lengthening in rapid jerks ... red and swollen in the dying sun, as though it were about to spout a load of granite seed" (19). In both works, then, the depleted landscape is linked to the exhaustion of its inhabitants, but in *Miss Lonelyhearts* the connections are painfully askew, brutishly constituted, and suggestive of rape as West draws out Eliot's imagery to extreme manifestations.

The motifs of *Miss Lonelyhearts*—stones, spring rain, a thrush, crowds of people, and so on—are shaped from those that comprise *The Waste Land*, but West disrupts the poem's balance between human and nonhuman, hopefulness and despair. Examining this balance and characterizing Eliot's poem as a "ceaseless hermeneutic," Helen Davidson discusses the absence of precise linguistic connections and logic as Eliot's strategy for suggesting allusive and paratactical fullness. As readers do not sense a rigorous unitary design, they accept the poem's subtle, multitudinous possibilities. The five sections of Eliot's poem, hermeneutically expansive but determinedly balanced, register and distribute emotions in the scenes and personae that form its landscape. For Eliot, this balance or equilibrium between the singular and the general, the settings and the landscape, suggests a step toward resolution.

The Waste Land's objects—its stony places, cracks that burst the violet air, whistling bats with baby faces—contain and communicate the powerful emotions generated by the poem and function as objective correlatives. In his essay on Lancelot Andrewes, where Eliot illustrates the usefulness of the correlative by contrasting Andrewes's sermons with Donne's, he cites Andrewes for a nearly perfect "equation" between personal expression and literary image. "Andrewes's emotion," Eliot writes, "is purely contemplative; it is not personal, it is wholly evoked by the object of contemplation, to which it is adequate; his emotions wholly contained in and explained by its object ..." (186–87). Donne's sermons, in contrast, are more "dangerous" than those written by Andrewes. The "objects" in his writing are not always "adequate" to absorb his personal feelings, and thus Donne, the individual, breaks through the surface of his sermons. Eliot insists that personal expression be displaced into correlatives; and he manages this in The Waste Land by displacing and dispersing it throughout the poem's five sections, all of which absorb personal and autobiographical elements into nearly endless hermeneutical possibilities.

Lacking Eliot's desire for emotional containment, West rewrites the death/life dichotomy, which in the poem settles into a pervasive apathy. In Miss Lonelyhearts apathy explodes into sadistic aggression. Lonelyhearts's acts of priestly benevolence go haywire; his activities with his "congregation" are spasmodic gestures that veer away from communality and order; and his treatment of the women who implore his help deteriorates into misogyny. The most enduring impression of West's fiction, according to Jan Gorek, "is not that of the artist's shaping hand working mass into form," but rather the "massive machinery of illusion, slipping out of control of its manipulators and its audience alike" (78). Against the suffering of his personae Eliot offers hope (though largely unrealized) in unexpected gusts of rain, snatches of song, and efforts to connect something with something although, as a voice in "The Fire Sermon" laments, "My people humble people" expect

WORKS CITED

Camus, Albert. *The Myth of Sisyphus*. New York: Vintage, 1955.

Conroy, Mark. "Letters and Spirit in *Miss Lonelyhearts*." *Nathanael West's "Miss Lonelyhearts"*: *Modern Critical Interpretations*. Ed. Harold Bloom. New York: Chelsea, 1987. 111–124.

DiStasi, Lawrence. "Aggression in *Miss Lonelyhearts*: Nowhere to Throw the Stone." *Nathanael West: The Cheaters and the Cheated*. Ed. David Madden. Deland: Everett/Edwards, 1973. 83–101.

Duncan, Jeffrey L. "The Problem of Language in *Miss Lonelyhearts*." *Iowa Review* 8 (1977): 116–127.

Hassan, Ihab. *Radical Innocence: Studies in the Contemporary Novel*. Princeton: Princeton UP, 1973.

Nelson, Gerald B. *"Lonelyhearts." Ten Versions of America*. New York: Knopf, 1972. 79–90.

Orvell, Miles D. "The Messianic Sexuality of *Miss Lonelyhearts*." *Studies in Short Fiction* 10.2 (1973): 159–167.

Raban, Jonathan. "A Surfeit of Commodities: The Novels of Nathanael West." *The American Novel and the Nineteen Twenties*. Ed. Malcolm Bradbury and David Palmer. New York: Arnold, 1971. 215–231.

Robinson, Douglas. "The Ritual Icon." *American Apocalpyses: The Image of the End of the World in American Literature*. Baltimore: Johns Hopkins UP, 1985. 198–232.

West, Nathanael. *Miss Lonelyhearts*. New York: New Directions, 1969.

MIRIAM FUCHS

Nathanael West's Miss Lonelyhearts: The Waste Land *Rescripted*

Nathanael West had studied T.S. Eliot's poetry and was reading Eliot's 1928 volume, *For Lancelot Andrewes: Essays on Style and Order,* while he was drafting his manuscript of *Miss Lonelyhearts.* Drawn to Eliot as well as to Pound, Crane, and Stevens, West had studied the collagist and mythic modes of the Modernist poets and written his own poetic sequence entitled "Burn the Cities."[1] He had traveled to Paris in 1927, where he skimmed expatriate circles and briefly met Eliot. When he returned to New York, West finished *The Dream Life of Balso Snell* and began a number of short stories. One story, in particular, makes explicit use of *Waste Land* materials. Entitled "The Adventurer," its protagonist daydreams adventures that include a Chapel Perilous, a wounded king, a desert landscape—elements of the *Waste Land* story as recounted by Jessie Weston in *From Ritual to Romance* and used by Eliot in *The Waste Land* (Martin, *NW: The Art of His Life* 161–68). West never completed "The Adventurer," but similar tropes, personae and thematic materials interestingly appear in the short work of fiction that he began in 1929—*Miss Lonelyhearts.*

Initially drawn to the bold experimentation of Eliot's poetry, West was starting to look cautiously at Eliot's attraction to ritual and to his growing ideological conservatism. Eliot had declared in *For Lancelot Andrewes* that henceforth his general point of view would be "classicist in literature, royalist

From *Studies in Short Fiction,* vol. 29, no. 1 (Winter 1992). © 1992 by Newberry College.

in politics, and anglo-catholic in religion" (vii), and insisting that he had "no claim to being modern," he rejected the role of vanguard and offered his own idea of "civilization" as an "alternative to modernity." Moreover, because Eliot expressed doubts "whether civilization [could] endure without religion, and religion without a church" (155), he concluded by conjoining civilization to Christianity.

Statements like these must have struck West with considerable force. He had criticized writers like Galsworthy, Bennett, and Wharton for their traditionalism and admired the Modernists, especially Eliot, for working toward an Anglo-American avant-garde. Eliot's ideas, even in the Introduction of *For Lancelot Andrewes*, indicated clearly that his early Modernist efforts to "make it new" were turning a corner back toward conservative traditions. West, having repudiated his own Judaism and having read extensively in the philosophy and history of religion, from De Labrialle's *History and Literature of Christianity* to Abelson's *Jewish Mysticism* to Weston's *From Ritual to Romance* (Martin 58), did not wish to promote another form of religion or to see Modernism moving toward an intellectual alliance with the Church. His treatment in *Miss Lonelyhearts* of Eliot's materials is thus largely critical and often parodic as West takes issue with Eliot and expresses his fear that ritual, modernized and commodified, would ultimately be a powerful form of seduction. At its most extreme, it would camouflage and legitimate the basest instincts of a culture's inhabitants.

Embedding *The Waste Land* within *Miss Lonelyhearts*, West parodies crucial elements of the poem in order to dramatize the dangers of authority outside of the self. He rewrites the death/life tensions of the poem into utter barrenness and critically examines the role of the quester/savior—merging it with his own Tiresian figure. But critics who have studied *Miss Lonelyhearts* in the context of Eliot's work have emphasized the derivative elements of West's novel rather than the critical stance that West takes in relation to Eliot. Edmond L. Volpe, for instance, cites numerous parallels to suggest that West must have culled *The Waste Land* for serviceable motifs and that in deference to Eliot and sharing his concerns, he created a central quester with whom readers would sympathize. According to Volpe, if Lonelyhearts wreaks havoc with the paradigmatic quest, his failure is not of his own making. Rather, it is caused by the inability of others to accept his sincere but imperfect message.

This argument cannot account for the fact that Miss Lonelyhearts, in the final chapters, luxuriates in a series of narcissistic and destructive hallucinations. Because Volpe believes that West wants readers to sympathize with his protagonist right to the end, Volpe is compelled to explicate the novel's concluding chapters as a loss of narrative control on West's part. It is more likely, however, given West's tendency toward satire and parody—and his explicit use of these techniques in his earlier *The Dream Life of Balso Snell* (1931)—that in *Miss Lonelyhearts* he *does* maintain narrative control and fully intends to expose Miss Lonelyhearts as a bogus, obsessive savior who, under the pretext of enacting a program for salvation, deforms the salvation dream into a sadomasochistic fantasy of empowerment.

West establishes a *Waste Land* context by writing into the first few pages of *Miss Lonelyhearts* a landscape that obviously draws upon the poem. However, he twists well known elements of "The Burial of the Dead" into violent and surreal permutations in order to deride Eliot's tentative projections of hope. The arid landscape in both works has the potential to rejuvenate, but in *Miss Lonelyhearts* it takes on a repugnant surreality through crude phallic symbolism. In the poem, April's efforts to breed life into the dead land and to instigate the seasonal cycle is persistent but gentle, achieved gradually by "stirring," "mixing," and "breeding." The poem's dichotomy between winter and spring, sterility and fertility operates in *Miss Lonelyhearts*, but the transition from winter to spring is a violent struggle between warring elements. Miss Lonelyhearts crosses a small city park:

> He walked into the shadow of a lamp-post that lay on the path like a spear. It pierced him like a spear. As far as he could discover, there were no signs of spring. The decay that covered the surface of the mottled ground was not the kind in which life generates. Last year, he remembered, May had failed to quicken these soiled fields. It had taken all the brutality of July to torture a few green spikes through the exhausted dirt. (4–5)

The ground is so desiccated that spring growth wrenched from the dirt is a violation of a landscape better left dead. In addition, West adds an unpleasant sexual twist to the scene. The grass consists of phallic spikes, the feminine earth is "dirt," and fertilization is tantamount to torture, caused by the brutal penetration of July. Leaning on a stone obelisk, Lonelyhearts finds that it offers no relief but erotically comes to life: "The stone shaft ... was lengthening in rapid jerks ... red and swollen in the dying sun, as though it were about to spout a load of granite seed" (19). In both works, then, the depleted landscape is linked to the exhaustion of its inhabitants, but in *Miss Lonelyhearts* the connections are painfully askew, brutishly constituted, and suggestive of rape as West draws out Eliot's imagery to extreme manifestations.

The motifs of *Miss Lonelyhearts*—stones, spring rain, a thrush, crowds of people, and so on—are shaped from those that comprise *The Waste Land*, but West disrupts the poem's balance between human and nonhuman, hopefulness and despair. Examining this balance and characterizing Eliot's poem as a "ceaseless hermeneutic," Helen Davidson discusses the absence of precise linguistic connections and logic as Eliot's strategy for suggesting allusive and paratactical fullness. As readers do not sense a rigorous unitary design, they accept the poem's subtle, multitudinous possibilities. The five sections of Eliot's poem, hermeneutically expansive but determinedly balanced, register and distribute emotions in the scenes and personae that form its landscape. For Eliot, this balance or equilibrium between the singular and the general, the settings and the landscape, suggests a step toward resolution.

The Waste Land's objects—its stony places, cracks that burst the violet air, whistling bats with baby faces—contain and communicate the powerful emotions generated by the poem and function as objective correlatives. In his essay on Lancelot Andrewes, where Eliot illustrates the usefulness of the correlative by contrasting Andrewes's sermons with Donne's, he cites Andrewes for a nearly perfect "equation" between personal expression and literary image. "Andrewes's emotion," Eliot writes, "is purely contemplative; it is not personal, it is wholly evoked by the object of contemplation, to which it is adequate; his emotions wholly contained in and explained by its object ..." (186–87). Donne's sermons, in contrast, are more "dangerous" than those written by Andrewes. The "objects" in his writing are not always "adequate" to absorb his personal feelings, and thus Donne, the individual, breaks through the surface of his sermons. Eliot insists that personal expression be displaced into correlatives; and he manages this in *The Waste Land* by displacing and dispersing it throughout the poem's five sections, all of which absorb personal and autobiographical elements into nearly endless hermeneutical possibilities.

Lacking Eliot's desire for emotional containment, West rewrites the death/life dichotomy, which in the poem settles into a pervasive apathy. In *Miss Lonelyhearts* apathy explodes into sadistic aggression. Lonelyhearts's acts of priestly benevolence go haywire; his activities with his "congregation" are spasmodic gestures that veer away from communality and order; and his treatment of the women who implore his help deteriorates into misogyny. The most enduring impression of West's fiction, according to Jan Gorek, "is not that of the artist's shaping hand working mass into form," but rather the "massive machinery of illusion, slipping out of control of its manipulators and its audience alike" (78). Against the suffering of his personae Eliot offers hope (though largely unrealized) in unexpected gusts of rain, snatches of song, and efforts to connect something with something although, as a voice in "The Fire Sermon" laments, "My people humble people" expect

"Nothing with nothing." Like Eliot, West assumes a correspondence between the natural and the human. But in denying that correspondence either harmony or balance, he symbolically releases his characters to enact decisions that reflect the unnatural developments of nature as well as perpetuate cultural violence.

Despite the fact that Lonelyhearts's quest is a series of sexual conquests that invert, rather than portray, the process of restoring harmony, critics invariably take Lonelyhearts's side. Their assumption is that these women misunderstand his benevolence and somehow deserve his abuse. If only they were more intelligent (Betty), or more compassionate (Mary Shrike), or more feminine (Mrs. Doyle), Lonelyhearts's efforts to ease their pain would have greater success. James Light presents this argument as he explains that "Miss Lonelyhearts, wishing to succor with love all the desperate of the universe and expecting to perform a miracle ... is shot by Doyle [in retaliation for having sex with Doyle's wife], destroyed, like Christ, by the panic and ignorance of those whom he would save" (75). Light's sympathy for Lonelyhearts is misplaced, for the journalist botches what he thinks is his calling so completely that comparisons to Christ—other than ironic ones—are inappropriate. West was inclined toward parody and satire from boyhood, had always used such techniques, and as Harold Bloom has written, parodies Lawrence, Melville, Hemingway, Fitzgerald, Maugham (6–8) and others throughout *Miss Lonelyhearts*. When he has the energy, Lonelyhearts indulges in selfish and predatory sexuality. When he is too weak to leave his bed, he dreams psychosexual-religious scenarios.

West's protagonist uses the privileged position of quester/hero as a pretext for exercising sexual dominance or giving in to misogynist desires. Betty takes him to a Connecticut farmhouse where she was born. The sharing of her "homeland" suggests that she is in some ways linked to authentic tradition, and as if establishing the possibility of harmony and beauty, the prose takes a rare lyrical turn ("the pale new leaves, shaped and colored like candle flames, were beautiful ... the air smelt clean and alive" [36]). West, however, splices the scene before it turns romantic or optimistic. Afterward, when the couple is about to make love, West's third-person voice returns to its customary clipped prose and traces a pantomime of fertility, sarcastically referring to Eve's original sin: "They each ate an apple, then put on their pajamas and went to bed. He fondled her, but when she said that she was a virgin, he let her alone and went to sleep" (37).

West subtly embellishes this failed "morning-after" scene with *The Waste Land*'s thrush ("Where the hermit-thrush sings in the pine trees / Drip drop drip drop drop drop drop"); but he parodies its song by giving it a repugnant, figurative twist: "Somewhere in the woods a thrush was singing.

Its sound was like that of a flute choked with saliva" (38). Ironically, it is the bird's reflexive gagging that excites the couple to make love. Extending the Edenic parody, Betty is naked on the grass. She hears the bird and turns provocatively to Lonelyhearts. Excited by the conjunction of the bird's suffering and Betty's sensuality, he runs toward her. This scene, which critics like Kingsley Widmar have oddly called a "pastoral," expresses West's denial that moments of mutual sympathy and intimacy—like the moment in Eliot's hyacinth garden—can produce an ameliorating effect. This "pastoral" takes place in a morbidly-described enclave with rotting foliage and "over everything a funereal hush" (38), and the intimacy is neither innocent nor sincere, at least for Lonelyhearts. He vanquishes Betty as the elements of nature, in an image that entangles voyeurism with militarism, watch over his exploitative triumph. Green, healthy leaves, "like an army of little metal shields," hang taut from the overhead tree as if to have a clear view of the couple on the ground (38).[2] From the gagging thrush to a pathetic recreation of Eden—also reminiscent of the hyacinth garden in *The Waste Land*—West's method is parodic, his vision pessimistic.

Miss Lonelyhearts's sexual exploitation of Betty is reiterated in Shrike's crude seduction of a Miss Farkis in a pantomime of aggression and conciliation that channels his own misogyny. Shrike introduces her by patting her on the "rump." He raises his fist as if to hit her, but when she recoils he changes the gesture to a caress. Potentially more adversarial than compliant, Miss Farkis is a powerful woman, but her strengths are jeeringly depicted. Her legs are strong, but her ankles are "thick"; her hands are "big"; her handshake "masculine"; her short hairstyle a "man's haircut." In other words, the third-person voice ridicules her strengths by warping them into sexually-charged insults. The battle concludes as Shrike burrows his face into her neck to assault her further, "like the blade of a hatchet in her neck" (7). Surrendering to her violation, she is relegated to an embarrassing stereotype.

Since the male approach to sexuality is exploitative and abusive, Mary Shrike's strategy is to marshal to her defense the weapon of titillation. This enables her to maintain power by denying any male the victory of consummation. By her own admission, she complements the "fakey" Spanish restaurant to which she asks Lonelyhearts to bring her and shows her appreciation by "offering herself in a series of formal, impersonal gestures. She was wearing a tight, shiny dress that was like glass-covered steel and there was something cleanly mechanical in her pantomime" (22). Mary does not dress, she masquerades, and the dazzling impenetrability of her uniform is meant to lure the enemy and fortify herself. Recalling Miss Farkis and Shrike in the speakeasy, the exchange between Miss Lonelyhearts and Mary in the restaurant illustrates how sex and violence are twisted into mutual aggression. Accused of wife abuse, Shrike insists that he is only an amateur, for "it's Mary who does the beating. Sleeping with her is like sleeping with a knife in one's groin" (21).

From Madame Sosostris in *The Waste Land* to Shrike in *Miss Lonelyhearts*, salvation is an artful strategy for self-promotion. In marketing their own prophecies, for instance, Shrike and Madame Sosostris share what Calvin Bedient in *He Do the Police In Different Voices* says is Sosostris's essential trait, "a vain, vulgar relation to reality as a system of readable (and profitably readable) object-signs" (57). For Shrike, the editor of the *Post-Dispatch*, reality consists of readable, writable, and, most essentially, of profitably writable signs. Mocking the New Testament, Shrike offers further text for Lonelyhearts's column: "Explain that man cannot live by bread alone and give them stones" (5). Lonelyhearts's first draft had alluded to the burning of lust and the attainment of peace, both fundamental processes to *The Waste Land*; but the chapter ends with Shrike's revisionary text, littered with parodies of biblical authority and Eliot's *Waste Land*.

West further expresses his criticism of Eliot's growing conservatism by reassigning the characters and images of *The Waste Land* a lesser status in his short novel. In effect, the objects from *The Waste Land* are the detritus of *Miss Lonelyhearts*. During a dream that serves as a negative and subtle metatextual reference to the poem, Lonelyhearts looks into a pawnshop window. There, in a recursive and reductive image for *The Waste Land* itself, he sees on display various mandolins and fishing tackle, reminiscent of the fisher king myths and specifically in "The Fire Sermon" of "the pleasant whining of a mandoline / And a clatter and a chatter from within / Where fishmen lounge at noon." But Lonelyhearts cannot conceive of the "inexplicable splendour" of Magnus Martyr, and recalls instead the sundry objects that slip out of control ("Mandolins strive to get out of tune") to assert their own impulses toward chaos ("All order is doomed ..." [31]). His dream is fueled by entropy; and his unconscious, ironically constituted by the trumpery in a pawnshop, is an unpleasant new site for the materials of Eliot's poem. Still dreaming, Lonelyhearts assembles watches, boots, and umbrellas into ancient symbols of diamonds, circles, triangles, and squares. One of these symbols goes out of alignment and its new configuration is a swastika.

West's pairing of the swastika with his character's "almost insane" need for his own version of cultural order is especially poignant in view of comments that Eliot would, in a few years, articulate in his 1939 book, *The Idea of a Christian Society*. Criticizing the "Liberal notion" that religion is a private matter (19) and looking only obliquely at Germany, Eliot does no more than acknowledge that objections could be raised "in the political and economic sphere." In fact, he chooses to remain silent until such time as "we set our own affairs in order." Wanting to promote his ideal Christian society, Eliot avoids any direct references to Nazi militarization and strategies for achieving cultural hegemony. Although West had given up his Jewish religion and has sometimes been called anti-Semitic, he was Jewish and would not have forgotten that both of his parents, fearful of Soviet rule and the revocation of basic freedoms, had fled Lithuania for America.[3] His depiction of Miss Lonelyhearts as obsessed with order and sadistically imposing his own solutions onto others who are less empowered than he assuredly had a contemporary political subtext.

By rescripting rituals and motifs from *The Waste Land*, West denies them regenerative potential and dramatically inverts Eliot's mythical framework. Eliot promoted its advantages in his essay on Joyce, "*Ulysses*, Order, and Myth," which he published in *The Dial*. Iterating his belief that myth could make the "modern world possible for art," Eliot describes Joyce's method in *Ulysses* as "a way of controlling, of ordering, of giving a shape and a significance to the immense panorama of futility and anarchy which is contemporary history" (177–78). A few years after the essay appeared, as Lawrence, Pound, and Eliot were refining their elaborate mythical structures, West was moving in an opposite direction. Denying that either order or form through reversion to collective myth is possible, West critically pitches his waste land text toward brutality and chaos.

The figure from myth that Eliot uses to link his disparate materials is, as he writes in his "Notes," "the most important personage in the poem, uniting all the rest."[4] That figure, Tiresias, "who sees the substance of the poem," is given heavy parodic treatment by West, who subjects his contemporary, Americanized version of the Greek seer from Ovid's *Metamorphoses* to failure and eventually to psychic breakdown. Tiresias's function and Eliot's apparent earnestness in footnoting the seer as *The Waste Land*'s central consciousness have been enduring critical issues. Earlier readers like Grover Smith and Elizabeth Drew, aligning themselves with Eliot's commentary, interpreted Tiresias as the most significant voice in the poem. More recently, in *He Do the Police in Different Voices*, Calvin Bedient analyzes Tiresias as just one of the central protagonist's numerous poses.[5] Helen Davidson views Tiresias as an important voice but denies that the poem has any single controlling protagonist. Although it is impossible to know specifically what West believed, as an early reader he probably accepted Eliot's explanation and adopted his own Tiresian figure in order to project a more pessimistic vision of his culture. Thus, West parodies Eliot's central figure in his own central figure, Miss Lonelyhearts.

Making his Tiresias almost ubiquitous, West distorts and hyperbolizes Eliot's seer. Eliot insists that Tiresias is *The Waste Land*'s most important "personage" despite only a brief appearance in "The Fire Sermon." In contrast, West blatantly centralizes and distributes his own Tiresias. Not just the novel's title, but all of its 15 chapters obsessively invoke his presence, repeating the generic name "Miss Lonelyhearts," and following it with a flat, satirical complement: "and the Dead Pan," "and the Fat Thumb," "on a Field Trip," "and the Party Dress." A few of the chapters have short, comic-book style titles: "Miss Lonelyhearts Returns," "Miss Lonelyhearts Attends a Party," "Miss Lonelyhearts Has a Religious Experience." Through this sardonic repetition West mocks the high seriousness with which Eliot treats the Tiresian "presence" (almost nowhere, but everywhere; not a "character," but a "personage"), and further insists on his physical presence by thrusting Lonelyhearts into frenetic motion unless he is immobilized in his bed. In this way, West subjects him to the same impulses toward disorder and violence as those whom Eliot would call the "characters" of the novel—Shrike, Mary Shrike, Betty, and the Doyles.

What Tiresias sees may or may not be the substance of *The Waste Land*. What West's newsman does is both the substance and the disaster of *Miss Lonelyhearts*. Known to his public as an unmarried (and consequently virginal) female, in his private life he carries on a series of disastrous heterosexual affairs. In fact, West's most compelling distortion of Tiresias's character is Lonelyhearts's inability to remain unaffected by human activity, to hold fast to his marginal but privileged position. His hermaphroditism has a modern, capitalist twist; he earns a living by projecting a female persona, and he spends his time by satisfying his male lust. Aware of his failure to manipulate either role separately or both roles simultaneously, he moves mechanically in opposite directions, in and out of the human arena. Unable or unwilling to renounce his desire, Lonelyhearts promotes himself as a form of spiritual therapy and concludes most of his transactions by violating the other person in some way, soon realizing that he has violated himself as well. After he arranges an appointment with Mrs. Doyle, a letter-writer, he exploits her. Sex with her, which is a "field trip" for him, offers the opportunity to indulge in role reversal since Lonelyhearts plays the passive sexual object while Mrs. Doyle dominates. Like Miss Farkis, she is derisively presented, her powerful body and her sensuality mocked. Through each rendezvous Lonelyhearts assures himself that he is searching for the right message, the exact wording, and signs of his humility and righteousness.

West's borrowings from "The Fire Sermon" and the controlling images of fire, water, and rock from "What the Thunder Said" provide *Miss Lonelyhearts* with its closing parodic moments. The poem alludes to Saint Augustine in Carthage, where he surveys its corruption and implores God to "pluckest me out." Lonelyhearts's experiences in the thickets of New York

City cause him, too, to wish for release. But his journey is inverted and delusionary—in his bed—and if Eliot's personae carry messages of salvation, in West's short fiction, the imperative to save turns inward and becomes an obsession for self-survival. Shrike's speech to the crowd about the purgation of lust through flames recalls the end of "The Fire Sermon." "You are afraid that even Miss Lonelyhearts, no matter how fierce his torch, will be unable to set you on fire.... Be of good heart, for I know that you will burst into flame" (52). But the only traits that burn are vestiges of altruism and benevolence, and soon Lonelyhearts is hallucinating that the people who have come to him for spiritual comfort are no more threatening than splashes of little waves that touch his feet, but never his heart.

West parodies the divine injunction of the Sanskrit words of the Thunder (Volpe 101) by transmitting its message through a debased medium, Shrike. "What the Thunder Said" holds out infinite promise: to dare a moment's surrender, to walk the white road together, to guide the sail and the oar, to allow one's heart to respond. In *Miss Lonelyhearts*, though, the voice, embedded in Shrike, instructs the quester to "Halt!" This enables Lonelyhearts to create himself in the image of his own desire, which is to make himself "perfect," perfectly impenetrable. Rather than give, sympathize, or control, he retreats into hallucinatory exile where God is neither Augustine's God nor Buddha. There is only the divine presence that Lonelyhearts creates in his frenzy, one that approves his cloistered delusion.

Looking broadly at his culture and more narrowly at Eliot's exposition of that culture, West constructs his short work from both literary sources and cultural references. He parodies the poem's classicism and offers capitalism. He divests Tiresias of privilege and omniscience. Aware of the poem's collagist design, he arranges his materials in abrupt segments that subordinate chronology and exaggerate disjunctions. He twists dominant elements like Tiresias as well as lesser ones like the mandolin and the thrush into violent, surreal permutations to deflate Eliot's projections of hope. The dominant metaphor and the seminal poem of the twentieth century are a crucial subtext for West, who critically subjects them to parody even as his refashioning of Eliot's tropes enriches his own short fiction, *Miss Lonelyhearts*.

Current debate over Eliot's politics, poetry, and life ranges from what Terry Eagleton calls his *arrière-garde* politics to what William Burroughs calls his avant-garde techniques, to what Cynthia Ozick insists was an "autocratic, inhibited, depressed, rather narrow-minded, and considerably bigoted fake Englishman" (121). In the midst of this debate, it may be useful to remember that West was one of the few American writers who recognized quickly the dichotomies of Eliot's career. Hemingway and Fitzgerald merely culled his work for serviceable motifs, and poets like Hart Crane and Wallace Stevens criticized *The Waste Land* and then remained silent as though it had never been published.[6] West chose to confront Eliot's commanding literary and intellectual presence and, in his own fiction, to take issue with Eliot's political and religious prescriptions. Looking back at *The Waste Land* with Eliot's recent essays in hand, West realized that Eliot's Modernism was diverging from his own version, which was founded on shock, negation, grotesque humor, ironic deflation, and exaggeration. Thus, in *Miss Lonelyhearts* he emphatically and ironically expresses his fears that ritual, modernized and thus commodified, could operate as a pretext for collective activity that could ultimately suppress individual freedoms. The reappearance in West's *Miss Lonelyhearts* of *Waste Land* prophets, corpses, conflicts and settings is twofold: a tribute to the undeniable force of *The Waste Land* and a measure of West's resistance.

NOTES

1. For additional biographical information as well as details concerning "Burn the Cities," see Martin, *NW: The Art of His Life* 107–10, 184–85, 329.

2. Widmar presents the ambiguities of this scene. He cites the negative elements (the funereal tone and the "army of little metal shields") and the positive ones ("the only bit of affectionate sex in West"). Still, he summarizes the scene as a "pastoral-sexual peace" and a "regenerative interlude" (43).

3. In his introduction to *Nathanael West*, Bloom discusses West as a deeply Jewish writer—through his negations and links with Jewish mysticism.

4. Eliot wrote in "The Frontiers of Criticism" that after the poem was published in the *Criterion* and the *Dial* without the Notes, it seemed "inconveniently short." Adding the Notes offered greater length for the British Hogarth edition and American Liveright edition. Eliot insisted they were a "remarkable exposition of bogus scholarship" and he regretted sending readers "on a wild goose chase after Tarot cards and the Holy Grail" (121–22). To what extent he actually did regret the Notes is, of course, debatable.

5. Disagreeing with critics who stress Tiresias's omniscient vision, Bedient writes that Tiresias sees far less" than the protagonist and is "only one of the protagonist's farewell performances, the dross he must leave behind before he consciously cultivates a form of seeing 'infinitely more disillusioned' than any suggested by Tiresias" (130). See 129–38 for Bedient's full discussion of Tiresias.

6. Studies of Eliot's influence include Carlos Baker's chapter "The Wastelanders" in his book on Hemingway. See also Bicknell, Gerstenberger and Olderman. In *Beyond the Waste Land*, Olderman traces the "generalized use" of the waste land metaphor in recent American novels. Asking Gorham Munson what he thought of Eliot's poem, Hart Crane offered his own panegyric in a 20 November 1922 letter, "It was good, of course, but so damned dead"(Weber 105). In 1950 Wallace Stevens was still explaining that Eliot's work had been instructive but only "as a point of departure, not as a model ... Eliot and I are dead opposites and I have been doing about everything he would not be likely to do" (677). Like Williams, both Crane and Stevens resort to death as metaphor to describe Eliot's achievement.

WORKS CITED

Baker, Carlos. *Hemingway: The Writer As Artist*. 4th ed. Princeton: Princeton UP, 1952.

Bedient, Calvin. *He Do the Police in Different Voices: The Waste Land and Its Protagonist*. Chicago: U of Chicago P, 1986.

Bicknell, John W. "The Wasteland of F. Scott Fitzgerald." *Virginia Quarterly Review* 30 (1954): 556–72.

Bloom, Harold, ed. *Nathanael West: Modern Critical Views*. New York: Chelsea, 1986.

Burroughs, William. "The Last European Interview." *Review of Contemporary Fiction* 4 (1984): 12–19.

Crane, Hart. *Letters of Hart Crane*. Ed. Brom Weber. New York: Hermitage, 1952.

Davidson, Helen. *T.S. Eliot and Hermeneutics: Absence and Interpretation in The Waste Land*. Baton Rouge: Louisiana State UP, 1985.

Drew, Elizabeth. *T.S. Eliot: The Design of His Poetry*. New York: Scribner's, 1949.

Eagleton, Terry. *Literary Theory: An Introduction*. Minneapolis: U of Minnesota P, 1983.

Eliot, T.S. *For Lancelot Andrewes: Essays On Style and Order*. 1928. New York: Doubleday, Doran, 1929.

———. *The Idea of a Christian Society*. 1939. London: Faber, 1967.

———. "Lancelot Andrewes." *For Lancelot Andrewes*. 3–24.

———. *Selected Prose of T.S. Eliot*. Ed. Frank Kermode. New York: Harcourt, 1972.

———. "*Ulysses*, Order, and Myth." *Selected Prose*. 175–78.

——— "The Waste Land." 1922. *The Complete Poems and Plays: 1909–1950*. New York: Harcourt, 1952.

Gerstenberger, Donna. "The Waste Land in A Farewell to Arms." *Modern Language Notes* 76 (1961): 465–66.

Gorek, Jan. *God the Artist: American Novelists in a Post-Realist Age*. Urbana: U of Illinois P, 1987.

Light, James L. *Nathanael West: An Interpretive Study*. 2nd ed. Evanston: Northwestern UP, 1971.

Martin, Jay. *Nathanael West: The Art of His Life*. New York: Farrar, 1970.

———. *Nathanael West: A Collection of Critical Essays*. Englewood Cliffs: Prentice-Hall, 1971.

Olderman, Raymond. *Beyond the Waste Land: A Study of the American Novel in the Nineteen-Sixties*. New Haven: Yale UP, 1972.

Ozick, Cynthia. "A Critic at Large: T.S. Eliot at 101." *The New Yorker* 20 Nov 1989: 119–54.

Smith, Grover. *T.S. Eliot's Poetry and Plays: A Study in Sources and Meaning*. Chicago: U of Chicago P, 1965.

Stevens, Wallace. *Letters of Wallace Stevens*. Ed. Holly Stevens. New York: Knopf, 1966.

Volpe, Edmond L. "The Waste Land of Nathanael West." *Renascence* 13 (1961): 69–77, 112. Rpt. in Martin, *NW: A Collection of Critical Essays*. 91–101.

West, Nathanael. *The Dream Life of Balso Snell*. New York: Moss and Kamin, 1931.

——— *Miss Lonelyhearts*. 1933. In *Miss Lonelyhearts and The Day of the Locust*. New York: New Directions, 1962.

Weston, Jessie L. *From Ritual to Romance*. 1920. Rpt. New York: Anchor, 1957.

Widmar, Kingsley. *Nathanael West*. Boston: Twayne, 1982.

Williams, William Carlos. *Autobiography*. New York: Random, 1951.

RICHARD P. LYNCH

Saints and Lovers:
Miss Lonelyhearts *in the Tradition*

Nathanael West's prose style was once described by William Carlos Williams as "plain American," and, perhaps because of his subject matter in *Miss Lonelyhearts* and *The Day of the Locust*, West has always been considered to be among the most American of novelists. It is peculiar, then, that *Miss Lonelyhearts* should so often be compared with the work of T.S. Eliot, the most European of poets. Whatever West may think of the literary works he alludes to, he does so much of it, and does it so self-consciously, that it is sometimes difficult to remember that he is an American writer. It is the prose style, indeed, that stamps *Miss Lonelyhearts* as American, just as the style of *The Loved One* reminds us that although its setting is Hollywood, its author is British.

   Miss Lonelyhearts, in fact, is to modern literary culture what Tiresias is in *The Waste Land* to the signs of modern decay: Tiresias sits in the center of Europe, a sensitive receiver reflecting for us the images of decay and dissolution that he picks up from the modern age; *Miss Lonelyhearts* contains such images, but like *The Waste Land*, it also invites comparison with more positive values in the literature with which it shares its main themes. West may, as Edmond L. Volpe suggests, have rejected Eliot's hope for a religious solution to modern ills, but that does not lead necessarily to Volpe's conclusion that "there is no hope of salvation."

From *Studies in Short Fiction*, vol. 31, no. 2 (Spring 1994). © 1994 by Newberry College.

If West had identified with his protagonist in some clear way, readers might be justified in considering the novel one of the most bleak pictures of human character in our time, but the author does not portray his character with sympathy, and the novel need not be read as a simple expression of despair. *Miss Lonelyhearts* is one of several key modern works that pit the ideal of human love against a longing for some spiritual or romantic ideal that does not require a relationship with another living, breathing, demanding human being. The longing for something more than love may be genuine in some instances and a mere evasion of the difficulties of love in others, but in sacrificing the possibility of human love, the protagonist almost always loses more than he gains. To say that there is no expression of hope in *Miss Lonelyhearts* is to deny its relationship to that abiding theme in modern literature. The very atmosphere of *Miss Lonelyhearts* and many of its characters assault the ideal of human love, and Miss Lonelyhearts himself fails to attain it, but that failure does not rob human love of its value.

The protagonist of *Miss Lonelyhearts* has come under attack recently, but not for the right reasons. Miriam Fuchs states that Miss Lonelyhearts "spends his time by satisfying his male lust." One must reject the word "satisfying" in this statement, however. There is nothing satisfying about any of Miss Lonelyhearts's relationships with women, nor does he expect any such result from them, even in anticipation. He goes to Betty the first time not for sex, not for a "conquest," as Fuchs puts it, but to regain his sense of order: "She had often made him feel that when she straightened his tie, she straightened much more" (11). The next day, in fact, when he is frightened by the shadow of the phallic monument, he realizes "he had completely forgotten sex. What he really needed was a woman" (19). When he went to visit Betty the day before, sex was simply not the goal. And where does he go when he decides that what he really needs is a woman? To Mrs. Shrike, the one woman he knows will not sleep with him. The only reason he gives for going to her is that her kisses make him feel "less like a joke." It is not only, however, that Mary Shrike refuses to sleep with him; Miss Lonelyhearts himself is incapable of responding to her kisses:

> He had been convinced that her grunts were genuine by the change that took place in her when he kissed her heavily. Then her body gave off an odor that enriched the synthetic flower scent she used behind her ears and in the hollows of the neck. No similar change ever took place in his own body, however. Like a dead man, only friction could make him warm or violence make him mobile. (19)

Miss Lonelyhearts tries to "excite himself into eagerness," but fails, and the end result is that he has once again just warmed her up for her husband. Whatever else Miss Lonelyhearts's relationship with Mary Shrike may be, it is not "satisfying."

Our hero does have sex with Mrs. Doyle, but he has to mythologize the experience first: "He thought of Mrs. Doyle as a tent, hair-covered and veined, and of himself as the skeleton in a water closet.... When he made the skeleton enter the flesh tent, it flowered at every joint" (26). The sea imagery associated with their actual encounter indicates that *Miss Lonelyhearts* is myth-making then, too. Volpe points out that West is parodying Eliot's use of water imagery as a symbol of regeneration. Far from being regenerated by this 15-minute experience, though, Miss Lonelyhearts becomes physically ill soon after Mrs. Doyle leaves.

Nor is satisfaction the end result of what some critics have referred to as the "idyll" in Connecticut with Betty. West labors a little with his imagery in this section to ensure that readers will not take the interlude too seriously. The "funereal hush" under the trees and the thrush's song like a "flute choked with saliva" are reminiscent of Thomas Hardy at his most intrusive. The important thing about the episode, though, is that they do make love, and that there are images of innocence as well as death, and that, in fact, the images of innocence seem less forced. The episode can legitimately be called idyllic, and it is important that it be seen that way, because the whole point is that it is not enough. Miss Lonelyhearts is not "cured" of his "Christ dream." Human love is not enough. What else is Betty's "limited" word, after all, but the offer of human love as it has traditionally been idealized in literature—an intimate relationship between two human beings? Too many critics have accepted Miss Lonelyhearts's dismissal of such a goal as an impossible solution for his problems, and I suspect that is because too many critics have taken seriously his ambition to be a modern Christ.

Finally, in what might loosely be called defense of Miss Lonelyhearts, he is not shot "in retaliation for having sex with Doyle's wife," as Fuchs asserts, but rather in retaliation for *refusing* to have sex with her. Actually, "retaliation" is not even the right word to apply, for, as Volpe notes, the shooting is accidental and "lacks the dignity of a deliberate act."

Fuchs is right, however, in focusing on Miss Lonelyhearts's relationships with women. Nathanael West does the same, after all, but for what purpose? To show Miss Lonelyhearts's inability to have a complete relationship with a woman? Or to show that even if he could have that kind of relationship, it would not be the answer to anything? In "Dover Beach," Matthew Arnold had suggested that there was little else left to modern human beings—only the personal relationship to shelter against the tide of human suffering and chaos, the same suffering and chaos Miss Lonelyhearts attempts to respond to. But the idealizing of such a relationship as the answer to human ills goes back further than the modern disillusion that began in Arnold's time. It goes back to the poet Arnold called in "Memorial Verses" the "physician of the iron age," the poet who most clearly identified the weaknesses of suffering humanity in the modern age.

Goethe chose love as the ultimate humanizing (and therefore saving) experience for Faust, the one force with which to counter Mephistopheles's nihilism. Shrike has been compared with other literary characters, but he reminds me of no one so much as Mephistopheles, who in Part One of Faust is constantly demeaning Faust's idealism, constantly attempting to degrade his relationship with Gretchen, reduce it to simple lust:

> Faust: My love is infinite.
>   I'm jealous of the Body of the Lord
>   When with her tender lips she touches it.
>
> Mephi: Well said, my friend! I've envied you indeed
>   Those twin delights that in the roses feed. (149)

Shrike degrades all women, as he ridicules all attempts at genuine emotion. His treatment of Miss Farkis is typical:

> "To the Renaissance! To the brown Greek manuscripts and mistresses with the great smooth marbly limbs.... But that reminds me, I'm expecting one of my admirers—a cow-eyed girl of great intelligence." He illustrated the word *intelligence* by carving two enormous breasts in the air with his hands. "She works in a book store, but wait until you see her behind." (6)

Miss Lonelyhearts lives in a general atmosphere in which women are demeaned or belittled. Most of his letters are from abused or deformed women. The conversation he hears in the bar among newspapermen is about teaching aggressive women writers a lesson by raping them. It is the same atmosphere Mephistopheles leads Faust to constantly, from the comparison between a suffering lover and a poisoned rat in "Auerbach's Cellar" to the obscene dance with naked witches on "Walpurgis Night," and above all in the degrading references to his "monkey," Gretchen.

Shrike ridicules all other possible avenues for seeking meaning in life: "My friend, I know of course that neither the soil, nor the South Seas, nor Hedonism, nor art, nor suicide, nor drugs, can mean anything to us.... God alone is our escape" (35). But Shrike has eliminated God, too, teaching Miss Lonelyhearts to "handle his one escape, Christ, with a thick glove of words" (33). If Shrike's sarcasm and parody of religion make it next to impossible for Miss Lonelyhearts to dream the Christ dream for long or take it seriously, then presumably his crude treatment of women and sexuality has a similar effect on Miss Lonelyhearts's relationships with women.

Again, the parallel with Mephistopheles is striking. Speaking to the Spirit of Earth in the "Forest and Cavern" episode, Faust laments the necessity of Mephistopheles, "so much his subtle word / Can sour and stifle all your gift of joy" (145). Mephistopheles treats Faust's idealism, his desire for genuine beauty and peace, with the same flippancy Shrike uses to undermine Miss Lonelyhearts's ideals. At the same time, there is a certain shared consciousness and shared guilt common to each of these relationships. Miss Lonelyhearts and Faust are thoroughly disillusioned souls, and in their despair, or near despair, they partake of some of the spiritual murkiness of their tormentors. Shrike's constant debunking of Miss Lonelyhearts's ideals is no excuse for the latter's treatment of Betty, any more than Faust can be excused for abandoning Gretchen. (There is another parallel here: Faust abandons the pregnant Gretchen for the sake of further attempts at ultimate experience and knowledge; Miss Lonelyhearts, in effect, abandons the pregnant Betty for the sake of fulfilling his Christ dream.)

Miss Lonelyhearts cannot legitimately be relegated to the status of a mere exploiter of women, then, but he is guilty of failing in his relationships with them. Perhaps the major difference between Faust and Miss Lonelyhearts is that Faust feels guilt; Miss Lonelyhearts does not, or claims not to.

Miss Lonelyhearts's position is that he has a higher goal than a mere relationship with a woman. The question still being debated is whether Nathanael West presented Miss Lonelyhearts in such a way as to indicate approval of this "higher goal." *Miss Lonelyhearts* explains his predicament in very clear terms to Betty:

> Perhaps I can make you understand. Let's start from the beginning. A man is hired to give advice to the readers of a newspaper. The job is a circulation stunt and the whole staff considers it a joke. He welcomes the job, for it might lead to a gossip column, and anyway he's tired of being a leg man. He too considers the job a joke, but after several months at it, the joke begins to escape him. He sees that the majority of the letters are profoundly humble pleas for moral and spiritual advice, that they are inarticulate expressions of genuine suffering. He also

discovers that his correspondents take him seriously. For the first
time in his life, he is forced to examine the values by which he
lives. This examination shows him that he is the victim of the joke
and not its perpetrator. (32)

Questions have been raised about the seriousness of this passage. It seems too
neat an analysis of the protagonist's situation, extraordinarily rational for a
character who is supposedly in the process of going mad. The question is not
merely whether we can take him seriously, but whether he takes himself that
way, or even whether he is sure that he is or is not serious.

The best evidence to judge by, one presumes, would be any actual
encounters between Miss Lonelyhearts and writers of these letters that have
so profoundly affected him. But there is only one such encounter in the
novel, and it is with Mrs. Doyle. Does she fit the analysis? Is her letter a
"humble plea for moral and spiritual advice"? Both Shrike and Miss
Lonelyhearts recognize it immediately as an offer of an adulterous affair. Is
Miss Lonelyhearts in this case "forced to examine the values by which he
lives"? Hardly. The actual experience is as routine and unemotional as his
response to her chatter afterwards: "He saw that she expected him to be
astonished and did his best to lift his eyebrows.... Her voice was as hypnotic
as a tom-tom, and as monotonous. Already his mind and body were half
asleep" (28–29). It is still possible that Miss Lonelyhearts's beliefs and his
analysis of them for Betty are sincere in the abstract, so to speak. After all, he
does attempt to "heal" the Doyles later on. But reality never seems to
correspond to the dream, and when Miss Lonelyhearts attempts to apply the
dream to it, he becomes "the victim of the joke" in more ways than one.

There are important similarities, in that respect, between Miss
Lonelyhearts and Dostoevsky's Underground Man. The Underground Man
makes impassioned speeches to the prostitute, Liza, at the same time that he
questions, even more self-consciously than Miss Lonelyhearts, his own
sincerity: "'Pictures, you have to go on painting that sort of pretty pictures!'
I thought to myself, although I swear I had spoken with real feeling" (95).
Miss Lonelyhearts engages in some of the same self-destructive behavior as
the Underground Man, too, and Betty and Liza, both ultimately rejected as
possible solutions, represent the same chance for the protagonist to save
himself from his miserable isolation.

There are differences between the two situations, but the similarities
help explain the peculiar relationship between Miss Lonelyhearts and Betty.
The Underground Man fears a real relationship with Liza, so he degrades
himself before her after she walks in on his petty argument with his servant,
Apollon, in an effort to make her hate him. Her reaction is not hatred or

disgust, however; she is still able to love him because she still believes in the genuineness of his emotions. Indeed, he tells us that after confessing to being a "vile worm," he "sobbed for a quarter of an hour in real hysterics" (117–18). Liza comforts him, but he cannot sustain genuine emotion for long, and begins to resent her for being superior to him, for forgiving him. They end by having sex: she assumes it is an expression of love, but he is merely taking revenge on her for being superior to himself by an expression of degrading lust. He gives her a five-rouble note afterwards to complete the insult.

Miss Lonelyhearts is not so melodramatic, but he makes similarly degrading and humiliating sexual gestures with Betty, and has the same reaction to her forgiveness and sympathy. Like the Underground Man, he is irritated by the woman's seeming superiority. He feels she is laughing at the insincerity he cannot hide, and surprises himself with the hatred in his voice when he refers to her as "Betty the Buddha":

> He remembered that towards the end of his last visit he had put his hand inside her clothes. Unable to think of anything else to do, he now repeated the gesture. She was naked under her robe and he found her breast.
>
> She made no sign to show that she was aware of his hand. He would have welcomed a slap, but even when he caught at her nipple, she remained silent.
>
> "Let me pluck this rose," he said, giving a sharp tug. "I want to wear it in my buttonhole."
>
> Betty reached for his brow. "What's the matter?" she asked. "Are you sick?"
>
> He began to shout at her, accompanying his shouts with gestures that were too appropriate, like those of an old-fashioned actor.
>
> "What a kind bitch you are. As soon as anyone acts viciously, you say he's sick. Wife-torturers, rapers of small children, according to you they're all sick. No morality, only medicine. Well I'm not sick. I don't need any of your damned aspirin. I've got a Christ complex. Humanity ... I'm a humanity lover. All the broken bastards...." (12–13)

The sexual gesture is not because he can think of nothing else to do. As his crude comments show, it is a clear attempt to demean her, and he cannot stand her calm reaction and concern for him. The gestures that are "too appropriate, like those of an old-fashioned actor," are like the Underground

Man's conscious playing of roles. The "humanity" that Miss Lonelyhearts loves is an abstraction, as abstract as the Underground Man's romantic dreams. Finally, neither protagonist can take the risk of a real relationship because neither is willing to give up the illusion of superiority. All of the Underground Man's relationships are characterized by the need for self-assertion, for feeling superior; there is no reason why he would deal with Liza any differently. That is why he cannot respond like a normal human being to her love. It would require breaking out of his self-contained world and making adjustments for another human being. And that is why Miss Lonelyhearts cannot respond to Betty's love: he is absolutely incapable of allowing another human being into an equal relationship with himself.

Love, as Edward Abood points out in *Underground Man*, requires faith, not necessarily religious faith, but belief in the other person and shared values. But the Underground Man can't give that kind of total assent to anything because, as he explains in the first part of *Notes from Underground*, he doesn't believe in anything (27). And that is precisely Miss Lonelyhearts's problem. He blames Shrike for his cynicism, but allows Shrike's mockery and crude jokes to determine his own views and his own ability (or inability) to be sincere.

Miss Lonelyhearts is not the last word on the conflict between human love and supposed higher ideals. One other work which can shed light on West's theme is Camus's novel, *The Plague*. West may not have been an existentialist, but that does not mean that his novel has no existentialist ideas in it. In one often quoted passage, Miss Lonelyhearts thinks of the metaphorical stone that has formed within his body: "If he could only throw the stone. He searched the sky for a target. But the gray sky looked as if it had been rubbed with a soiled eraser. It held no angels, flaming crosses, olive-bearing doves, wheels within wheels" (5). Volpe has said that this passage describes "that moment of complete despair that the French existentialist writers a few years later were to term *Nausée*, or The Absurd," but that the novel could not be read as existentialist because the author never moved beyond that despair (or never allowed his character to do so).

Whether West is consciously existentialist or not makes little difference, however, for he and Camus are dealing with the same basic themes. Like Dr. Rieux and Tarrou in *The Plague*, Miss Lonelyhearts is tormented by apparently meaningless and undeserved human suffering. They act more efficiently and more selflessly to relieve that suffering than he does, though it is unfair to say that Miss Lonelyhearts makes no attempt. He does try to reconcile the Doyles, though he fails miserably, and he resists Mrs. Doyle's last attempt to seduce him. Rieux and Tarrou do not defeat the plague either, however; they only put up what human resistance they can to it, until it withdraws. That withdrawal does not mean that they are free of plague, however, as Tarrou points out.

Humans are never free of it, any more than Miss Lonelyhearts can forget the letters and the Bronx slums by retreating to a Connecticut farm.

The specific parallel I would like to suggest is between Miss Lonelyhearts and Tarrou. Naturally, Tarrou is a more admirable character. He does not display the lapses in human compassion that Miss Lonelyhearts does, but then West's world is more gritty and realistic than that of Camus, despite the latter's graphic descriptions of the plague. What the two characters do have in common is their ambitions, and what they leave behind in order to pursue those ambitions. Miss Lonelyhearts wants to be Christ for his correspondents, wants to perform miracles and heal their suffering. Tarrou, as he explains to Dr. Rieux, has a similar goal:

> "It comes to this," Tarrou said almost casually; "what interests me is learning how to become a saint."
> "But you don't believe in God."
> "Exactly! Can one be a saint without God?—that's the problem, in fact the only problem, I'm up against today." (237)

Sainthood is the third category in Tarrou's list of human types, the category of the "true healers," the category of "peace"; and the path to peace is "the path of sympathy." Just as Tarrou wants to be a saint without believing in God, Miss Lonelyhearts wants to be Christ without believing in God. Tarrou's only other possibilities are his other two types: "murderers" and "innocent murderers"—those who acquiesce willfully in human suffering and those who do not do so willfully, but simply because they are unable to escape being human. Miss Lonelyhearts has no other road open to him, either, or at least none that he is able to see. For Miss Lonelyhearts, as for Tarrou, there are pestilences, those blind forces that cause human suffering, and there are victims, and he takes the victims' side.

More important than their goals, however, is what both characters give up in pursuit of them. Rieux alludes to it, and in so doing, provides us with helpful material to analyze the ambiguity of Miss Lonelyhearts's position:

> "But, you know, I feel more fellowship with the defeated than with saints. Heroism and sanctity don't really appeal to me, I imagine. What interests me is being a man."
> "Yes, we're both after the same thing, but I'm less ambitious."
> Rieux supposed Tarrou was jesting and turned to him with a smile. But, faintly lit by the dim radiance falling from the sky, the face he saw was sad and earnest. (238)

Unlike Rieux, Miss Lonelyhearts sees no contradiction between "fellowship with the defeated" and sainthood, but there is, and that is why his position is impossible. Saints cannot be men, not in Rieux's sense, and Tarrou knows that. He also knows, in his sadness, that sainthood may not be the higher achievement.

What both Tarrou and Miss Lonelyhearts look beyond and in a sense despair of is human love. Rieux compares the two goals after Tarrou's death:

> But for those others who aspired beyond and above the human individual toward something they could not even imagine, there had been no answer. Tarrou might seem to have won through to that hardly-come-by peace of which he used to speak; but he had found it only in death, too late to turn it to account. If others, however ... had got what they wanted, this was because they had asked for the one thing that depended on them solely. And as he turned the corner of the street where Grand and Cottard lived, Rieux was thinking it was only right that those whose desires are limited to man and his humble yet formidable love should enter, if only now and then, into their reward. (279–80)

Miss Lonelyhearts is offered human love, but he rejects it in favor of his Christ dream, or what he imagines to be a higher attainment in life. That "higher attainment" excludes human love, because it generalizes all further relationships with humanity. "I'm a humanity lover," he explains to Betty, and in the same scene realizes that he feels no guilt at having proposed to her two months earlier and then ignored her. Miss Lonelyhearts wants to have a relationship with humanity, but cannot form a relationship with another single human being. The Doyles, the only correspondents with whom he has a physical relationship, are not individual human beings in Miss Lonelyhearts's mind, but general symbols of unmerited suffering, abstractions.

The brief "idyll" with Betty in Connecticut is possible because it does not happen in the real world from Miss Lonelyhearts's point of view. Once he has had his "experience," however, riding his bed for three days and becoming the "rock," he can promise Betty anything because he has generalized her, too, made her an abstraction: "He was not deliberately lying. He was only trying to say what she wanted to hear" (55). After she announces she is pregnant, he again proposes to her:

> He begged the party dress to marry him, saying all the things it expected to hear, all the things that went with strawberry sodas

and farms in Connecticut. He was just what the party dress wanted him to be: simple and sweet, whimsical and poetic, a trifle collegiate yet very masculine.... He did not feel guilty. He did not feel. (56)

Betty has been reduced to her attributes, her party dress and the associations it calls up in Miss Lonelyhearts's mind; and this is possible because it is now a "simplified" mind, a mind that need no longer attempt to deal with the complexities of other individual human beings. He can deal with Betty, in fact, the same way he has dealt with the disembodied correspondents to his newspaper column: by telling her what she wants to hear, whether it's the truth or not, and ignoring the consequences. All complexities are absorbed by the rock, which absolves him of any further responsibility.

Finally, Miss Lonelyhearts rejects the same solution to modern ills that Eliot rejected: redemption through a warm, loving relationship between two human beings. Both Eliot and West paint the disease of the modern age substantially as the decay of human love. The tawdry, emotionless affair between the typist and the clerk witnessed by Tiresias in "The Fire Sermon" is perfectly reflected in the casual, animal-like encounters of *Miss Lonelyhearts*. And yet Eliot's solution is not a revival of genuine love, but a revival of religious faith—the solution of Miss Lonelyhearts the character, but not *Miss Lonelyhearts* the novel. West may have made Miss Lonelyhearts a more sympathetic figure than Shrike, but the reader cannot give too much sympathy to a man who treats other human beings with almost as much brutality as Shrike, who feels no guilt, and who ultimately retreats from the life that troubles him and rejects any form of responsibility: "What goes on in the sea is of no interest to the rock" (53). It is here that Miss Lonelyhearts becomes the complete opposite of Tarrou. Tarrou feels guilty, implicated by the very fact of being human in the suffering of others. Miss Lonelyhearts finds a way out, and the way out abandons all those for whom he would be Christ.

All of the protagonists discussed here think of themselves, or represent themselves, as "saviors" in one way or another, and three out of the four ruin the women they might have saved. Tarrou avoids such a mistake because he alone has an acute sense of the harm a single human being can do, and is constantly on the alert to do as little harm as possible. Surely, West's short novel is, quite consciously, one of a series of warnings to the modern age: not warnings out of fear that we will not be saints, but out of fear that we will not do what humans can do. And along with the warning against allowing love between individual human beings to degenerate goes a warning against the condition that is both cause and effect of such a disaster, echoed in Miss

Lonelyhearts and best expressed by the Underground Man: "We even find it difficult to be human beings, men with real flesh and blood of our own ... we are always striving to be some unprecedented kind of generalized human being.... Soon we shall invent a method of being born from an idea" (123). Miss Lonelyhearts, one might argue, is reborn from an idea, but it does not support his new life for long.

WORKS CITED

Abood, Edward. *Underground Man.* San Francisco: Chandler and Sharp, 1973.

Camus, Albert. *The Plague.* Trans. Smart Gilbert. New York: Vintage, 1948.

Dostoevsky, Fyodor. *Notes from Underground.* Trans. Jessie Coulson. New York: Penguin, 1972.

Fuchs, Miriam. "Nathanael West's *Miss Lonelyhearts.* The Waste Land Rescripted." *Studies in Short Fiction* 29 (1992): 43–55.

Goethe, Johann. *Faust, Part One.* Trans. Philip Wayne. New York: Penguin, 1949.

Volpe, Edmond L. "The Waste Land of Nathanael West." *Nathanael West: A Collection of Critical Essays.* Ed. Jay Martin Englewood Cliffs, NJ: Prentice, 1971. 91–101.

West, Nathanael. *Miss Lonelyhearts.* [1933]. *Miss Lonelyhearts and The Day of the Locust.* New York: New Directions, 1962.

MARIAN E. CROWE

The Desert, the Lamb, the Cross: Debased Iconography in Nathanael West's Miss Lonelyhearts

You're morbid, my friend, morbid. Forget the crucifixion, remember the
Renaissance. There were no brooders then.

—*Miss Lonelyhearts*

Much of the criticism of Nathanael West's *Miss Lonelyhearts* has centered
on the question of the extent to which this short, trenchant novel undercuts
Christian belief. West himself described the novel as "the portrait of a priest
of our time who has a religious experience" ("Notes" 67). Yet the irony of the
novel calls into question the religious nature of Miss Lonelyhearts'
experience, the genuineness of his priesthood, and the feasibility of any
religious faith in the modern world. My purpose in this essay is not to judge
the genuineness of Miss Lonelyhearts' religious experience or to claim him
as either saint, martyr, or Satan figure.[1] On the contrary, my concern is with
the distorted Christian symbols that run throughout the novel and that
convey a sense of why Miss Lonelyhearts' "Christ dream" (39) is impotent,
distorted, and eminently worthy of the satire Shrike heaps upon it.

Most critics see the book's critique of Christianity as centered on, or
even equivalent to, the character of Miss Lonelyhearts and the authenticity
of his religious faith. Some, like Thomas M. Lorch, view him as a kind of
moral hero: "Miss Lonelyhearts's religious commitment leads him to grow in

From *Christianity and Literature*, vol. 45, no. 3–4 (Spring-Summer 1996). © 1996 by the
Conference on Christianity and Literature.

faith and saintliness in a way which compensates at least in some degree for the limitations placed upon him" (108). Marcus Smith argues that, although Miss Lonelyhearts is a "deliberate non-believer" (80) in the beginning of the book, in chapter 13 he "has obviously been reborn" (81). More recently, Janet St. Clair has maintained that Miss Lonelyhearts is "a hero of sorts" and that his "'Christ complex' betrays neither madness nor naiveté, but rather the supremely human attempt to locate and incorporate a dimension of meaning lying beyond the mundane physical plane" (147).

Other scholars, however, contend that Miss Lonelyhearts' so-called religious experience is impotent, sham, inauthentic. Randall Reid proposes that Miss Lonelyhearts lacks genuine faith: "His dilemma is that of a man with a religious vocation ... in which he cannot believe" (83). Arthur Cohen suggests that what drives Miss Lonelyhearts is not religious faith at all but what the character himself accurately describes as a "Christ complex," a "fixation of the mind, a conviction that only if Miss Lonelyhearts himself becomes the shoulders of the world ... will humanity be healed" (277). Both Cohen and James F. Light locate the failure of Miss Lonelyhearts' "religious experience" largely in terms of the unbelieving world, which makes faith impossible. Cohen maintains that "the saint can communicate only when there is a community to address, when people are at least bound by common affections and belief, when they share sources of feeling and devotion. The saint cannot speak when absolutely nobody listens" (278). Thus, for many of these critics Miss Lonelyhearts' experience is normative for the viability of Christian faith in the modern world.

Regardless of how literally or how ironically West may have intended his description of Miss Lonelyhearts as "a priest of our time," the imagery of the book strongly undercuts the possibility of reading as genuine the priesthood and religious experience of the novel's protagonist. Especially for a reader with some knowledge of the Christian tradition and theology, the particular way in which these symbols are mutilated and distorted conveys a sense of what is wrong, sham, inauthentic about Miss Lonelyhearts' attempt to live the "Christ dream."

St. Clair focuses on the inadequacy of the Christian symbols in her analysis of Miss Lonelyhearts' inability to read them, which she describes as "eviscerated," although they "once connected humanity with its sources of transcendent power" (147). She suggests that Miss Lonelyhearts' problem is not so much the contemporary world as the fact that "either our shopworn symbols or our shallow and imbalanced modes of perceiving them perhaps no longer afford us access to transcendent power" (150). Thus, according to St. Clair, the failure of the symbols is both in themselves—they are "shopworn"—and in Miss Lonelyhearts' capacity for understanding them.

The claims which Paul Ricoeur makes for symbolic language in his essay "The Language of Faith" can be made for Christian symbols as well: "The dimension of language in which preaching is deployed, in which, therefore, the *kerygma* is able to be spoken and myth able to be preserved, is from end to end a symbolic dimension" (232). Symbolic language, according to Ricoeur, "says more than what it says, ... says something other than what it says and ... consequently, grasps me because it has in its meaning created a new meaning. Here the words I use have a semantic charge which is, properly speaking, inexhaustible." Although Ricoeur is speaking explicitly of symbolic *language* in this essay, surely the central Christian symbols affect the Christian—or the potential Christian—in the same way. They are "an exploratory instrument of [one's] existential possibilities, of [one's] situation in being" (233).

The fractured and distorted symbols in *Miss Lonelyhearts*, which can be seen as a kind of reverse *kerygma*, are an important part of West's surrealistic method. Surrealism juxtaposes startling images that are designed to induce "the strange intangible forces lying at the depths of the rational man" (Light 42). Thus, for the Christian reader, these symbols connect with a deeply felt level of religious faith, a level which is not *ir*rational but which is deeper than rational. They still carry a "superabundance of meaning" (Ricoeur 234), and they call into question the existential possibilities for one who holds Miss Lonelyhearts' "Christ dream."

At this point it is imperative to draw a clear distinction between author and character. As the son of a Baptist minister, Miss Lonelyhearts would, of course, be very familiar with the Bible and the Christian creed. On the other hand, his Baptist background would probably make him more literalist in his approach to the Bible than he would be were he from a Catholic, Orthodox, or other strongly liturgical tradition. West, however, was neither Baptist nor Catholic but Jewish. His parents were Jewish immigrants who "conceived of themselves less as Jews than as Russians" (Light 17). Religion was less important to them than education, and West grew up with little formal religious training or practice. Jay Martin claims that they "gave up their Judaism with their emigration" (25). However, during his college years at Brown University, West had to face the fact of his Jewishness when it excluded him from fraternities. He subsequently changed his name from Nathan Weinstein to Nathanael West. He may, in fact, have known more about Catholicism than about Judaism. As a student at Brown, he was fascinated with Catholic mysticism. According to Light,

There was a strong interest in Catholicism among the students at this time, and West occasionally contributed to the bull sessions some of the lore that he had accumulated from his considerable reading in the lives of the saints. Like many such readers he had gained a thorough knowledge of the mystical experience, but he read, and discussed what he read, with skepticism, not so much for spiritual Inspiration as for "the perversities and oddities in the medieval Catholic writers." (25)

In addition, West read James Joyce extensively, thus familiarizing himself even more with Catholic tradition and symbolism. One of his friends said of him, "'On the subject of Catholicism ... he could talk for hours. He had an incredible array of facts, from earliest Church history to the present'" (qtd. in Martin 58). His first novel, *The Dream Life of Balso Snell*, in which a flea named St. Puce lives upon the body of Jesus, includes a strong satire of Catholicism. While the satire shows a completely irreverent attitude toward what Christians consider most sacred, it also shows great familiarity with the tradition.

Perversions of Scripture, liturgy, and Christian iconography are replete in *Miss Lonelyhearts*. From Shrike's parody of a litany on the very first page—

Soul of Miss L, glorify me.
Body of Miss L, nourish me.
Blood of Miss L, intoxicate me.
Tears of Miss L, wash me. (1)

—to his mockery of the Lord's Prayer—"'Give us this day our daily stone'" (5)—to the medal Mary Shrike wears provocatively low on her chest, and which turns out to be a prize for a 100-yard dash (20, 23), this extremely short novel is amazingly rich in distorted Christian imagery. By far the most important instances of this imagery are the three major symbols in the Judeo-Christian tradition: the desert, the lamb, and the cross.

The desert is a richly evocative image for Jews and Christians alike. It is the locus of the Exodus, the formative theophanic experience of the Hebrew people; the place of transition from bondage to freedom; the place where the Hebrews experienced Yahweh's protection, learned His name, and received His law. The desert is also central in the life of Jesus, the place where he was tempted and where he repeatedly went to pray. The desert also figured prominently in the beginnings of Christian monasticism. We know that West was familiar with this part of early Christian history, for he read and was "deeply affected by Flaubert's *The Temptation of St. Anthony*" (Light 43). In the second and third centuries after Christ, the Desert Fathers chose to live an ascetic life in Egypt, Palestine, Arabia, and Persia. They fled the decadence of the late Roman Empire out of a profound conviction that only in the austerity and simplicity of desert life could they live out their vocation and remain close to Christ. Thomas Merton explains:

> What the Fathers sought most of all was their own true self, in Christ. And in order to do this, they had to reject completely the false, formal self, fabricated under social compulsion in "the world".... Not that they rejected any of the dogmatic formulas of the Christian faith: they accepted and clung to them in their simplest and most elementary shape. (6)

The desert, then, represents the passage from bondage to freedom. It is a place of waiting, of learning patience, of suffering, of temptation; it is a place where one learns the name of God and is given the opportunity to embrace His law. Although the desert is a place of theophany in the Judeo-Christian tradition, it also holds special risks. Merton adds a cautionary note:

> The hermit had to be a man mature in faith, humble and detached from himself to a degree that is altogether terrible. The spiritual cataclysms that sometimes overtook some of the presumptuous visionaries of the desert are there to show the dangers of the lonely life-like bones whitening in the sand. The Desert Father could not afford to be an illuminist. He could not dare risk attachment to his own ego, or the dangerous ecstasy of self-will. (8–9)

Miss Lonelyhearts thinks of his surroundings as a desert: "A desert, he was thinking, not of sand, but of rust and body dirt, surrounded by a back-yard fence on which are posters describing the events of the day. Mother slays five with ax, slays seven, slays nine" (25). The novel is filled with images of sterility, stunted and decayed vegetation, violence and death. As critics have noted, West's portrayal of this desolate landscape undoubtedly owes much to T.S. Eliot's *The Waste Land* (Martin 184). Yet it also resonates with some of the connotations of the biblical desert, thus setting up the expectation of some kind of theophany preceded by suffering, trial, and temptation. As Miss Lonelyhearts leaves the newspaper office, he sees a landscape inimical to the growth of vegetation: "The decay that covered the surface of the mottled ground was not the kind in which life generates. Last year, he remembered, May had failed to quicken these soiled fields. It had taken all the brutality of July to torture a few green spikes through the exhausted dirt" (4–5). Later, when Miss Lonelyhearts and Betty go for a walk in the woods, "in the deep shade there [is] nothing but death—rotten leaves, gray and white fungi, and over everything a funereal hush" (38). Furthermore, although Miss Lonelyhearts spends little time alone, his sense of alienation from his friends and associates makes him *feel* as isolated as any third-century ascetic hiding out in a desert cave. These two components of the desert experience—the sterility of the environment and the sense of isolation—are obvious. The third part, spiritual renewal and theophany, is more problematic.

One problem is with the place itself; the other is with the disposition Miss Lonelyhearts brings to it. A desert can provide two kinds of emptiness: a pregnant emptiness or a barren emptiness. Miss Lonelyhearts' desert is inimical to life, but it is not sparse and clean and open. It is not a pregnant and receptive emptiness, open to transcendence, but a cluttered and violence-ridden, fenced-in enclosure. Even this kind of "desert" could perhaps facilitate an encounter with God, but Miss Lonelyhearts clutters his life with so much noise—meeting his friends in speakeasies, going to parties—that he forestalls the likelihood of such an encounter. In order for a desert experience to be theophanic, it must be characterized by patience, openness, and discipline.

The image of the lamb recalls both the paschal lamb of the Old Testament as well as Jesus, the new Lamb of God. The lamb is for Jews and Christians the archetypal image of the sacrificial victim, its blood a sign of God's special protection, its flesh reverently consumed in a sacred communal meal. In *Miss Lonelyhearts* the lamb figures prominently in a scene that, even though it is a dream, is shocking in its brutality. Miss Lonelyhearts dreams that he and some friends sacrifice a lamb after a night of drinking. There is no reverent, ritual slaughter and no prayerful, communal meal but rather a messy, sadistic, gory killing:

> When they had worked themselves into a frenzy, he brought the knife down hard. The blow was inaccurate and made a flesh wound. He raised the knife again and this time the lamb's violent struggles made him miss altogether. The knife broke on the altar. Steve and Jud pulled the animal's head back for him to saw at its throat, but only a small piece of blade remained in the handle and he was unable to cut through the matted wool.

The lamb manages to run away, and Miss Lonelyhearts eventually finds it. "He crushed its head with a stone and left the carcass to the flies that swarmed around the bloody altar flowers" (10). This sentence ends the episode and the chapter. There is no nourishment, no communion, no taking away of guilt by participation in the purity of the victim. This is sacrifice gone awry.

The brutality of this act, the gratuitousness of the violence, and the intoxication of the "priest" are all powerful signs of the way in which the very notion of sacrifice has been distorted in Miss Lonelyhearts' world. Ideally sacrifice is an attempt to restore a balance that has been lost and to appease and/or please a more powerful being. The sacrificial victim is not the cause of the imbalance or offense but serves as a *substitute* for the real source of the evil. That is why the lamb was always seen as such an ideal symbol for Christ. What seems to be driving Miss Lonelyhearts in this scene, however, is rage at the defenseless and innocent lamb. His action here exemplifies what is portrayed elsewhere in the novel: his passionate, desperate, at times wild attempt to stomp out evil. Unlike correct sacrifice, however, Miss Lonelyhearts' attempts lack discipline, restraint, acknowledgment of his own guilt and reverence for a higher being.

By far the most pervasive and powerful Christian symbol in *Miss Lonelyhearts* is the cross. In the third chapter of the novel, Miss Lonelyhearts' room is described:

> The walls were bare except for an ivory Christ that hung opposite the foot of the bed. He had removed the figure from the cross to which it had been fastened and had nailed it to the wall with large spikes. But the desired effect had not been obtained. Instead of writhing, the Christ remained calmly decorative. (8)

One of the most striking features of this paragraph is the phrase "the desired effect," suggesting that Miss Lonelyhearts' primary concern is aesthetic. On the other hand, the word "writhing" is curious. Most crucifixes depict Christ looking inert, as if he might already have died. His physical suffering, though clearly evident, is not stressed. Why does Miss Lonelyhearts want to emphasize Christ's agony by having him appear to writhe? Moreover, why does he think that separating the image of Christ's body (traditionally referred to as the corpus) might produce the desired effect?

Whereas Miss Lonelyhearts wants a corpus without a cross, the early Christians used a cross without a corpus. The separation of the corpus from the cross is significant in light of the latter's iconographic history. The earliest known uses of the image featured a simple geometric sign with no human figure on it. Even this simple representation was problematic for the early Christians, since they associated shame with the manner of Christ's death. George S. Tyack in *The Cross in Ritual, Architecture, and Art* explains:

The Christians of the first two centuries, however, seldom
employed any material image of the Cross, and never the
Crucifix.... In days when crucifixion was still in use as the most
degrading of all forms of punishment, and the cross to the world
at large a more infamous figure than the gallows is now to us, it
must have been difficult even for the followers of the Crucified to
rise entirely above the common sentiment of their age. (4)

In time Christians became more open about displaying the sign of the cross,
especially after Constantine's dream that he would conquer under that sign.
Eventually the cross came to be seen as a sign of victorious power but also a
"sign of the wisdom of God, which as 'the foolishness of God' in the Pauline
formula, was wiser than any vaunted human wisdom" (Pelikan 102).
Eventually some crosses were made with a figure of a lamb superimposed on
them. It was only in the sixth century that crucifixes as we know them, with
a human figure superimposed on the cross, came into common usage.

In 692 at the Council in Trullo the Greek Fathers articulated what was
coming to be a more clearly felt sense of the theological importance of the
image that combined corpus and cross: "'We order that, instead of the
Lamb, our Lord Jesus Christ shall be shown hereafter in His human form in
the images; so that, without forgetting the height from which the Divine
Word stooped to us, we shall be led to remember his mortal life, His passion,
and His death, which paid the ransom for mankind'" (qtd. in Tyack 21). In
other words, the complete image provides a visual emblem of the Incarnation
and the Atonement, holding together divinity and humanity in this image of
kenosis.

Although the crucifix featuring a realistic representation of a crucified
Jesus superimposed on the cross eventually became common in Western
Christianity, the Eastern tradition "bejewelled its crosses and displayed them
without a corpus to emphasize the triumph of Christ over the cross"
(Cunningham 152). The Western Church, however, stressed the physical
sufferings of Christ, especially during the medieval period. The history of
the iconography of the cross thus discloses a tension at the heart of Christian
piety in relation to its central icon. Only gradually and with some reluctance
did Christians endorse the use of this image; and even when they did, there
was always the question of whether to emphasize the glorious triumph of the
kingly Christ or the physical suffering of the human Christ. Both aspects are
clearly essential to a complete understanding of Christ's redemptive death,
but no single work of visual art can express them both.

The image of the cross haunts Miss Lonelyhearts' imagination. He
dreams that he is in the window of a pawnshop filled with all kind of

paraphernalia in disarray. The lack of order depresses him, and he tries to form the objects into some kind of shape. He forms a phallus, geometric shapes, and a swastika. Finally, in desperation he begins to make a gigantic cross.

> When the cross became too large for the pawnshop, he moved it to the shore of the ocean. There every wave added to his stock faster than he could lengthen its arms. His labors were enormous. He staggered from the last wave line to his work, loaded down with marine refuse—bottles, shells, chunks of cork, fish heads, pieces of net. (31)

In this dream sequence Miss Lonelyhearts seems obsessed with the cross as a shaping form, a way of holding the disparate objects of the world into some coherent and meaningful form. Here Jaroslav Pelikan's remarks on the form of the cross are relevant:

> The very shape of the cross symbolized its comprehension of all the ways of God, the vertical and the horizontal bars representing the height and the breadth of the universe, and their point of convergence where the head of Christ was laid representing the unification and ultimate harmony of all in Christ crucified. For the cross was, on the one hand, the most evident of all proofs for the power of evil in the world.

Pelikan emphasizes that the "true wisdom of the cross" is "the ability to hold both of these together, neither ignoring the presence and power of evil ... nor allowing the presence and power of evil to negate the sovereignty of the one God" (105). In his dream Miss Lonelyhearts' cross lacks this shaping ability, this power to impose a measure of coherence and to contain evil within some kind of bounds. Evil, in the form of refuse, simply proliferates. It is out of control, not unlike Miss Lonelyhearts' own life. The fact that evil in this dream sequence escapes all efforts to control it may be due not so much to its own inherent power as to Miss Lonelyhearts' failure to *see* its power accurately, to take it seriously enough.

This is not to say that Miss Lonelyhearts is not emotionally moved by the suffering he sees. He is profoundly, painfully moved by it—especially in comparison with Shrike, who mocks it, and Betty, who insulates herself from it. However, a crucial aspect of Miss Lonelyhearts' approach to evil is conveyed by the phrase "Christ dream." In his obsession he seems bent on dreaming away or wishing away the evil in the world by resorting to tawdry sentimentality. "Life, for most us, seems a terrible struggle of pain and heartbreak, without hope or joy," he writes to one of his correspondents. "Oh my dear readers, it only seems so. Every man, no matter how poor or humble, can teach himself to use his senses. See the cloud-flecked sky, the foam-decked sea" (26). This sentimentality is not an adequate shaping principle. It is powerless to impose any order or coherence upon the chaos of evil. It is also part of what W.H. Auden called West's Disease, "a disease of consciousness which renders it incapable of converting wishes into desires." Auden asserts that a wish is a kind of lie:

> A wish is fantastic; it knows what is the case but refuses to accept it. All wishes, whatever their apparent content, have the same and unvarying meaning: "I refuse to be what I am." A wish, therefore, is either innocent and frivolous, a kind of play, or a serious expression of guilt and despair, a hatred of oneself and every being one holds responsible for oneself. (241)

Auden's analysis helps to explain why Miss Lonelyhearts' behavior is so erratic, why one moment he is embracing a suffering person and the next throttling him. His rage directed at suffering people is not only a classic instance of displacement; it also points to his failure to understand redemptive suffering and to recognize his own complicity and guilt. For one suffering from West's Disease, the cross does not work as a shaping image.

The cross is not a flight from evil. Nor is it a charm that transforms evil into something else. True, Christians do believe that the cross *leads* to the Resurrection, but only by way of the cross. Suffering remains an essential part of the paradigmatic Christian experience. When Light asserts that "Miss Lonelyhearts is shot by Doyle, destroyed, like Christ, by the panic and ignorance of those whom he would save" (94–95), he implies that the Crucifixion was a tragic accident that sabotaged Christ's *real* intent. Christians, however, believe not only that Christ willingly embraced suffering but that he *came* to die. The Passion is the most elaborately detailed narrative sequence in all four gospels; it is definitely portrayed as the culmination and crowning achievement of Christ's ministry. Louis A. Ruprecht, Jr., writing on Mark's gospel, explains the primacy of the cross: "The way to new life takes us through death, and it is only through the loneliness of Gethsemane and the coronation on a cross that Christ came into his Kingdom" (19-20). Hans Urs von Balthasar also insists that suffering must "really be taken seriously in Christianity" and that "Christ's Cross is to be allowed the absolute seriousness of God-forsakenness" (154).

Miss Lonelyhearts may appear to hold the same belief when he writes in a letter, "Christ died for you.... His gift to you is suffering and it is only through suffering that you can know Him. Cherish this gift, for...." However, he breaks off in mid sentence, exclaiming that for him Christ is "a vanity" (39). The truncated sentence represents his inability or unwillingness to follow the thought through to its completion, to give serious enough consideration to what might follow the "for." The choice of the word "vanity" is striking. Although it is true that Miss Lonelyhearts' "Christ complex" (13) probably contributes to his egotistical view of himself as a kind of savior (reflected in Shrike's sarcastic reference to Christ as "the Miss Lonelyhearts of Miss Lonelyhearts" [6]), "vanity" here probably has more of the nuance used in English translations of the first chapter of the Book of Ecclesiastes: "Vanity of vanities! All things are vanity! What profit has man from all the labor which he toils at under the sun? ... All speech is labored; there is nothing man can say" (1:2–3, 8). Most commentaries explain that "vanity" here is best understood as a "puff of vapor."[2] In fact, Miss Lonelyhearts does not really believe in Christ, for when trying to decide how to respond to Mrs. Doyle's letter he muses, "If he could only believe in Christ, then adultery would be a sin, then everything would be simple and the letters extremely easy to answer" (26). After typing the above words about Christ's death and gift of suffering, Miss Lonelyhearts gives dramatic expression to his genuine attitude when he snatches the paper out of the typewriter (39).

The corpus that Miss Lonelyhearts has nailed to his wall is the focal point for what many critics refer to as his mystical experience. It occurs in the last chapter of the novel titled "Miss Lonelyhearts Has a Religious Experience."

> He fastened his eyes on the Christ that hung on the wall opposite his bed. As he stared at it, it became a bright fly, spinning with quick grace on a background of blood velvet sprinkled with tiny nerve stars.
>
> Everything else in the room was dead—chairs, table, pencils, clothes, books. He thought of this black world of things as a fish. And he was right, for it suddenly rose to the bright bait on the wall. It rose with a splash of music and he saw its shining silver belly. (56–57)

The result of this experience is that Miss Lonelyhearts feels "clean and fresh. His heart was a rose and in his skull another rose bloomed." The account of this incident is replete with floral imagery, striking in a novel that has emphasized a sterile and decaying nature. Miss Lonelyhearts feels united to

God: "His identification with God was complete. His heart was the one heart, the heart of God" (57). Some critics clearly see this as a genuine mystical experience, a profound religious moment (see Light 94). Of course, the assertion of Miss Lonelyhearts' union with God is narrated through his viewpoint. The reader may remain skeptical. Most of the great authorities on mysticism—the author of *The Cloud of Unknowing*, St. John of the Cross, St. Theresa of Avila—as well as Buddhist, Hindu, and Muslim masters stress that genuine revelation or spiritual understanding comes after long, arduous, and disciplined practice in prayer and contemplation. The author of *The Cloud of Unknowing* cautions that "it is hard work and no mistake for the would-be contemplative; very hard work indeed, unless it is made easier by a special grace of God" (94). He also warns that "the earthly and physical fancies of inventive imaginations are very fruitful of error" (121). In fact, he cautions, the devil may be involved.

I shall not attempt to determine whether or not Miss Lonelyhearts' strange vision in this episode is truly a mystical encounter with Christ, a demonic visitation, or simply the perfectly natural result of exhaustion and illness. But as the culminating image of the cross in the novel, the spinning cross is the opposite of the symbol that Pelikan describes as stabilizing and inclusive, holding together a realistic acknowledgment of both good and evil but centered on the saving power of Christ. The spinning cross lacks form. It is not a readable symbol.

The poet William Everson, in an essay titled "Dionysus and the Beat Generation," could be describing Miss Lonelyhearts as well as the young people of his time. Everson argues that the Beat Generation was attempting

> to fuse Eros and Agape in a profane synthesis, but by settling for ecstasy at any price, it rove[d] restlessly from the delirium of sensational licentiousness to compulsive flights at the infinite through drugs or dithyrambic aestheticism.... But because in its protest against stodginess it repudiate[d] true order, not simply the Apollonian order of contingent effects, but the veritable order of interior synthesis, it oscillate[d] between an orgiastic sexuality and an incoherent elation. The way of perfection is hard, rigorous, and disenchanting, as the great religions have ever taught. (25)

Without "the veritable order of interior synthesis," Miss Lonelyhearts' "Christ dream" remains just that—a *dream*. St. Clair suggests that the Christian symbols in *Miss Lonelyhearts* may be "shopworn," implying that they are somehow worn out or old-fashioned. I would prefer to say that the ways in which they are fractured, fragmented, and distorted point to the failure of Miss Lonelyhearts and his contemporaries to understand their true significance or to respond with the "hard, rigorous, and disenchanting" self-discipline and self-knowledge required to read them correctly.

In the Judeo-Christian story the desert, a place inimical to the flourishing of life, becomes the place of spiritual refreshment and renewed commitment, but the place of theophany is also the place of law. Essential to the desert experience are patience, prayer, and discipline. The unblemished paschal lamb and the innocent Lamb of God pointed out by John the Baptist signify the purity, innocence, and self-sacrifice that command reverent attention and inspire the choice to endure the hardships required to escape from slavery. Finally, the cross—especially the icon of the crucifix—images the central mystery of the Incarnation, the God-Man emptying himself in *kenosis*. In Miss Lonelyhearts' world, however, the desert is the cluttered, noisy, and decaying modern wasteland that militates against an encounter with God. The lamb is the poor, suffering creature that, although pitied, is destroyed in an act of meaningless and violent rage. The corpus of Jesus without the cross indicates a loss of the insight that only gradually came to the worshiping Christian community: one cannot have a sweet, sentimental Jesus without facing the hard truth of prayer, patience, discipline, and redemptive suffering. One cannot separate Christ from his cross.

Such a reading does not contradict St. Clair's assertion that Miss Lonelyhearts is "a hero of sorts," nor does it necessarily imply the correctness of Cohen's interpretation that Miss Lonelyhearts' fervor is not religious faith at all but an egotistical obsession with his own messianic role (277). Miss Lonelyhearts may be sincere and well intentioned, and his inability to read the Christian symbols may be caused by the disorder in his life that, to a certain extent, is engendered by the modern world. But the novel also suggests that, disconnected from the community of memory, which is the Church, and divorced from the context of liturgy that reenacts the saving stories, the symbols may become, finally, illegible. The distortions in the presentation of these symbols and the deferral of the expectations they raise clarify the essentially false nature of Miss Lonelyhearts' obsession with Christ and ultimately affect the novel's ability either to undercut or to affirm the possibility of Christian faith.

NOTES

1. Jones, for example, argues that Miss Lonelyhearts is a "restless Satan" and Shrike "the true modernist Christ" (201).

2. See, for example, Fischer 71.

WORKS CITED

Auden, W.H. "Interlude: West's Disease." *The Dyer's Hand*. New York: Vintage, 1968. 238–45.

Balthasar, Hans Urs von. *Truth Is Symphonic*. Trans. Graham Harrison. San Francisco: Ignatius P, 1987.

The Cloud of Unknowing and Other Works. Trans. Clifton Wolters. New York: Penguin, 1978.

Cohen, Arthur. "Nathanael West's Holy Fool." *Commonweal* 64 (1956): 276–78.

Cunningham, Lawrence S. *The Catholic Experience*. New York: Crossroad, 1987.

Everson, William. "Dionysus and the Beat Generation." *Earth Poetry*. Ed. Lee Bartlett. Berkeley: Oyez, 1980. 21–27.

Fischer, James A. Song of *Songs, Ruth, Lamentations, Ecclesiastes, Esther*. Collegeville Bible Commentary No. 24. Collegeville: Liturgical P, 1986.

Jones, Beverly. "Nathanael West's *Miss Lonelyhearts*." *Critical Essays on Nathanael West*. Ed. Ben Siegel. New York: G.K. Hall, 1994. 195–202.

Light, James F. *Nathanael West: An Interpretative Study*. 2nd ed. Evanston: Northwestern UP, 1971.

Lorch, Thomas M. "West's *Miss Lonelyhearts*: Skepticism Mitigated?" *Renascence* 18 (1966): 99–109.

Martin, Jay. *Nathanael West. The Art of His Life*. New York: Farrar, 1970.

———, ed. *Nathanael West. A Collection of Critical Essays*. Englewood Cliffs: Prentice, 1971.

Merton, Thomas, trans. *The Wisdom of the Desert: Sayings of the Desert Fathers of the Fourth Century*. Boston: Shambala, 1994.

Pelikan, Jaroslav. *Jesus Through the Centuries*. New Haven: Yale UP, 1985.

Reid, Randall. *The Fiction of Nathanael West: No Redeemer, No Promised Land*. Chicago: U of Chicago P, 1967.

Ricoeur, Paul. "The Language of Faith." *The Philosophy of Paul Ricoeur. An Anthology of His Work*. Ed. Charles E. Reagan and David Stewart. Boston: Beacon, 1978. 223–37.

Ruprecht, Louis A., Jr. "Mark's Tragic Vision: Gethsemane." *Religion and Literature* 24.3 (1992): 1–25.

Smith, Marcus. "Religious Experience in *Miss Lonelyhearts*." Martin, *Critical Essays* 74–90.

St. Clair, Janet. "Timid Defender of the Faith: The Prophetic Vision of Miss Lonelyhearts." *Renascence* 46 (1994): 147–61.

Tyack, George S. *The Cross in Ritual, Architecture, and Art*. London: Williams Andrews, 1900.

West, Nathanael. *Miss Lonelyhearts & The Day of the Locust*. New York: New Directions, 1962.

———. "Notes on *Miss Lonelyhearts*." Martin, *Critical Essays* 66–67.

Chronology

1903	Born October 17 as Nathan Weinstein, first child of Anna and Max Weinstein, then a prosperous New York City building contractor.
1917–20	Irregularly attends DeWitt Clinton High School, New York City, but does not graduate.
1921	Enters Tufts College with a doctored high school transcript. Fails all courses and leaves at end of first semester.
1922–24	Transfers to Brown University using someone else's transcript. Receives Bachelor's degree in English. Becomes close friend of S.J. Perelman.
1924–26	Intermittently employed in father's construction business, while reading widely and writing.
1926–27	Lives in Paris from October through January; legally changes name to Nathanael West. Called home as parents' prosperity declines due to building slump.
1927–29	Through relatives obtains job as night manager of New York City hotel. Meets Edmund Wilson and writes for *The New Yorker*.
1930–32	Becomes manager of Sutton Hotel and provides free lodging for indigent writer friends. Publishes *The Dream Life of Balso Snell* in 1931 in limited edition. Becomes

	friends with William Carlos Williams and associate editor of his magazine *Contact* from 1931–32.
1933	With sister and her husband, S.J. Perelman, becomes co-owner of farmhouse in Erwinna, Pennsylvania. Publishes *Miss Lonelyhearts*, but publisher goes bankrupt, preventing wide distribution of the book. Becomes contract scriptwriter in Hollywood for Columbia Studios.
1934	Returns to Erwinna. Publishes *A Cool Million*.
1935	Returns to Hollywood in search of employment. Suffers from poverty and illness.
1936–38	Scriptwriter for low-budget films for Republic Pictures. Active in Screen Writers Guild.
1939	*The Day of the Locust* published. Does well-paid script work for a number of studios.
1940	Marries Eileen McKenney on April 19 in Beverly Hills, California. Friendship in Hollywood with F. Scott Fitzgerald. Collaborates on several highly paid movie scripts, as well as other scripts. On December 22, is killed with wife in car crash near El Centro, California.
1957	*The Complete Works of Nathanael West* published.

Contributors

HAROLD BLOOM is Sterling Professor of the Humanities at Yale University. He is the author of over 20 books, including *Shelley's Mythmaking* (1959), *The Visionary Company* (1961), *Blake's Apocalypse* (1963), *Yeats* (1970), *A Map of Misreading* (1975), *Kabbalah and Criticism* (1975), *Agon: Toward a Theory of Revisionism* (1982), *The American Religion* (1992), *The Western Canon* (1994), and *Omens of Millennium: The Gnosis of Angels, Dreams, and Resurrection* (1996). *The Anxiety of Influence* (1973) sets forth Professor Bloom's provocative theory of the literary relationships between the great writers and their predecessors. His most recent books include *Shakespeare: The Invention of the Human* (1998), a 1998 National Book Award finalist, *How to Read and Why* (2000), *Genius: A Mosaic of One Hundred Exemplary Creative Minds* (2002), and *Hamlet: Poem Unlimited* (2003). In 1999, Professor Bloom received the prestigious American Academy of Arts and Letters Gold Medal for Criticism, and in 2002 he received the Catalonia International Prize.

KINGSLEY WIDMER taught remedial English at San Diego State College for many years and also has taught at several other institutions in the U.S. and abroad. He is the author of numerous publications, among *them Edges of Extremity: Some Problems of Literary Modernism, The Literary Rebel,* and titles on D.H. Lawrence, Melville, and Henry Miller.

MARK CONROY teaches English at Ohio State University and is the author of *Muse in the Machine: American Fiction and Mass Publicity* and *Modernism and Authority*, a study of Flaubert and Conrad.

DOUGLAS ROBINSON has taught at the University of Tampere in Finland and is the author of *John Barth's* Giles Goat-Boy: *A Study, American Apocalypses,* and *Ring Lardner and the Other.*

ROBERT EMMET LONG is the author or editor of numerous books, including titles on Henry James and Fitzgerald. He has been drama critic of the *North American Review* and has reviewed books for the *Saturday Review, The Nation, Commonweal,* and a variety of other periodicals.

JOHN KEYES has taught English at Ryerson Polytechnical Institute.

ROBERT WEXELBLATT has been Professor and Chairman of the Division of Humanities for the College of Basic Studies at Boston University. He is the author of books of short stories and a book of essays.

BEVERLY J. JONES has been a high school English teacher for many years in various states. She is the author of an essay on *Miss Lonelyhearts* that appeared in G.K. Hall's *Critical Essays on Nathanael West.*

MIRIAM FUCHS teaches English at the University of Hawaii, where she has also been Director of the Honors Program in English. She is the author of *Text is Myself: Women's Life Writing and Catastrophe* and co-editor of *Breaking the Sequence: Women's Experimental Fiction.* She has also published works on Hart Crane, Dante Gabriel Rosetti, Hilda Doolittle, and others.

RICHARD P. LYNCH is Professor of English and has been Chair of the English Department at College Misericordia.

MARIAN E. CROWE has been Lecturer in English at St. Mary's College. Her work has appeared in *New Oxford Review* and *Commonweal.*

Bibliography

Auden, W.H. "Interlude: West's Disease." In *The Dyer's Hand and Other Essays*. New York: Random House, 1956.

Bloom, Harold. *Nathanael West*. New York: Chelsea House, 1986.

Butler, Rebecca R. "Todorov's Fantastic, Kayser's Grotesque, and West's *Miss Lonelyhearts*: Selected Essays from the First International Conference on Fantastic in Literature and Film." In *The Scope of the Fantastic: Theory, Technique, Major Authors*, edited by Robert A. Collins and Howard D. Pearce, 41–48. Westport, CT: Greenwood, 1985.

Ciancio, Ralph A. "Laughing in Pain with Nathanael West." In *Literature and the Grotesque*, edited by Michael J. Meyer, 1–20. Amsterdam: Rodopi, 1995.

Daniel, Carter A. "West's Revision of *Miss Lonelyhearts*." *Studies in Bibliography* 16 (1963): 232–243.

Devlin, James E. "Nathanael West Borrows from Erskine Caldwell." *Notes on Contemporary Literature* 17, no. 4 (September 1987): 2–3.

DiStasi, Lawrence. "Aggression in *Miss Lonelyhearts*: Nowhere to Throw the Stone." In *Nathanael West: The Cheaters and the Cheated*, edited by David Madden, 83–101. Deland: Everett/Edwards, 1973.

Duncan, Jeffrey L. "The Problem of Language in *Miss Lonelyhearts*." *Iowa Review* 8 (1977): 116–127.

Edenbaum, Robert I. "To Kill God and Build a Church: Nathanael West's *Miss Lonelyhearts*." *The CEA Critic* 29 (June 1967): 5–7, 11.

Harrington, Gary. "*Miss Lonelyhearts* and *Pylon*: The Influence of Anxiety." *ANQ* 6, no. 4 (October 1993): 209–211.

Hattenhauer, Darryl. "West's *Miss Lonelyhearts*." *Explicator* 49, no.2 (Winter 1991): 120–121.

Hickey, James L. "Freudian Criticism and *Miss Lonelyhearts*." In *Nathanael West: The Cheaters and the Cheated*, edited by David Madden, 111–149. Deland, Florida: Everett/Edwards, 1973.

Hyman, Stanley Edgar. *Nathanael West*. Minneapolis: University of Minneapolis Press, 1962.

Jackson, Thomas H. *Twentieth-Century Interpretations of Miss Lonelyhearts*. Englewood Cliffs, NJ: Prentice-Hall, 1971.

Jones, Beverly J. "Nathanael West's *Miss Lonelyhearts*." In *Critical Essays on Nathanael West*, edited by Ben Siegel, 195–202. New York: G.K. Hall, 1994.

Keyes, John. "Nathanael West's 'New Art Form': Metamorphoses of Detective Fiction in *Miss Lonelyhearts*." *English Studies in Canada* 8, no. 1 (March 1982): 76–86.

Light, James F. *Nathanael West: An Interpretative Study*. Evanston: Northwestern University Press, 1971.

Madden, David. "The Shrike Voice Dominates *Miss Lonelyhearts*." In *Critical Essays on Nathanael West*, edited by Ben Siegel, 203–212. New York: G.K. Hall, 1994.

Martin, Jay, ed. *Nathanael West: A Collection of Critical Essays*. Englewood Cliffs: Prentice-Hall, 1971.

Mayer, D.R. "West's Parody of the *Anima Christi* in *Miss Lonelyhearts*." Explicator 34, no. 2 (1975): Item 11.

Nelson, Gerald B. "Lonelyhearts." In *Ten Versions of America*. New York: Knopf, 1972.

Orvell, Miles D. "The Messianic Sexuality of *Miss Lonelyhearts*." *Studies in Short Fiction* 10, no. 2 (1973): 159–167.

Poznar, Walter. "The Apocalyptic Vision in Nathanael West's *Miss Lonelyhearts*: Selected Papers from Eighth and Ninth Annual Florida State University Conference on Literature and Film." In *Apocalyptic Visions Past and Present*, edited by JoAnn James and William Cloonan, 111–119. Tallahassee: Florida State University Press, 1988.

Prasad, Suman Prabha. "The Sympathetic Misogynist: A Consideration of the Treatment of Women in Nathanael West's *Miss Lonelyhearts*." In *Modern Studies and Other Essays in Honor of Dr. R.K. Sinha*, edited by R.C. Prasad and A.K. Sharma, 72–79. New Delhi: Vikas, 1987.

Raban, Jonathan. "A Surfeit of Commodities: The Novels of Nathanael West." In *The American Novel and the Nineteen Twenties*, edited by Malcolm Bradbury and David Palmer, 215–231. New York: Arnold, 1971.

Rahim, R. Abdul. "Nathanael West's *Miss Lonelyhearts*: A Parody of Modern Life." *Indian Journal of American Studies* 22, no. 2 (Summer 1992): 107–112.

Ratner, Marc L. "'Anywhere Out of This World': Baudelaire and Nathanael West." *American Literature* 31, no. 4 (January 1960): 456–463.

Reid, Randall. *The Fiction of Nathanael West: No Redeemer, No Promised Land.* Chicago: University of Chicago Press, 1967.

Richter, David H. "The Reader as Ironic Victim." *Novel* 14, no. 2 (Winter 1982): 135–151.

Rozelle, Lee. "Ecocritical City: Modernist Reactions to Urban Environments in *Miss Lonelyhearts* and *Paterson*." *Twentieth-Century Literature* 48, no. 1 (Spring 200): 100–115.

Schoenewolf, Carroll. "Jamesian Psychology and Nathanael West's *Miss Lonelyhearts*." *San José Studies* 3, no. 3 (1981): 80–86.

Schoening, Mark. "Dr. Lonelyhearts." *American Literary History* 5 (Winter 1993): 663–685.

Scholem, Gershom. "Redemption Through Sin." In *The Messianic Idea in Judaism and Other Essays on Jewish Spirituality*. NY: Schocken Books, 1971.

Simons, John L. "A New Reading of the End of West's *Miss Lonelyhearts*." *Notes on Modern American Literature* 5, no. 3 (Summer 1981): Item 16.

St. Clair, Janet. "Timid Defender of the Faith: The Prophetic Vision of *Miss Lonelyhearts*." *Renascence* 46, no. 3 (Spring 1994): 146–161.

Tseng, An-kuo. "'Good Reasons for Not Laughing': Humor as Violence in Nathanael West's *Miss Lonelyhearts*." *Euramerica* 28, no. 4 (December 1998): 173–213.

Veitch, Jonathan. "'Lousy with Pure/Reeking with Stark': Nathanael West, William Carlos Williams, and the Textualization of the 'Real.'" *Prospects* 21 (1996): 123–148.

Volpe, Edmond L. "The Waste Land of Nathanael West." *Renascence* 3 (1961): 69–77.

Walsh, Joy. "*Miss Lonelyhearts*: The Problem of Touching and the Primary Need for Fictions." *Notes on Modern American Literature* 6, no. 1 (Spring–Summer 1982): Item 4.

West, Nathanael. "Some Notes on *Miss Lonelyhearts*." *Contempo* 3 (May 15, 1933): 1–2.

Wexelblatt, Robert. "*Miss Lonelyhearts* is a Novella." *Lamar Journal of the Humanities* 15, no. 1 (Spring 1989): 3–10.

Acknowledgments

"The Religious Masquerade: *Miss Lonelyhearts*" by Kingsley Widmer. From *Nathanael West*, pp. 26–50. © 1982 by Twayne Publishers. Reprinted by permission of The Gale Group.

"Letters and Spirit in *Miss Lonelyhearts*" by Mark Conroy. From *The University of Windsor Review*, vol. 17, no. 1 (Fall–Winter 1982), pp. 5–20. © 1982 by The University of Windsor Review. Reprinted by permission.

"The Ritual Icon" by Douglas Robinson. From *American Apocalypses: The Image of the End of the World in American Literature*, pp. 213–232. © 1985 by The Johns Hopkins University Press. Reprinted by permission.

"*Miss Lonelyhearts*: The Absurd Center of the Dead World" by Robert Emmet Long. From *Nathanael West*, pp. 44–83. © 1985 by Frederick Ungar Publishing Co., Inc. Reprinted by permission of the Continuum International Publishing Group.

"Inarticulate Expressions of Genuine Suffering? A Reply to the Correspondence in *Miss Lonelyhearts*" by John Keyes. From *The University of Windsor Review*, vol. 20, no. 1 (Fall–Winter 1987), pp. 11–25. © 1987 by The University of Windsor Review. Reprinted by permission.

"*Miss Lonelyhearts* and the Rhetoric of Disintegration" by Robert Wexelblatt. From *College Literature*, vol. 16, no. 3 (1989), pp. 219–231. © 1989 by West Chester University. Reprinted by permission.

"Shrike as the Modernist Anti-Hero in Nathanael West's *Miss Lonelyhearts*" by Beverly J. Jones. From *Modern Fiction Studies*, vol. 36, no. 2 (Summer 1990), pp. 218–224. © 1990 by the Purdue Research Foundation. Reprinted by permission.

"Nathanael West's *Miss Lonelyhearts*: *The Waste Land* Rescripted" by Miriam Fuchs. From *Studies in Short Fiction*, vol. 29, no. 1 (Winter 1992), pp. 43–55. © 1992 by Newbery College.

"Saints and Lovers: *Miss Lonelyhearts* in the Tradition" by Richard P. Lynch. From *Studies in Short Fiction*, vol. 31, no. 2 (Spring 1994), pp. 225–235. © 1994 by Newberry College.

"The Desert, the Lamb, the Cross: Debased Iconography in Nathanael West's *Miss Lonelyhearts*" by Marian E. Crowe. From *Christianiaty and Literature*, vol. 45, no. 3–4 (Spring–Summer 1996), pp. 345–358. © 1996 by the Conference on Christianity and Literature.

Index